FRANCIS MARION:

The Swamp Fox

Books by Hugh F. Rankin

Rebels and Redcoats
   (with George F. Scheer)
The American Revoluton
The Theater in Colonial America
Criminal Trial Proceedings in the
   General Court of Colonial Virginia
The Golden Age of Piracy
The North Carolina Continentals
Francis Marion: The Swamp Fox

Leaders of the American Revolution Series
North Callahan, EDITOR

FRANCIS MARION:

The Swamp Fox

HUGH F. RANKIN

Thomas Y. Crowell Company
NEW YORK   Established 1834

Designed by Ingrid Beckman

Manufactured in the United States of America

ISBN 0–690–00097–9

1   2   3   4   5   6   7   8   9   10

Library of Congress Cataloging in Publication Data

Rankin, Hugh F
  Francis Marion: the Swamp Fox.

  (Leaders of the American Revolution series)
  Bibliography: p.
  1. Marion, Francis, 1732–1795. I. Title.
E207.M3R36   973.3′092′4 [B]   73–10062
ISBN 0–690–00097–9

For Jane Hogan

Preface

The life of Francis Marion was something like a sandwich—a highly spiced center between two slabs of rather dry bread. Admittedly this study begins a bit slowly, but with two or three exceptions, Marion's life until well into his forties was rather mundane. And after the Revolution, worn out by the vicissitudes of war, he slid back into relative obscurity. His claim to fame rests primarily upon his actions for two and one-half years.

Legends have been built on this American Cincinnatus, beginning early in the nineteenth century. Peter Horry, who served with him, produced a manuscript on Marion which, on December 19, 1803, he presented to the Georgetown, South Carolina, Literary Society on the condition that they print it at their own expense. Some five weeks later a committee suggested that since Horry now had been offered the use of the Marion manuscripts and might want to make changes, the proposal be postponed. Apparently Horry made some use of these papers, for on April 27, 1804, the president of the Society, John Keith, again put forth the idea of printing Horry's manuscript; a committee appointed to investigate the cost advised against it.

Somewhere along the way, during the next three years, Horry met Mason Locke "Parson" Weems, an ordained Anglican minister who was then a traveling book salesman for the publisher Mathew Carey of Philadelphia. Weems had already written the highly successful *Life and Memorable Actions of George Washington,* published anonymously around 1800, which was to run through seventy editions. In the fifth edition he had added the famous cherry tree story. At the time he met Horry he was casting about for another romantic figure on whom to focus his vivid imagination. Marion seemed to fit his needs, and Horry allowed Weems to rewrite the manuscript.

In December 1807 Weems wrote Horry, "Knowing the passion of the times for Novels, I have Endeavoured to throw some Ideas & facts about Genl. Marion into the Garb & Dress of a military Romance." The following June he was reporting that he would need another three weeks for revision and "to polish & Colour it into a Style that will I hope sometimes Excite a Smile & sometimes Call forth a Tear." The result was a highly romantic Marion, clad in shining armor, smiting the Philistines both to the right and the left. When he saw what Parson Weems had wrought from his manuscript, a saddened Peter Horry wryly commented, "Most certainly, 'tis not my history but your romance." And thus was the Marion legend created. Yet I have used the Horry and Weems volume when there has appeared to be some basis of fact struggling upwards through the florid prose.

Others followed along the trail blazed by Horry and Weems. William Dobein James, who as a lad of fifteen had joined Marion's brigade, pulled together the reminiscences of others as well as his own and published them in 1821 under the title *A Sketch of the Life of Brig. Gen. Francis Marion and a History of His Brigade.* The passage of the years had dimmed his memory and the chronology of events is sometimes confused, but he also added to the Marion legend.

When William Gilmore Simms wrote and published his *Life of Francis Marion* in 1844, the South Carolina novelist claimed that he had a manuscript written by Peter Horry. Perhaps it was because the South so desperately needed heroes to counter the flood of antislavery criticism leveled at her during the era before the Civil War that Simms's biography went through at least ten editions. It is perhaps fitting that three years later Simms published *The Life of Chevalier Bayard*, cast in the same mold as his life of Marion. And so the legend grew.

Since then others have written of the man, some perpetuating the legend, others placing him on a lower pedestal and adding a bit of tarnish to the image. This is not to say that Marion was undeserving of such tarnish, for he was a feisty and sensitive individual, subject to all those emotional disturbances common to men when they are engaged in a civil war and counting as enemies those who had formerly been friends and neighbors. Yet he cannot be dismissed as a romantic, for the very nature of his operations earned him his legend and his romantic aura.

In bringing this book together I am grateful to a number of people. Mrs. Elizabeth H. Drew of New York City, while working with me on another project, gave generously of her time in searching out isolated Marion items. My colleague Dr. Bennett H. Wall was kind enough to go through the materials in the Huntington Library when he was in California. Richard Batt kept an eye out for such materials while he was working on his own project on the Maryland Continental Line, and Dr. John Sellers of the Library of Congress was more than generous with his time. There is not enough space to list the many fine people who man the search rooms of such depositories as the William L. Clements Library, the Southern Historical Collection, the North Carolina Department of Archives and History, the Tulane Library, the South Carolina Department of Archives, the South Caroliniana Collection, the Library of Congress, the National Archives, the New York Public Library, and the New-York Historical Society. But to them all I am most grateful.

HUGH F. RANKIN

Illustrations

Maps

Chapter I

A small man in physical stature, Francis Marion stood tall in the eyes of the age in which he lived. His primary thrust into history lasted no longer than three years, yet his name was, and still is, bestowed upon uncounted babies, while some twenty-nine towns and seventeen counties throughout the land have been named for him. In one sense this is an extraordinary recognition when it is remembered that he fought in only three major military operations of the American Revolution: the 1776 siege of Charleston, the assault against Savannah, and the battle of Eutaw Springs. Although he performed well in each, his activities were not such as would have earned his niche in history. In general, these skirmishes that he fought might be termed the froth of battle. But as early as 1775, one British general had seen in such engagements the seeds of defeat when he wrote, "Our army will be destroyed by damned driblets . . . America is an ugly job . . . a damned affair indeed." And six years later the staid *Annual Register* was to voice its opinion from London:

Most of these actions would in other wars be considered as skirmishes of little account, and scarcely worthy of a detailed narrative. But these small actions are as capable as any of displaying military conduct. The operations of war being spread over that vast continent, by the new plan that was adopted, it is by such skirmishes that the fate of America must be necessarily decided. They are therefore as important as battles in which a hundred thousand are drawn up on each side.

His early years in the South Carolina Continental Line, other than the siege of Charleston and the attack on Savannah, were relatively quiet. Although he did attain the rank of lieutenant colonel, Francis Marion was not particularly outstanding nor did he hold exceptional promise as a military leader. Perhaps "steady" would be the best term to apply to those years. True, he was an important cog in a sizable military machine, but cogs seldom stand out, no matter how important their functions. Marion did not emerge into real prominence, either in a military or civil capacity, until he had reached the September of his life.

Despite an appearance that can at best be described as uninspiring, he was able to instill discipline and devotion among those who followed him. Yet he was a man with a short fuse, and oversensitive, especially when he fell into one of his deep and black moods. He resented taking commands from those of equal rank. He was greatly troubled when he sometimes had to deal with the swollen egos of those who served with him, but he forced himself to make what he considered to be the best decision, even though it might lead to the breaking up of a valued friendship. In truth, Francis Marion became more than a partisan leader; to those who rode with him he was an emotional experience.[1]

When he was born, sometime during the winter of 1732, Francis Marion didn't appear to be a child a father could do much bragging about. It has been stated that he was so tiny and puny that he was "not larger than a New England lobster, and might easily enough have been put in a quart pot." Both ankles and knees were somewhat malformed from birth.[2]

Francis was the youngest of the six children born to Gabriel and Esther Marion, the others bearing the names of Esther, Isaac, Gabriel, Benjamin, and Job. The parents were of French extraction, with the grandparents among those Huguenots who had fled France in 1690 after the revocation of the Edict of Nantes. They had been among the seventy or eighty families who had settled along the Santee River and who had started a new life for themselves by grubbing a living from the soil. By the time John Lawson, surveyor for the Lords Proprietors of Carolina, traveled through the area in the early 1700s he was able to note that the settlers lived "as decently and happily, as any Planters in these Southward Parts of America." [3]

Yet these Huguenots seemed to prefer to live more simply than their counterparts who had settled in and around Charleston. They continued to live modestly even after some became prosperous; few preferred to build pretentious mansions to display their wealth. [4]

For his first five or six years Francis Marion lived with his parents on his birthplace, Goatfield Plantation, in St. John's Parish, Berkeley County, South Carolina. For the scrawny youngster life was a steady process of work and learning, for the Huguenots were great believers in education. Yet his formal learning must have been thin, for there were few opportunities to polish the basic facts he was taught. It has been assumed that most of the children of the district were taught at home by their parents, most of whom kept alive the traditional Huguenot reverence for things cultural as they fought to scrape a living from the soil. Certainly Francis's letters in later life suggest that his education did not proceed too far beyond the bare essentials. And most of the soldiers from the district who later served under Marion showed a fairly high degree of literacy—for the eighteenth century. [5]

He was no more than six years old when his family moved to a plantation on Winyah Bay in Prince George Parish. There is a

3

possibility that he may have attended school in nearby George-town, if such facilities were available.

Georgetown was a port, and it must have been the bellying sails of ships as they sought the open sea that stirred Marion's imagination into ambition. For a youth in his teens, any life was better than the drudgery of the farm. He was about fifteen years old when he could no longer resist the call of the sea. With his parents' consent, he shipped aboard a schooner bound for the West Indies. The outward-bound voyage was uneventful, but on the return passage trouble rose up out of the sea. For some reason a whale attacked the schooner, ramming the hull with such force that the planking was opened and the seams sprung. Water poured into the hold, and the captain and his six crewmen took to the ocean in an open boat. As they pulled away from the foundering vessel, a little dog leaped overboard and swam to the boat. For five days the men suffered excruciating thirst as the rays of a brassy sun bore down upon them. As the days dragged past, they finally brushed inhibitions aside and killed the pet, drinking the blood and gulping down the raw flesh. On the sixth day two of the crewmen died; on the seventh the survivors reached land.[6]

This experience was enough to give young Marion his fill of the sea, his dreams of adventure having disappeared with the schooner. Yet, according to reports, the voyage, despite the or-deal of shipwreck, had been good for his health. Life on the farm now appeared more attractive. He remained behind on the fam-ily farm as his elder brothers and sisters married and moved away to homes of their own. About 1750 Gabriel, senior, died and the youngest Marion assumed the management of the plantation and the support of his mother.

Francis was twenty-five when his military career began. Al-though the French and Indian War had been going on for several years, the fighting had not yet touched South Carolina. As the war neared its end, the Cherokees began to act up along the frontier. Governor William Henry Lyttleton enlarged the militia in the face of the threat. Captain John Postell of the Winyah Bay area began recruiting his company from among the Huguenots. Francis and Gabriel, for whom he always felt the closest affection of all his brothers, enlisted on January 31, 1756 in the company of Upper St. John Parish. Soldiering was learned, after a fashion, at the periodic militia musters.[7]

When the Cherokees did begin their war, Gabriel secured a commission as captain and recruited a cavalry company in St. John's. Francis enlisted, but his company was disbanded when Governor Lyttleton concluded a treaty with the Indians. Gabriel moved away to St. Stephen's Parish, but he had no more than settled in his new home than the Cherokees rose again and began to stain the frontier with blood. Lieutenant Colonel Archibald Montgomerie led his Highland Regiment (British regulars stationed in Charleston) and the South Carolina militia over into the valley of the Little Tennessee. Near the Indian town of Echoe he stumbled into a Cherokee ambush. He drove them back and then fell back to Fort Prince George, beating off two additional attacks along the way.

Lieutenant Governor William Bull, acting as chief executive of the colony, requested assistance from Lord Jeffery Amherst, commander in chief of British forces in North America. On January 6, 1761, Lieutenant Colonel James Grant and 1,200 British regulars disembarked in Charleston. Colonel Thomas Middleton, Lieutenant Colonel Henry Laurens, and Major John Moultrie, all prominent in South Carolina political affairs, were authorized to recruit a regiment of militia to provide support for the regulars. The first lieutenant of Captain William Moultrie's company of infantry was Francis Marion.[8]

In June the long columns began their winding marches up the Santee and Congaree. Reaching Fort Prince George in the northwest section of the province, Grant turned northward into North Carolina and toward the Cherokee town of Echoe. The Indian scouts ranging out in front of the column reported that the Cherokees had once again laid an ambush in the defile in which they had surprised Montgomerie. They had to be driven out before the army could advance. A detachment under Marion was given the task of clearing the pass.

Cautiously the green lieutenant led his thirty men into the tangle of trees. The Indians waited until they were well within range before loosing a blistering fire. Marion's advance was slowed as his men sought the protection of trees. But even as the savages whooped, the lieutenant led his men forward, advancing from one tree to another. By the time the Indians had been driven off and Marion and the survivors made it through the pass, twenty-one of his thirty men had been either killed or wounded. Grant's column crashed through and charged up the hill on which the main body of Indians lay. The Cherokees gave fierce resistance and were not dislodged until noon, when they finally broke and ran.

Grant pushed forward to burn Echoe. Moving down the Tennessee and Tuckaseagee valleys, he destroyed more than fifteen Indian towns and either burned or cut down their crops. So relentlessly did Grant move through the countryside that the Cherokee chieftain Attakullakulla, sometimes known as "Little Carpenter," came in and sued for peace. After a thirty-day campaign, Grant marched back to Charleston.[9]

When Middleton disbanded his regiment, Marion returned to the farm. It had been a hard campaign, but Marion had gained insofar as his future was concerned. Accounts of his behavior had filtered back, and from this time on he was accorded greater respect by the people along the Santee. He had also soldiered with men who were, or were destined to become, prominent in South Carolina affairs and who had noted his conduct. On the expedition there had been not only Middleton, Laurens, and Moultrie but Andrew Williamson, Isaac Huger, and Andrew Pickens. William Moultrie, his immediate commander, stated that "He was an active, brave and hardy soldier, and an excellent partisan officer." [10]

On the surface, however, there seemed to be little chance that Marion would further distinguish himself throughout the remainder of his life other than as a prosperous planter. He farmed leased lands along the west bank of the Santee and became an integral part of the social life of his community. He loved to hunt and fish and grew to know the area as well as a person could. By 1773 he had accumulated enough wealth to purchase his own plantation. It was located on the Santee, four miles below Eutaw Springs, and just above "Walnut Grove," the home of his brother Benjamin. Francis called his place "Pond Bluff" because of a pond at the foot of a bluff facing the river. [11]

The records suggest that Francis Marion participated but little in the resistance against British Parliamentary measures during the Revolutionary crisis. Yet he must have taken a fairly active role, albeit on a local scale, for when the people of St. John's Parish elected delegates to South Carolina's first Provincial Congress, they chose Francis and his brother Job as two of their representatives. This extralegal body, convening in Charleston on January 11, 1775, chose Charles Pinckney as its president and Peter Timothy, publisher of the *South Carolina Gazette*, as secretary. If he had hoped for drastic action (which he probably did not), Marion was disappointed, for the Charleston Congress did little other than rubber-stamp the Continental Association prohibiting the importation of merchandise from England. They did debate the issue of nonimportation, but it was little more than an exercise in semantics. The body also appointed Committees of Safety for the various parishes as a means of keeping the revolutionary spirit alive. The group adjourned with an address to the crown, professing loyalty to the king, which they presented to Lieutenant Governor William Bull.

The mood was soon to change. General Thomas Gage, commanding general of the British forces in North America, had sent his redcoats marching out from Boston, and there had been fighting in the Massachusetts villages of Lexington and Concord and along the way back into the city on April 19, 1775. Riders on swift horses carried the news from town to town, with Isaac Marion one of those forwarding the news as it passed through the Little River settlement on the North Carolina border. Henry Laurens, president of the South Carolina General Council of Safety, issued a call for the Provincial Congress to convene in Charleston on June 1, 1775.

There was more excitement for the delegates as they assembled. From Arthur Lee, Virginia-born lawyer in London, came a letter saying that the British were considering inciting the Indians to warfare. This letter, coupled with the "bloody scene of the 19th of April last, near Boston," had the effect of changing the Provincial Congress from a debating society to a legislative body. In response to a resolve of the Continental Congress on June 6, the South Carolinians voted to raise two regiments of infantry and one of cavalry to be composed of five hundred men each. These Provincial troops, eventually to be taken into the Continental Line, or regular army, were to perform as a nucleus around which the militia of the colony could act. Then, too, there was the question of militia officers, for they held royal commissions and had sworn allegiance to the British crown. Throughout the proceedings of the congress Marion seems not to have taken a strong role, but he apparently was well known to the members, and it is to be suspected that he let it be known that he would not be unhappy if selected to act in some military capacity.[12]

On June 12 the congress ballotted for officers. So great was the military zeal and ardor at this time that more than four times the number needed offered themselves for military commissions. In the voting for captains, Charles Cotesworth Pinckney and Barnard Elliot received 140 votes each, while Francis

Marion and William Cattell each received 135. The Horry cousins, Daniel and Peter, were each given 131. In the regiments the captains were to be ranked according to the votes they received in the Provincial Congress.

The First and Second regiments were to be infantry units, while the Third was to be cavalry, or mounted "Rangers." William Thomson was selected as colonel of the Third Regiment. The field officers of the First Regiment included Christopher Gadsden as colonel, Isaac Huger as lieutenant colonel, and Owen Roberts as major.

William Moultrie was chosen as colonel for the Second Regiment, with Isaac Motte as lieutenant colonel and Alexander McIntosh as major. Among the ten captains assigned to this regiment was Francis Marion. The officers were assigned seniority according to the votes they had received in the congress. In this balloting Marion had tied for third out of twenty. In the Second Regiment he was ranked second captain behind Barnard Elliot. Peter Horry was fifth captain.[13]

On June 18 the new royal governor, Lord William Campbell, came ashore in Charleston. In contrast to pomp and ceremony usually accompanying such occasions, his reception was rather cool. A delegation from the Provincial Congress waited upon him with a declaration of principles and urged him to disabuse the king's mind of the idea that they were disloyal subjects possessed of a lust for independence. Campbell, in a rather curt reply, assured them that he knew of no representatives of the people other than the legally constituted General Assembly.[14]

With formalities past, Colonels Gadsden and Moultrie set about organizing their regiments on June 21. The first thing that Moultrie had his officers do was to uniform themselves properly in blue coats with linings, facings, and cuffs of red. Buttons were white, as were waistcoats and breeches. Their hats were to carry a silver crescent and a plume.[15]

With two captains remaining in Charleston to set up receiving depots, Moultrie sent his remaining officers out into the country-side on recruiting missions. Barnard Elliot roamed as far south as Georgia drumming up recruits. The recruiting parties were fairly large, with Elliot's numbering thirteen people, including the musicians who were to play at the "Virginia hops" given for likely prospects. Other lures included barbecues, patriotic ha-rangues, and one would suspect less-publicized bonuses, for El-liot noted that he "enlisted two females for the services. . . ." Among those he recruited in Georgia on July 7, 1775, was one William Jasper,[16] a plain fellow who didn't seem the hero he was to become.

Marion's territory was along the Santee, Black, and Peedee rivers. Excitement was running high in those areas and his task was not difficult. He was able to sign sixty men, among them his nephew Gabriel Marion, who was listed as a "Cadet." Just as soon as his recruits could be assembled in Charleston, Marion began their training. By September he felt they were ready to take the field.[17]

In the meantime, a flag had been designed for the regiment. At the direction of the Council of Safety, Moultrie had designed a banner "for the purpose of signals," but it was soon adopted as a regimental banner. It was a blue flag and held the silver crescent after the emblems worn by the officers of the First and Second Regiments on their hats. He added the word "Liberty" on the blue background.[18]

No sooner had Marion declared his company ready for action than he was given a mission. On September 13, President Henry Laurens (of the Council of Safety) ordered Moultrie to detach 150 men to slip out of town and take Fort Johnson on James Island. This post occupied a commanding position insofar as the entrance to Charleston Harbor was concerned and could, to a degree, control all water traffic.

Moultrie ordered Captains Pinckney (of the First Regiment), Elliot, and Marion to select fifty men from each of their companies and hold them in readiness to move on a moment's notice.

At twelve that night the three captains, under the overall command of Lieutenant Colonel Isaac Motte, embarked aboard a "packet" at Gadsden Wharf. An hour later the captain of the transport dropped anchor a mile from shore, refusing to approach nearer the fort because of a low tide and his fear of the artillery mounted on the walls of Fort Johnson. The men had to be rowed ashore in two small boats capable of holding only fifteen men each trip. By dawn only Pinckney's and Elliot's commands had reached shore. Without waiting for Marion's men they rushed forward.

They met with no resistance. During the night Colonel Alexander Innes, secretary to Governor Campbell, had taken the garrison out to the two sloops of the Royal Navy anchored offshore, the *Tamar* and the *Cherokee*. When the fort had been rushed, the attackers had found the gates hanging open, the guns dismounted and off their platforms, and only a small housekeeping force of five men within the walls.

Nothing happened for the remainder of that day, but during the evening Innes appeared as a messenger from Governor Campbell and demanded to know by what authority a military installation of His Majesty had been seized. Refusing to allow Innes within the gates, Pinckney's blunt reply was, "By the authority of the Council of Safety." As a precautionary measure, Colonel Moultrie alerted all South Carolina troops for immediate action.

The following morning the *Tamar* and *Cherokee* moved in toward James Island. But Colonel Motte had kept his men working, and by the time the sloops swept in, three of the cannon had been remounted. The sight of their black muzzles and 150 men lined up along the parapets ready for action was enough to discourage the captains. They pulled off out of range and dropped their hooks in the anchorage known as Rebellion Road.

A short time later the governor was taken aboard and carried off by the *Syren,* a frigate of the Royal Navy.[19]

The two sloops hovered offshore. Near dawn on November 12 they tacked in nearer the town and lobbed 160 shells towards the city, but these were ineffective, causing more fright than damage.[20]

But the presence of the *Tamar* and *Cherokee* was enough to persuade the Provincial Congress to increase their military manpower, hasten work on the defenses of Charleston, and order "every military operation to oppose the passage of any British military armaments." Out of a fear that there might be a sudden British raid, a depot was established at Dorchester, thirty miles up the Ashley River near the head of navigation. Not only military supplies, but all public records were deposited there.

And there was danger from another quarter. The people of the west had never embraced rebellion so readily as those of the tidewater. Their isolated position gave them few reasons for grievances against British wrongs; conversely, they held strong feelings against the low country for the many delays in granting them courts and representation in the legislature. The latest leader to rise among the backcountry loyalists was Colonel John Scofield.

Because of the scarcity of any kind of arms and ammunition, the arsenal at Dorchester could prove an attractive objective for Colonel Scofield and his Tories. Although Moultrie referred to Scofield as a "stupid, ignorant blockhead," he was a formidable enough opponent to cause some alarm, especially after the rumor that Scofield and his men were down out of the uplands to seize arms. Because the Dorchester stores were guarded by only the local militia, the Council ordered Moultrie to send an officer with sufficient troops to secure the depot.

Since early November, when South Carolina had organized an artillery regiment and Elliot had been promoted to major in that unit, Marion had been the ranking captain of the Second Regiment. On November 9 Marion was selected to command the two companies detached to Dorchester. Not only was he to take special care in guarding and defending the "cannon, Gunpowder, Stores & Publick Records," but his orders stated that the Committee of Safety at Dorchester was to provide enough slaves to move the cannon "lying by the Water side, to a Spot more safe. . . ." In addition to the sixty men from his own unit, he was strengthened by twenty-nine privates from Captain Francis Huger's company. Three lieutenants made up the remainder of the officers.[21]

In the early stages of the tour, the possibility of an attack by Scofield and his Tories lent excitement to the duty. But as the dull, gray days of November and December followed one upon the other, the men grew restless and irritable. By December 10 forty-five men of his command were either on the sick list or had deserted. Marion requested that he be recalled. Before leaving he expressed his thanks to the militia officers who had served under him, "Except Capt. Wigfall." The post was turned over to the militia of Colonel Samuel Elliot and by dusk on December 18 his command was back in Charleston.[22]

His new assignment in Charleston, however, proved equally boring: remounting the guns and repairing the walls of Fort Johnson. By Christmas 1775 work was started on the fortifications on Haddrell's Point behind Sullivan's Island. On February 10, 1776 Marion's command was there, perhaps engaged in constructing a battery. Several companies of militia had been detached under his command to speed the work.

It was during this period that John Rutledge, newly elected President of the Council of Safety, decided that Sullivan's Island should be fortified. Because of the additional manpower needed to man the fortifications, the South Carolina Congress had authorized the formation of two new rifle regiments; Major McIntosh of the Second Regiment was transferred to the First Rifle Regiment and promoted to lieutenant colonel. Francis Marion, as senior captain, was elevated to major in the Second

Regiment on February 22, 1776 by the Provincial Congress. On March 1 the Second Regiment was also ordered to construct the fort on Sullivan's Island. It was just another work detail insofar as the men were concerned. But spring was coming and spring was the time for war.[23]

For some time the deposed royal governors of the southern colonies, Josiah Martin of North Carolina and William Campbell of South Carolina, had been writing to London urging that a strike be made against their former provinces. They assured Whitehall that these areas were now ripe for the picking. Then, too, they argued, Charleston would be a particularly valuable acquisition, for that port was the most important in the southern colonies; if Charleston fell, the rebels would be deprived of supplies from the outside world and the town could be used as a base from which a campaign for the subjugation of the southern colonies could be launched.

Because of the insistence of Governor Martin, the first assault was to be made against North Carolina, where it was expected that a large number of Scots Highlanders and the former Regulators in the backcountry (who had rebelled against the tidewater in 1771) would support the royal cause. After North Carolina had been secured, an attack against Charleston could be launched overland while the British fleet battered the town from the sea. The British ministry approved the plan. A junction with the North Carolina loyalists was to be made in the Cape Fear by a small detachment from Boston under General Henry Clinton and a larger force from Ireland under Charles, Lord Cornwallis. Clinton was to have the overall command of the military operations.

Nothing seemed to go right for the British. A premature uprising by the Highlanders resulted in their defeat and dispersion at the battle of Moore's Creek Bridge, February 27, 1776. Bureaucratic fumblings, foul weather, and other mishaps so delayed the sailing of Cornwallis's command that the vanguard did not

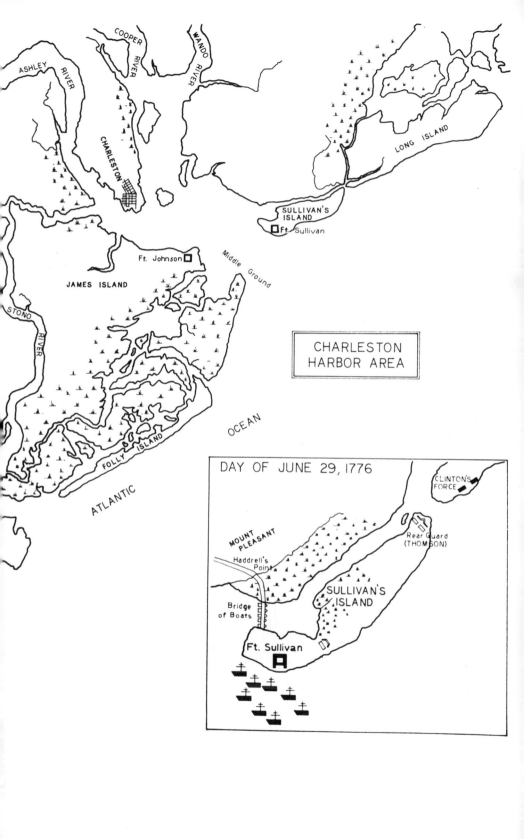

ASHLEY RIVER

COOPER RIVER

WANDO RIVER

CHARLESTON

LONG ISLAND

SULLIVAN'S ISLAND

☐ Ft. Sullivan

Ft. Johnson ☐

JAMES ISLAND

Middle Ground

STONO RIVER

FOLLY ISLAND

OCEAN

ATLANTIC

CHARLESTON HARBOR AREA

DAY OF JUNE 29, 1776

CLINTON'S FORCE

Rear Guard (THOMSON)

MOUNT PLEASANT

Haddrell's Point

SULLIVAN'S ISLAND

Bridge of Boats

Ft. Sullivan

limp into the Cape Fear until the middle of April and it was not until May 3 that the entire expedition was assembled. Because of their defeat at Moore's Creek Bridge there was no loyalist force with which to make a junction. Sir Peter Parker, commanding the fleet, persuaded Clinton that they should sail to Charleston and take that port.[24]

Back in November 1775 the Continental Congress, foreseeing a possible attack upon the port, had resolved that Charleston be fortified "immediately." But the work there had gone slowly, perhaps because that same resolution had decreed that "the expence [is] to be paid by the said Colony." [25]

The confluence of the Ashley and Cooper Rivers formed the arrowhead-shaped peninsula on which Charleston lay, thereby restricting the approach to the city by land. Bordering the mainland were low, sandy islands, most of them overrun with a tangled mass of palmettos, myrtle thickets, and scrub oaks. Usually they were separated from the mainland by turgid inlets, meandering streams, and grassy marshes. Some six miles out was the entrance to the harbor, protected by its massive sandbar, effectively blocking the passage of heavily loaded vessels of deep draught except at high tide. On the south side of the harbor lay James Island, on which stood Fort Johnson, now heavily armed and protected by an additional battery; in all there were a total of forty-three guns on the island.

Nearer Charleston, on the north side of the harbor, was Sullivan's Island, a sandy strip four miles long and only about a mile wide at high tide. To the north of Sullivan's, separated by a narrow inlet termed the "Breach," lay unfortified Long Island. To the rear of Sullivan's, at Haddrell's Point, there was a small battery. Other batteries and strongpoints had been thrown up at strategic places around the town.[26]

In late May Charleston began to take on the appearance of an armed camp. Reinforcements had come in, including a number of Virginia and North Carolina Continentals. But the aid that the South Carolinians looked forward to most was in the person of one man, Major General Charles Lee, recently appointed commanding general for the Southern Department. Lee had been a lieutenant colonel in the British Army and at one time had been a major general in the Polish Army. His arrogance had been mistaken for military talent by some who had allowed themselves to become convinced that he was the secret weapon by which the war was to be won. When the lank, sarcastic general arrived, trailed by his ever-present pack of dogs, he "excited the public ardour." Some were irritated by Lee's eccentricities, perhaps best expressed in the observation of C. C. Pinckney: "General Lee appears very clever, but is a strange animal; however . . . we must put up with ten thousand oddities in him on account of his abilities and his attachments to the rights of humanity." Others grumbled when the general sharply criticized the local soldiery who refused to do manual labor on the fortifications until forced. Still others displayed their unhappiness when he ordered buildings on the wharves to be dismantled and replaced with earthworks and other military "mince-pies."

Although work on Fort Sullivan had begun in January, it was no more than half completed in early June. The walls had been constructed of two parallel rows of palmetto logs sixteen feet apart, the interval filled with sand. The rear of the fort was as yet incomplete and invited encirclement. This redoubt and its supporting batteries contained thirty-four pieces of artillery, their sizes ranging from nine to thirty-one pounders. The Second South Carolina Regiment of 413 men and twenty-two men of the Fourth Artillery Company manned the guns and the parapets. About the middle of April Colonel William Moultrie had assumed command of the post. There was a feeling of confidence in the fort: Thomas Pinckney assured his mother, "We are now all prepared for the Reception of these Gentry whenever they may be hardy enough to attack us."

Lee had made it obvious that he didn't like Fort Sullivan,

which he had termed a "slaughter pen." Not only was there danger of encirclement, but he insisted that there was no proper route of retreat. To provide the latter, he proposed a crude pontoon bridge of planks supported by empty barrels; it proved impracticable after the bobbing structure was tested by 200 North Carolina Continentals and it sank so low in the water that they were obliged to return.[27]

There was little doubt that the British objective was Charleston. By April 26 Captain Peter Horry's company of light infantry had been stationed on Bull's Island to prevent enemy landing parties from coming ashore for fresh water or cattle.[28]

Even as defensive preparations went forward, the British fleet, estimated to be fifty-one sail, had been rocking at anchor on the far side of the bar since June 4. Over two weeks were required to remove the heavy guns from the two largest men-of-war until they rode high enough in the water to make it across the shallows.

There was a flurry of military etiquette when a boat bearing a flag of truce coming into Sullivan's Island was fired upon by an "ignorant Centry." Captain Francis Huger was sent out to make amends; his apology was accepted.[29]

A large group of infantry under Clinton and Cornwallis had been landed on Long Island on June 8. Their intelligence had suggested that the "Breach" could be forded, but now they discovered that the water was too deep to allow such a crossing, even at low tide. To oppose their passage, Lee had sent forward Colonel William Thomson's Third Regiment of South Carolina Rangers, the First North Carolina Continental Regiment, two hundred South Carolina militia, and the South Carolina "Raccoon" Company of fifty riflemen. They were supported by two artillery pieces.

On June 28, at ten in the morning, in a movement almost majestic in execution, the British fleet moved in toward the town. The naval vessels, with springs on their cables, dropped anchor some four hundred yards off Sullivan's Island and then opened up on the fort with the full force of their firepower. All that sultry June day Fort Sullivan and the enemy warships traded broadsides. Parker's ships shuddered as the balls from Moultrie's guns plowed into their hulls. British shot, on the other hand, buried itself in the sand and the spongy wood of the palmetto logs making up the walls of the fortification.

Major Francis Marion was in command of the heavy guns on the left. He, as did other officers, pointed the pieces before they were fired. All of Moultrie's guns fired slowly and deliberately, for the Colonel had only 5,400 pounds of gunpowder, and he wished to conserve the supply. At one time there was an hour's lull in the firing from the fort when they ran low on powder and many of the onlooking townspeople became convinced that the defenders had given up the fight. According to one account, it was Marion leading a small party who left the fort and removed the powder from the armed schooner *Defence* then lying in Stop Gap Creek. This allowed the fort to continue a slow methodical fire until a supply was brought over from town. It was said that Marion directed the fire of the guns in his sector with great skill.

At one time during the fight, General Lee came across to the Island "to encourage the garrison by my presence; but I might have saved myself the trouble; for I found, on my arrival, they had no occasion for any sort of encouragement: I found them cool to the last degree."

Above the fort, from an old ship's mast, flew the blue flag with its silver crescent and the word "Liberty" as designed by Moultrie. A cannonball carried away the staff, and the banner fluttered to the ground outside the walls. Sergeant William Jasper of the Grenadier Company of the Second Regiment leaped through an embrasure, fastened the flag to a sponge staff used to swab the cannon, and then, climbing back into the fort, he raised it above the walls. The watching townspeople, who had feared that the garrison had struck its colors, gave forth with a mighty cheer.

Around nine-thirty that evening the battered British vessels slipped their cables and pulled back out of range. Some said that Marion personally gave them a "parting shot" that ripped through the hull of Sir Peter Parker's flagship, the *Bristol.* In later years Peter Horry said the cannoneer was Captain Richard Shubrick. Unbeknownst to the defenders of Charleston, the ex-royal governor, Lord William Campbell, served as a volunteer commander on the second gun deck of the *Bristol* and during the action received the "contusion" that was a factor in his death two years later.

General Lee was amazed at the strong defense put up by the South Carolinians, and he fairly strutted in his dispatches. He lavished praise on Moultrie's defense of Fort Sullivan and was forced to admit that it "astonished me; it was brave to the last degree." He did not admit, however, that on the morning of the battle he had sent Colonel Francis Nash of the North Carolina Continentals to relieve Moultrie, but the British had opened fire before the exchange could take place.[30]

The British fleet in the words of Lee, "sheared off the next morning like earless dogs," and dropped down to their former anchorage. There they lay for over three weeks, patching their damaged ships before taking to the open sea. Lee, in the meantime, kept the troops working on the fortifications.

There had been a total of thirty-six casualties within Fort Moultrie. The Second Regiment had suffered a loss of ten killed and twenty-three wounded. Those who had witnessed the battle had been impressed by the "Immortal Glory of the 2d Regiment. . . ."[31]

On June 30, Marion participated in the parade as Moultrie marched his command in review before General Lee. On July 4, President Rutledge of the Provincial Congress inspected the garrison at Fort Sullivan and presented his personal short sword to Sergeant Jasper. The sergeant was also offered a lieutenant's commission but declined, giving as his reason the fact that he could not write and "was not fit to keep officers' company, being only bred a sergeant." When Mrs. Barnard Elliot presented "an elegant pair of colors" to the regiment her words were recorded in Marion's Orderly book: "Your gallant behaviour in Defense of Liberty & your Country Entitles you to the Highest Honours. Accept of these two Standards as Reward justly Due to your Regiment, I make not the least Doubt under heavens Protection you will stand by them as Long as they can wave in the Air of Liberty." Colonel Moultrie and Lieutenant Colonel Motte accepted the flags on behalf of the regiment. A resolution of the Continental Congress which praised the defenders of Charleston was followed by a letter of commendation from General Washington. General Lee sent over a hogshead of rum for the refreshment of the Second Regiment. Yet not every ceremony had been in praise of gallantry. On July 2 four soldiers who had gone absent without leave on the day of the battle were flogged with two hundred lashes each while "dress'd in Petticoats & Caps." [32]

But all in all, it was a most satisfactory way to begin a war.

Chapter II

There was little time to celebrate the victory or savor the praise. The Georgia frontier was under almost constant harassment by raiders operating out of St. Augustine and Pensacola. Florida Tories swung across the border to carry off cattle and slaves, murdering those who were so bold as to offer resistance. The Georgians cried for relief, but the South Carolinians offered little, for they well knew that the Virginia and North Carolina Continentals soon would be returning to their homes and they wished to keep their own troops at hand for their own protection. Nor were the North Carolinians and Virginians eager to march farther south; they argued that the South Carolinians should go to the aid of Georgia, just as they had come to the defense of Charleston.

The question was finally resolved with the decision that a regiment each from North Carolina and Virginia, supported by the Second South Carolina Regiment under Moultrie, would march into Georgia. As soon as Lee was positive that the British were leaving South Carolina, he began his preparations for the Georgia campaign. By late July there were frantic messages reporting British ships off Savannah. The North Carolinians under Brigadier General Robert Howe and the South Carolinians under Isaac Huger were ordered to move down to Purysburg on the Savannah River. Although he did not confide his project to many of the officers under his command, Lee was planning an expedition into East Florida as a means of relieving some of the enemy pressure on Georgia.[1]

It was during these preparations that the news arrived, on August 5, 1776, that the Continental Congress had declared the colonies independent of England. The celebration in Charleston assumed a dignified air as the chief civil authorities and high military officials paraded slowly through the street, and, said Henry Laurens "amidst loud acclamations of thousands who always huzza when a proclamation is read." The Second Regiment may have participated in the festivities, for on July 22 they had been ordered over to Charleston from Fort Sullivan.[2]

Although the Continental Congress had taken the South Carolina regiments into the Continental Army on June 18, President John Rutledge seemed reluctant to allow them to take the field on a regular army basis for fear Lee would order them out of South Carolina. The regiments were brought near full strength when Lee allowed some of the men from the North Carolina Continentals to be "translated" into the South Carolina and Georgia Continental regiments. Enough men took advantage of an additional enlistment bonus, so that Edward Rutledge, John's brother, was to later state, "We raised our complement of men in the neighboring colonies."[3]

In Georgia, those troops that had already marched suffered in the August heat. Those North Carolina Continentals stationed at Sunbury were poorly supplied, while many were clad in little more than rags. Some fourteen or fifteen died each day as a result of disease. In the midst of his preparations for his expedition, Lee was recalled to the northern army. First James Moore of North Carolina, and then after his death on April 15, 1777, Robert Howe, also of North Carolina, both major generals, were appointed commanding generals of the Southern Department. Howe had little use for the Georgia venture, terming it "a fatiguing, pointless expedition." The troops who had survived the disastrous campaign straggled back into Charleston.[4]

In November Marion received another promotion. After the South Carolina regiments had been taken into the Continental establishment, Colonels Christopher Gadsden and William Moultrie were elevated to brigadier generals. Now, on November 23, 1776, in Howe's general orders, Isaac Motte was announced as colonel of the Second Regiment, replacing Moultrie, with Francis Marion promoted to lieutenant colonel and Peter Horry as major.[5]

The regiment spent much of its time in strengthening the defenses of the town. Fort Sullivan, now renamed Fort Moultrie, was completed, and as the palmetto logs had proved so effective during the British attack, they were now placed before Fort Johnson. Because of the shortage of weapons, especially bayonets, the men were trained in the use of spears. But the boredom of such routine was getting to many of the officers of the South Carolina line, and an uncommon number of them submitted their resignations. This epidemic of resignations led Howe to declare in his general orders, November 26, 1776, "Local advantages . . . and temporary inconvenience, are but contemptible pleas for retirement. . . ."[6]

On February 23 a dispatch rider reined his heaving mount to a halt in front of General Howe's headquarters in Charleston. He brought the news that fifty men of the South Carolina Rangers under Captain Richard Winn stationed at Fort McIntosh on the Satilla River in Georgia were being attacked by the Tories and Indians. Howe ordered a detachment under Motte and Marion to relieve the post at Fort McIntosh. Howe rode off posthaste to Savannah. On February 28 Marion followed, leading six hundred men with four field pieces and an adequate supply of ammunition, entrenching tools, and provisions in several schooners. Before they reached Savannah, Winn had been forced to surrender to a British force under Major General Augustine Prevost. But the British had been checked at Ogeechee Ferry and had failed in an attempt to take the works at Sunbury. In Savannah on March 18 Motte loaded his men aboard transports and carried them back to Beaufort, from where they marched overland back to Charleston.[7]

Other than the little flurries of excitement, such as the attack on Fort McIntosh, the year 1777 was relatively quiet in the South. The regiment spent most of its time in the vicinity of Charleston. So monotonous was garrison life that the regiment dwindled in numbers, many of the men refusing to reenlist once their original terms had expired; some deserted. Colonel Motte was frequently absent from the regiment and Marion was left in command.

Marion spent most of his time training and disciplining the troops. He held a passion for tidiness, order, and discipline, and his orders constantly referred to the absence of all three in the regiment. Although basically a kind man, he was also a stern disciplinarian. His men were strangers to cleanliness and ordinary practices of good hygiene and health, and they were constantly enjoined to be as "Clean as possible." Both officers and men were cautioned not to appear at roll call barefooted. He hated the manner in which the men allowed their hair to grow. Time and time again he admonished them to wear their hair no longer than the tops of their shirt collars, for "long hair gathers filth, and takes a great deal of time and trouble to keep clean and [in] good order. . . ." For those who refused to comply in cutting, plaiting or tying up their hair there was the warning: "Any soldier who comes on parade with Beards, or hair uncomb'd, shall be dry shaved immediately, and have his hair dressed on the parade." Other practices that disturbed him were the wanton firing of weapons, drunkenness, straying away from sentry duty, plundering the inhabitants, selling military articles, and disobedience of orders. But it was the personal hygiene of the soldiers that seemed to concern him most. Repeatedly, orders similar to the one below appeared in his orderly book:

This filthy custom of the Soldiers doing their Occasions in and around the fort has already made a Disagreeable smell in Garrison which must bring Disorders on every individual if not prevented— all Officers to be particular in bringing every man to a Court Marshal who are guilty of such vile practices.

There were frequent courts martial.[8]

His men, according to Peter Horry, loved him and "Marion wished his officers to be gentlemen. Whenever he saw one of them acting below that character, he would generously attempt his reformation." At times he was strict with his officers, enough so that one young lieutenant was led to characterize him as "an ugly, cross, knock kneed, hook-nosed son of a bitch." Moultrie noted that Marion was the "architect of the Second Regiment." Yet, despite his efforts, the Colonel was not too sure of his men. When on June 28, 1777, in celebration of the anniversary of the victory over the British, the ladies of the town gave a "Genteel dinner" for the men, and the officers added a hogshead of claret and three barrels of beer for the troops, there was a note of apprehension in regimental orders:

Col. Marion hopes the men will behave with Sobriety & Decency in honour to those Ladies who have been so kind as to give them so genteel a treat, for Soldiers being seen in the Street Drunk or Riotous, will be a scandal to the Regiment, and prevent any firther notice being taken of them. He hopes they will keep in the Barracks, and not a man go in town that day & should any man be Overtaken in liquor, the Sergeants & Corporals will have them put quietly in their Barracks. . . .[9]

On September 23, 1777, Colonel Motte resigned the command of the Second Regiment. Although Marion was elevated to the command, his rank still remained lieutenant colonel. The active commanders of British regiments were lieutenant colonels, for most of the regular colonels now held the rank of general, and this, in turn, complicated the exchange of prisoners. When the British refused to exchange a captured Continental colonel for a British lieutenant colonel, the Continental Congress, on May 28, 1778, resolved to cease promoting regimental commanders to colonel. This was to remain Marion's rank as a Continental officer until September 1783.

For the remainder of the year the Second Regiment remained on garrison duty at Fort Moultrie. This was something of a post of honor, for it was felt that the British would attempt to erase the humiliation of their defeat at Charleston and that Fort Moultrie would be their initial objective. Marion still drilled his men in the ways of soldiers, with both officers and men on the parade ground every afternoon. He still worked at having them appear more soldierlike, even to having the men on guard duty powder their hair. The sound of the lash was heard frequently on the parade, as miscreants—especially deserters—received their 99 or 100 with a cat o' nine tails or a switch. The regiment was understrength with only 214 men, and recruiting parties roamed the state. An increasing number of officers resigned and Marion's orders were they were "no longer to be respected and obeyed as a Continental Officer."

There was a slight change in the uniforms of the regiment. On June 12, 1778, General Moultrie issued orders that all officers were to acquire leather caps according to the pattern left with one Callahan, a saddler in Charleston. Moultrie also issued another order that was to change Marion's personal habits. The general ordered regular portions of vinegar to be issued to the regiment because of its medicinal value. It has been said that from this time on Marion's favorite drink became a mixture of vinegar and water, a brew some called the "drink of the Roman soldier."

There was one bit of sorrow when, on October 26, his friend Barnard Elliot died. The following day Marion served as a pall-bearer while the Grenadier Company of the Second Regiment acted as honor guard. The silk standards presented to the regiment by Elliot's wife were carried in the funeral procession.[10]

Despite the tedium of garrison duty, there was promise of action in the near future. From the Continental Congress came warnings that the British were probably contemplating making the southern states the object of their next major offensive. Some guessed this to be the result of a longing by "General Clinton to gratify a personal picque, to convince the world of his prowess & to wipe away the stain which the British had suffered in a former attempt upon Charlestown. . . ." In late December 1778, there had also been the report of one William Haslan, a North Carolina loyalist who had served aboard the British transport, *Neptune*. Haslan stated that the British fleet was recently reported to have sailed from New York for Savannah. Orders issued just before they sailed, reported Haslan, were "to burn and destroy all who would not submit." [11]

There had also been a change in the top level of command in the South. For some time South Carolina politicians had been unhappy with Robert Howe, and as early as August 20, 1777, the State Assembly had passed a resolution questioning Howe's right to command in that state. In addition, there was the general's unhappy quarrel with Christopher Gadsden, with Gadsden becoming so inflamed that he had resigned his military commission. When Gadsden refused to retract his criticism of Howe's operations, the affair had come to a climax in August 1778, when the two had decided to settle their differences on the field of honor. Howe's bullet had grazed Gadsden's ear, while the latter had fired into the air. Yet some whispered that

Howe's recall was because of a "little ridiculous matter he has been concerned with in South Carolina, with regard to a female, [which] has induced the Delegates of Georgia and South Carolina to desire his recall." Major General Benjamin Lincoln of Massachusetts was appointed Howe's successor in command of the Southern Department.[12]

In September 1778, Howe had been notified of his recall and ordered north to join Washington's army as soon as possible after Lincoln's arrival. But because the Tories and Indians were acting up in Georgia, Howe went down to Savannah instead.

While he was there a British fleet transporting 3,500 troops from New York under Lieutenant Colonel Archibald Campbell dropped anchor off Savannah. They attacked the town on December 29, 1778. Howe put up as good a defense as he could, with troops numbering one-fourth of those of the enemy and with no cooperation from local authorities. However, he was forced to withdraw and give up the town to the enemy.[13]

Lincoln, in the meantime, arrived in Charleston in early December, and sometime around the first of January 1779, started marching toward Georgia. When Moultrie left with Lincoln, he appointed Marion temporary commandant of Charleston and also charged him with sending on men and supplies to the army. Major Peter Horry commanded the regiment.

When Lincoln came within twenty-eight miles of Savannah he received a dispatch from Howe informing him that the town had fallen to the enemy. Lincoln then proceeded to gather an army of Continentals and militia at Purysburg. Marion experienced difficulty supplying Lincoln's troops, for, among other things, it was difficult to "git" a commissary who would accept such a low-paying position. Wagons were equally hard to come by. On February 22 Moultrie had ordered that 150 men be detached from the Second Regiment under the command of Horry and marched to Purysburg. Captain Motte took over the command of what was left of the regiment. Lincoln needed all the reinforcements that he could get, for a portion of his force, mostly militia under John Ashe of North Carolina, was routed at Brier Creek on March 2, 1779.[14]

Lincoln refused to allow this setback to deter him; in fact, he began to grow ambitious as reinforcements flowed into his camp. Leaving approximately a thousand men under General Moultrie to defend the base at Purysburg, on April 23 Lincoln crossed the Savannah River and marched for Augusta with a design for cutting the British line of communications with the backcountry and forcing the enemy in close to Savannah so that the Georgia Legislature, scheduled to meet in Augusta the first of May, might be free of molestation.

General Augustine Prevost, commanding British troops in Georgia, kept a close watch on Lincoln's movements. To draw Lincoln out of Georgia, Prevost, with 2,400 men and a large number of Indians, slipped across the Savannah into South Carolina on April 29. As Prevost swung toward Moultrie at Purysburg, the South Carolina general retreated, destroying bridges as he fell back. Riders were dispatched to advise Lincoln of this development and to warn the citizens of Charleston. Lincoln was not too alarmed, for he was convinced that the British thrust was little more than a diversion "to divide, distract and perplex us in our operations." During the night of May 7, 1779, Moultrie marched into Charleston, to be received in happy acclaim by the terrified inhabitants, who had fallen into "a strange consternation in Town, people frightened out of their wits. . . ."[15]

Had Prevost driven straight through to the gates of Charleston, the city might well have fallen to him. But the plantation homes along his route, with their promise of booty, were as effective in slowing the British march as a strong rear-guard action. Prevost even went so far as to weaken himself by detaching men to escort flour and other plunder back to Georgia. Not until May 9 did the British vanguard of eight hundred men cross the Ashley and move down Charleston Neck, there to be confronted by hastily thrown up earthworks and abatis. Marion and a hundred men of the Second Regiment had been pulled out of Fort Moultrie and had been stationed in a redoubt anchoring the left flank of the defensive line. Shortly afterward they were returned to Fort Moultrie in case the British attempted to come into Charleston by water.

Not much in the way of military action developed. Count Casimir Pulaski, the volunteer Polish nobleman who had but recently arrived with his ill-disciplined legion of infantry and mounted troops, went out from Charleston to meet the enemy on the morning of May 11. Setting up an ambush, he sallied forth with eighty men in an attempt to lure enemy dragoons into his trap. The plan failed miserably; Pulaski received a sound thrashing when some of his men broke from their concealment too soon and gave the plan away. The only other action occurred one night when a detachment under Major Benjamin Huger went out to strengthen a gap in the lines by placing wagons as temporary barricades. Someone neglected to inform Moultrie of the venture, and when the activity was spotted, the defenders of the town opened with artillery and small arms fire. Major Huger and seven or eight of his men were killed.[16]

John Rutledge, now Governor of South Carolina, suggested to Moultrie that a parley be arranged with the enemy. The flag that went out carried the message: "General Moultrie, perceiving from the motions of your army that your intentions are to besiege the town, would be glad to know on what terms you would be disposed to grant a capitulation should he be inclined to capitulate."

Prevost's reply that he would accept only an unconditional surrender of the town was countered by the amazing proposal of

Governor Rutledge: the city would be turned over to the enemy if Prevost would guarantee the neutrality of the harbor and the rest of South Carolina for the remainder of the war!

Prevost again replied that unconditional surrender was the only terms he would consider. While his answer was being discussed at the Governor's quarters, Captain Thomas Dunbar rode in with a message from Lieutenant Colonel Marion. He reported that the British had noted the continuing work on the fortifications during the exchange of messages, and Prevost had sent in a warning that unless the work came to an immediate halt, he would attack.

Before Prevost could muster an assault, however, an intercepted letter from General Lincoln revealed that he was making a forced march to come to the relief of Charleston. Should he come up on Prevost's rear while an attack upon the city was in progress, the British risked being caught between two fires. During the night of May 12, Prevost filed off to camp on Johns Island to await water transportation back to Georgia. To protect his rear, earthworks were thrown up on the mainland at Stono Ferry.[17]

Shortly after the withdrawal of the enemy, Lincoln arrived in the vicinity of Charleston and his army went into camp at Dorchester. Although the Second Regiment was pulled out of Fort Moultrie and held in readiness to march at a moment's notice, it sat idle in Charleston. By June 16 Prevost began to embark his army in transports. The great bulk of the booty and slaves gathered on the march through South Carolina was first put on board. A detachment of nine hundred regulars, Hessians, and Tories was left to man the redoubt and cover the embarkation. On June 15 Lincoln met with his officers and Governor Rutledge and decided to move against the enemy at Stono Ferry. But Lincoln was never a man to make a hasty move, and it was not until June 19 that a council of officers decided the attack should be made the following day.

Moultrie, as Lincoln's second in command, was to lead a force from Charleston and move down to James Island, where he could be seen by Prevost, who could then send no reinforcements to Stono. The South Carolina Continentals under his command included the First, Third, and Sixth Regiments formed into a brigade under Charles Cotesworth Pinckney. Of Marion's command, 210 troops remained in Fort Moultrie; others were stationed in Charleston. Boats were carried by Moultrie's men to ferry themselves over to John's Island to "tread on their heels if possible," and to cooperate with Lincoln's main force once the attack on the redoubt began. For some reason Moultrie did not immediately execute his orders; it was whispered that his procrastination was deliberate so that he might enjoy the conviviality of a social event in Charleston that evening. Moultrie's excuse was that he was awaiting boats from Ashley Ferry. By the time his detachment reached James Island (a different island), they had lost the tide in Wappoo Inlet and the current was flowing too swiftly to use the small boats. Some complained that "from mismanagement they did not reach their place of destination until the action was over."

In the meantime, in an engagement lasting over two hours, Lincoln had thrown his force against the British redoubt at Stono Ferry. He finally drew off his men as each side harassed the other by a desultory long-range fire. Moultrie partially atoned for his late arrival by sending out two large row galleys from James Island to capture a British schooner loaded with plundered household goods. Three days after the battle the enemy moved down to Port Royal Island, thereby ending the threat to Charleston.[18]

For Marion and the men of the Second Regiment back at Fort Moultrie, the routine of garrison duty followed this flush of excitement. Activity was mostly confined to the mounting of guards and hours of drill under a hot sun, which was made more intense as it was reflected off the white sand.

Farther to the south, it appeared that Georgia had once again become a British colony, so much so that Sir James Wright had returned to reassume his duties as royal governor. Savannah was garrisoned by 2,400 troops, a large number of whom were loyalists.

All during the late spring and early summer of 1779, the Continental Congress, General Lincoln, Governor Rutledge, and the French Consul at Charleston, Monsieur Plombard, had sent urgent appeals for aid to Admiral-General Count Charles Hector Théodat d'Estaing, commanding the French fleet in the West Indies. The admiral had returned to the islands after the dismal failure of the joint French-American attempt to dislodge the British from Rhode Island in August 1778. His standing orders allowed him to extend aid to the Americans when he deemed it wise. In fact, General Washington also expected to receive some help in his northern operations from the eccentric Frenchman.

But Count d'Estaing was a man of many whims and sudden impulses, and he suddenly decided to go to the southern mainland. Word was dispatched to Charleston, by five ships, that he was sailing for Savannah with thirty-three naval vessels and four thousand soldiers. He was firm in his insistence that he would operate in American waters for only two weeks, for to remain longer would expose his ships to the possible dangers of the hurricane season.[19]

This announcement, on September 3, 1779, took Lincoln and everyone else by surprise. Rising from a sickbed, the general gathered every available man and marched southward through the piney woods toward Savannah. The 214 men of Marion's regiment had been alerted on September 5, and his orders were to provide his men with sixty rounds of ammunition and hold them ready to march at a moment's notice. The ninety North Carolina Continentals then in Charleston were placed under his command, although Marion complained they were "Intirely

Naked, none have any Shirts or Shoes." On September 16 Lincoln's column marched into the Frenchman's camp, pitched beneath the moss-hung oaks some three miles below Savannah. His own command encamped at Bard's Plantation a mile nearer the town.

To Lincoln's consternation, he discovered the haughty admiral had already summoned the garrison to surrender to the "Army of His Most Christian Majesty," omitting any reference to his American allies. But in Augustine Prevost, d'Estaing found a master of procrastination, who asked for, and received, twenty-four hours to consider the terms. He also requested that the women and children be allowed to leave the town. This gave time for him to strengthen his works and for additional troops to come from Beaufort under the command of Lieutenant Colonel John Maitland, who was guided into the city by a black Gullah fisherman who had led them through a watery wasteland described by a newspaper as seldom traveled before "but by bears, wolves and runaway Negroes." This reinforcement raised Prevost's command to 3,200 men. It was then that he began to act "strong and so very saucy," and sent out word that he would fight.

Even d'Estaing was forced to admit that allowing time was "an unpardonable mistake, which decided the ill success of the expedition." When the Frenchman's actions were first reported to Marion, he flew into an intense rage; Peter Horry was "actually afraid he would have broken out on General Lincoln." But when he discovered it was d'Estaing who had acted so rashly, Marion burst out with, "My God! Who ever heard of anything like this before? First allow an enemy to entrench and then fight him!" [20]

No sooner was the truce over than it began to rain, the ground becoming a quagmire, making the task of moving heavy artillery forward a more difficult task. At first Moultrie urged an immediate assault upon the town before the British managed

35

to further strengthen it, but d'Estaing decided, apparently unsupported by Lincoln, that a siege would be the most prudent course of action. As soon as the soggy ground had dried, siege lines were opened on September 23. Artillery was muscled forward fourteen miles from the landing place into the lines. On October 1 the guns began a methodical fire that saturated the town.

The arrogance of d'Estaing and many of his officers led to increasing friction between the allies. Even those inside the town became aware of the growing animosity. Colonel John Harris Cruger of the New York Volunteers, noted that the Americans were "so much despised by the french as not to be allowed to go into their Camp, no communication together."

Marion seemed equally disgusted with his own men. Once they were away from garrison duty, the troops of the Second Regiment had reverted to their old sloppy manners. Now they were wearing their hats uncocked and going barelegged. Their hair had grown long and many refused to shave, all of which, Marion complained made "them appear more like wild Savages than Soldiers."

As the days dragged by, d'Estaing grew impatient with the monotony of siege operations and was perhaps a bit chagrined that Prevost had outwitted him in the early negotiations and was now apparently withstanding the siege. His naval captains were urging that the siege be abandoned, for the fleet needed repairs, the hurricane season was at hand, and an average of thirty-five seamen were dying every day of scurvy. Although ten days had elapsed of the fifteen that d'Estaing had now allowed for the siege, the lines were still incomplete and French engineers estimated that at least another ten days' work would be needed to complete them. Over the angry protests of Lincoln and a number of French army officers, d'Estaing decided to make an all-out frontal attack upon the town. There was little that Lincoln could do but agree with the mad scheme.

During the early morning hours of October 9, 1779, five columns, three of them French, were to advance against the town with a total force of 3,500 Frenchmen and 1,500 Americans. One of the American columns was to be made up of the First and Fifth South Carolina Continentals, supported by a few Georgia regulars, all under the command of Brigadier General Lachlan McIntosh. The second, composed of Marion's Second South Carolina Continentals and the Charleston militia, would be under the command of Brigadier General Isaac Huger and Colonel John Laurens. Marion's Second Regiment was to act in support of Laurens and the light infantry.

From the very beginning one error compounded another until it became obvious that without a miracle the venture could end only in disaster. A deserter—some say it was Sergeant Major James Curry of the Charleston militia—saw to it that the enemy was informed of the time and nature of the attack. The Frenchmen were late in arriving at the line of departure, and when they did finally come up, d'Estaing led them to the attack before the other two columns were properly in position. A heavy fog blanketed the field. Little mistakes and the lack of communications made the situation even more confusing. The French columns advanced and were thrown back by a galling fire, their ranks riddled by grapeshot.

The objective of the South Carolina Continentals and militia was the strong Spring Hill redoubt. Marion's Second Regiment was now moved forward and spearheaded the attack as his and Laurens's men flung themselves against the ramparts. This work was defended by dismounted dragoons and Lieutenant Colonel Thomas Brown's regiment of South Carolina loyalists. By the time that Laurens's command had started forward, the enemy had been alerted by the French effort and the American column was subjected to a heavy frontal and enfilade fire. Marion led his men across the moat and into the abatis amidst a hail of musketry. Lieutenant James Bush carried forward the blue banner of the Second Regiment. He was felled by a shot from the redoubt. As he dropped he handed the flag to Sergeant William Jasper. Jasper started forward. He fell, mortally wounded, but at the same time handed the flag back to Bush who was once again on his feet. As Bush staggered forward he was hit a second time, falling into the ditch with the banner beneath his body. Before he was killed, Lieutenant James Gray planted the Regiment's second banner, a red one, on the berm, the ledge between the ditch and base of the parapet. A French soldier also managed to take the fleur-de-lis of France to the walls of the Spring Hill redoubt.

The parapet was found to be too steep and too high to scale while under fire. The retreat was ordered. Before he fell back, Sergeant Allen McDonald grabbed the red flag and dashed back down the hill with the other South Carolinians. As Laurens's men began to retreat, the British counterattacked with a small company of marines and the grenadiers of the Sixtieth Regiment. In fierce hand-to-hand fighting they managed to dislodge those tenacious few who had managed to cling to forward positions. Lachlan McIntosh brought up his troops in support, but because of the retreat and general confusion of the moment, he was also forced to withdraw.

It had been a bloody fight, and a British officer reported that "many hung dead and wounded on the abatis," while "the plain was strewed with mangled bodies." Between them, the casualties suffered by the allies numbered sixteen officers and 228 rank and file killed, and sixty-three officers and 521 men wounded— almost one-fifth of the total force engaged in the assault. Among those receiving a mortal wound was the colorful Pole, Count Pulaski. He had been attempting to lead his cavalry in a foolhardy charge between the Spring Hill redoubt and the works to the west and had been caught in the abatis. Colonel Daniel Horry had assumed the command and had attempted to complete the mission, but he was unable to stem the retreat that began when Pulaski fell.

The South Carolinians lost about one-fourth of those engaged. The dead were buried in one great common grave. Prevost later reported that he buried 203 rebels around the Spring Hill redoubt and twenty-eight over to the left of that post. There had been 116 pounded prisoners taken, many of whom died later. Both William Jasper and Pulaski were put aboard ships to be transported back to Charleston; both died at sea.

British losses were comparatively small, with General Clinton's official returns listing sixteen killed and thirty-nine wounded. Figures given in other sources report that there were forty killed, sixty-three wounded, and fifty-two missing.[21]

Despite the outcome, there was a feeling that the town could be taken. Charles Cotesworth Pinckney wrote his mother that "This Repulse seems not to dispirit our Men, as they are convinced it was only owing to a mistake of the Ground." Lincoln wished to continue the siege, but d'Estaing, who had been wounded, wanted nothing more to do with Savannah. His crews were sick and his army had suffered a mauling. Lincoln's pleas fell on deaf ears, and on October 18 the siege was lifted. The following day Lincoln pulled his troops back across the Savannah. The next day the French began their evacuation and, as one British officer noted, "descended to a degree of civility we had hitherto been strangers to."

The Continental failure to retake Savannah meant that the British now held a base from which an extensive campaign could be launched against the southern states. Yet, in retrospect, had the attack succeeded and the enemy been forced to give up the town, Francis Marion would still probably have received little notice except as the capable commanding officer of a South Carolina Continental regiment. Without Savannah, the British might well have abandoned their plans for a southern campaign.[22]

After crossing the Savannah, Lincoln had halted briefly at Ebenezer Heights and then had encamped on Bull's Plantation at Sheldon. He continued to Charleston, leaving the South

Carolina survivors of Savannah at Sheldon under the overall command of Lieutenant Colonel Francis Marion. There they continued for the next three months.

The duty was more monotonous than garrison duty in Charleston, for Sheldon offered little in the way of amusement for the soldiers. Most of the activity was confined to scrounging provisions and hunting down deserters who had fled up the Savannah River. By early December Marion was reporting the "Destress of the Soldiers, for want of Shoes, they are without & doing Duty in the field, in Exceeding Cold & frost." The men were kept busy building huts of logs and earth against the chill of winter. There was some trouble when the men started pulling down the local church to secure bricks for their shelters. They were too weak to attack and could not easily retreat because there were no baggage wagons. The militia under Marion's command were constantly harassed and plundered by wandering bands of Negroes, leading to several "Scrimages" with the blacks, but without loss on either side. He also managed to capture some South Carolina whites who held a "Plundering pass" issued by Prevost. On Christmas day, Marion issued an angry reprimand when the men celebrated the holiday by firing their muskets. Although Lincoln could offer him little help, he was impressed with the "pains you have taken to Accomodate the Men."

There was also a dispute involving rank, when Colonel Garden of the South Carolina militia, because of his higher rank, attempted to assume the command of the Continentals. He had no right to do this and Marion resisted and was upheld by both Moultrie and Lincoln.[23]

There was a bit of business to get out of the way. The Continental Congress had directed that the six South Carolina regiments on the Continental establishment, none of which had their full complement of men, be reduced to three. On Governor Rutledge's suggestion, Marion called the officers together to seek their opinions as to the reduction and reorganization of the regiments. By January 20, 1780, it had been decided that the three regiments would be commanded by Lieutenant Colonels Francis Marion, William Scott, and William Henderson, with Isaac Harleston, Edmund Hyrne, and Thomas Pinckney as majors. Those twenty-seven captains who were to serve in the reorganized regiments were selected on the basis of seniority. Some of those who were chosen were unhappy with the reorganization and refused to return to their commands, preferring to sulk at their homes.

Those officers who were not selected for the new units were declared supernumerary and were to return to their homes until there was a vacancy in their rank. Among those declared supernumerary was thirty-two-year-old Peter Horry, who had served with Marion since the formation of the Second Regiment. As a captain he had commanded the light infantry; later he had risen to major and was Marion's second in command. On October 19, 1779, when the Fifth Regiment had been formed, he had been given command of that unit and promoted to lieutenant colonel. In the consolidated regiments he could not be considered for the command of any one of the three, for his date of rank as a lieutenant colonel was too recent. Horry rode off to his home to await a call to return to duty.[24]

Marion had grown tired of Sheldon and wanted to return to Charleston. He had not long to wait.

Chapter III

Now that they held Savannah, it was fairly certain that the next major objective of the British would be Charleston. Word had been received from the Continental Congress suggesting that this was the case. Washington had also detached the North Carolina and Virginia Continentals from the Northern army; even now they were marching to the defense of Charleston.

Fearing that the British might strike overland from Savannah, Lincoln ordered Marion to secure intelligence of British operations in the Savannah area. From his post at Sheldon, Marion constantly sent patrols across the Savannah River.

By December 24, 1779, the first British transports had weighed anchor in New York and had dropped down to Sandy Hook. It had not been given out as to where they were going, but Henry Laurens wrote "their Destination is so well ascertained as to be out of Doubt. . . ." The weather worked to the advantage of the Charlestonians. The fleet had cleared Sandy

Hook on December 26, but the following voyage of thirty-eight days was made horrendous by turbulent weather. North Edisto Inlet, just south of Charleston, had been their original destination, but that landing had been by-passed in favor of putting into Savannah for repairs and allowing the troops an opportunity to regain their health. By January 30, 1780, the first arrivals were rocking at anchor off Tybee Island.

On January 23, a British cargo vessel had been "decoyed" into Charleston harbor and captured. Her papers indicated that Charleston was definitely the object of British attention. This was confirmed less than a week later when Commodore Abraham Whipple, in command of the tiny fleet of Continental vessels in Charleston, captured and brought in two sloops that had been transporting around fifty British dragoons. From them and the latest intelligence reports it was learned that the enemy's plans called for a complete subjugation of both Carolinas by May and that the attack upon Charleston could involve a different strategy than that employed in 1776. Clinton, it was reported, "will make a Rigorous push for it, for . . . he thinks it necessary to do something to distinguish himself before he returns to England." [1]

On January 31, in an effort to consolidate his strength, Lincoln recalled all outlying units, leaving only a little over 200 light infantry and cavalry in the field to observe British operations in Georgia and possibly give the alarm should they make a push from that quarter. The light infantry were to be organized from 227 of the best men under Marion's command at Sheldon, and he was to command them until the arrival of Lieutenant Colonel William Henderson, after which he was to return to Charleston.

It wasn't much of a regiment that he led back to Charleston. Because of the hard duty in Georgia and the depreciation of the Continental currency with which the soldiers were paid, the Second Regiment was only one-third of its authorized strength. Governor Rutledge called out the militia and ordered Moultrie to establish a receiving station at Bacon's Bridge near Dorchester. In February Marion was dispatched to this post by Lincoln, his mission to properly train these occasional soldiers, and "in his hands they lost the rude and inefficient character, the inexpert and spiritless manner, which, under ordinary commanders always distinguish them." [2]

Marion didn't stay long at Bacon's Bridge. On February 11, to the accompaniment of alarm guns in Charleston, British transports hove to off North Edisto Inlet and began disembarking troops on Simmon's Island. A post was secured at Stono Ferry and from there Sir Henry Clinton gradually worked his troops on to James Island. On March 6 Fort Johnson was taken by an attack from the rear. By February 19 Marion was back in command of his regiment, working his men at strengthening the fortifications around the city which, "like mushrooms . . . sprang from the soil." [3]

With the approach of the British, the State Assembly, sitting in Charleston, hastily adjourned. Before they did, they delegated almost dictatorial powers to Governor Rutledge, justifying their action with, "Whereas, in times of danger and invasion, it has always been the policy of republics to concentrate the powers of government in the hands of a supreme magistracy for a limited time." Until ten days after the meeting of the next legislature, Rutledge, and such members of his council as were available, were endowed with "a power to do every thing necessary for the public good; except the taking away the life of a citizen, without a legal trial." This body also approved a resolution of the Continental Congress "to defend the town to the utmost extremity." Rutledge had almost immediately put his new authority into effect, impressing some six hundred slaves and putting them to work on the fortifications. [4]

The approach of the enemy was not allowed to interfere with Charleston social life. About March 19 Moultrie's adjutant general, Captain Alexander McQueen, gave a dinner party at his home on the corner of Orange and Tradd streets. Among the invited guests was Francis Marion. McQueen liked to give parties, and apparently his idea of a good time was to get roaring drunk along with all of his guests. Following a custom of the day, he locked the doors after dinner and began to propose innumerable toasts to liberty and victory. Marion was a light drinker; in fact one source typed him as "abstemious." He also was an obstinate individual who had no intention of being forced into any personal activity of which he did not approve. Rather than create a scene, he began to look around for a way to escape the party. A second-story window stood open. He dropped from it to the ground below, striking the ground at an awkward angle. One of his already weak ankles was broken "in a shocking manner." Peter Horry was to note that "When the story got about in Charleston, most people said he was a great fool for his pains, but the event soon proved Marion was in the right, and there is no policy like sticking to a man's duty." [5]

On March 20 Admiral Marriott Arbuthnot had lightened his heavy ships enough to start bringing them across the bar. On the 29th Clinton crossed the Ashley River in force, and on April 1 he began laying out the saps and parallels in the classic manner of European siege warfare.

On April 12 Lincoln persuaded Governor Rutledge and some of his council to leave town "to preserve the Executive Authority of the State." Lieutenant Governor Christopher Gadsden and five members of the Council remained behind to carry on the functions of civil authority. The general also issued orders directing "all supernumerary officers and all officers who are unfit for duty" to leave Charleston. Among the latter was Francis Marion, and, with his usefulness temporarily at an end, he was carried out of town on a litter.

He went into hiding among his relatives along the Santee River and, said Moultrie, was "obliged to sculk from house to house among his friends, and sometimes hide in the bushes until

45

he grew better." He was by no means safe, for British detachments rode through the countryside rooting out rebels. But he remained safely hidden until news came that, on May 12, 1780, Charleston had surrendered when, in the words of one British officer, "Lincoln limped out at the head of the most ragged rabble I ever behold." This disaster in turn endangered Marion's personal safety, for it now meant that additional troops could be released to search out suspected rebels and eradicate the last vestiges of rebellion.[6]

Peter Horry put on his uniform to prevent his being taken and accused of being a spy, and then rode 120 miles to Camden to offer his services to Governor Rutledge and Brigadier General Isaac Huger who were there. They advised him to travel on into North Carolina and join the army under Baron de Kalb, the ranking American Major General in the South after Lincoln's capture.[7]

Although his ankle was still so painful that he had to be helped on and off his horse, Marion had also dressed himself in his uniform and with Oscar, his faithful black body servant, crossed the Santee. At Little River he stopped for a visit with his brother Isaac and then rode on into North Carolina, hoping to catch up with that remnant of the Southern Army that had been marching to the relief of Charleston when that city surrendered. Along the way he was joined by several friends. Behind them they left a state that had been caught up in the throes of one convulsion after another and, despite British claims, was not so complacent under the heavy heel of the conqueror as appeared on the surface.

Marion probably left at a good time, for the British were attempting to consolidate their gains and wipe out any pockets of resistance that might still be active. Shortly after the fall of Charleston, Sir Henry Clinton sent three columns into the interior of South Carolina to strengthen the British hold upon the state. One group moved westward toward the village of

Ninety Six, while another marched southward toward Augusta. The main column was under Clinton's second in command, Charles, Lord Cornwallis, major general in His Majesty's Army and the man scheduled to replace Clinton as commanding general in the South when Clinton returned to New York.

On May 18 Cornwallis, with 2,500 infantry and mounted troops and five field pieces, moved from the East branch of the Cooper River northward toward the Santee. His destination was Camden, his mission to investigate the rumors that a rebel force was gathering there. While he was awaiting boats to ferry his command across the river, Banastre Tarleton and his green-jacketed British Legion were detached to Georgetown on the strength of a rumor that a group of insurgents were assembling in the vicinity. Tarleton's dragoons swept through the area, dispersing rebels and collecting oaths of allegiance from those who had not fled. Discovering the rumor to be false, Tarleton rejoined the army.

Cornwallis found that the force supposed to be collecting at Camden was retreating northward. It had been composed of a brigade of North Carolina militia under Brigadier General William Caswell, along with 350 Virginia Continental dragoons commanded by Colonel Abraham Buford, who had been marching to the relief of Charleston when they heard of that city's capitulation. The combined force split, with the militia falling back on Cross Creek, while Buford's command started marching for Hillsborough in North Carolina.

Cornwallis felt that there was little to fear from the North Carolina militia and paid little attention to Caswell's command. Tarleton, however, was sent in pursuit of Buford. Mounting the infantry of his legion behind his cavalry, he covered 154 miles in fifty-four hours, a number of his horses dying under the strain of carrying their double burden. He caught Buford in the community known as the Waxhaws near the North Carolina border. Tarleton sent forward a demand that Buford surrender before he actually came in sight of his quarry. Not knowing the size of Tarleton's force, Buford refused. That afternoon, May 29, Tarleton came up with Buford in open woods and charged in amongst the Virginians. After the British swept through them, Buford raised the white flag and had his men ground their arms. Paying no attention to this request for quarter, Tarleton led his men forward with bayonet and saber. Buford and a few of his men managed to escape the slaughter; 113 of the Virginians were killed and over 200 wounded. Tarleton's losses were 5 killed and 14 wounded.

In his pursuit of Buford, Tarleton had almost bagged Governor Rutledge, who was staying at Clermont, the home of Colonel Henry Rugely, twelve miles north of Camden. Although holding a commission in the loyalist militia, Rugely was also conscious of the obligations of a host. When he heard Tarleton was coming, he awakened his guest and suggested that he be on his way. Rutledge galloped off toward Charlotte, North Carolina.[8]

Tarleton was not a man to win loyalty and respect for the British cause. Two days after the massacre in the Waxhaws, one of his lieutenants cut down a Quaker lad in his own front yard. That same day two young boys were accused of firing upon the column; one was hanged, the other forced into the British Army as his punishment.

But the population appeared quiescent. From around South Carolina came such reports as: "The most violent Rebels are candid enough to admit the Game is up and are coming in to make their submission in great numbers." Charleston's *Royal Gazette* boasted that there was "NOT A REBEL IN ARMS IN THE COUNTRY." Some militiamen, it was reported, were taking and bringing in their former officers as prisoners to the British. Some of the more violent rebels, ran the story, had fled their homes and gone to live among the Catawba Indians. And on June 10 Alexander MacDonald wrote home to Scotland, "This

Country is now intirely conquered; the People crowd in from all quarters to deliver up their arms. . . ." Yet as among all conquered peoples, there was a seething undercurrent of hatred in the South awaiting an opportunity to surface.[9]

Clinton, on May 22, issued a proclamation offering a pardon to all those who came and professed allegiance to the crown and indicating there would be eventual self-government under which the people would be taxed only by their own Assembly. Many persons, convinced that they had been abandoned by the Continental Congress, flocked in to take the oath, especially since there was a recurring rumor that the Congress was going to cede the three southernmost states to Great Britain. So strong did the rumor become that on June 23, 1780 the Congress was forced to resolve "that the said report is insidious and utterly devoid of Foundation."

But there was unhappiness, especially among many of those whom the British had elevated to power. As a means of keeping the rebels down and the loyalists in control, on June 3 Clinton issued a new proclamation. Those paroles previously granted were pronounced void, and those who refused to take "an active part in settling and securing His Majesty's government" would be considered enemies. Then, on June 8, 1780, satisfied that South Carolina was back safe within the royal fold, he and Admiral Arbuthnot sailed back to New York, leaving Lord Cornwallis in command of southern operations. A number of his officers in the field felt Clinton's last proclamation to be "unfortunate" and some feared "unfavourable consequences," while Cornwallis declared that it "did not at all contribute to the success of my operations." [10]

Despite optimism on the part of the British, the second revolution in South Carolina had begun within two weeks after the fall of Charleston. When the home of Thomas Sumter near Statesburgh was burned by Captain Charles Campbell of Tarleton's Legion, said William James, he "roused the spirit of a lion." On May 28 Sumter left his smouldering home and took to the field. He moved through the Catawba lands collecting a partisan force, disrupting British foraging parties, and disarming loyalists. He was soon joined by a force under Colonel William Hill. On June 14, 1780 Sumter's followers had elected him as their general, although Governor Rutledge was not to commission him as brigadier general of militia until October 6. Their numbers swelled after Captain Christian Huck of Tarleton's legion burned the Aetna Iron Works operated by Hill and Isaac Hayne. On July 11, in a pitched battle at James Williamson's plantation, they met and defeated a party under Captain Huck, killing between thirty and forty, including Huck, and wounding about fifty. Only twelve of Huck's party escaped (some say as many as twenty-four). Sumter had one man killed. His success led many to come in to join him, swelling the total number under his command to about six hundred men.

Huck's defeat had upset Cornwallis's evaluation of the situation. On July 4 the general had written his brother William that the "Province of South Carolina has totally submitted, and American affairs wear a better aspect than they have done for some time." His optimism had led him to overlook the rebellious attitude that was seeping through other areas of the state.[11]

Admiral Arbuthnot, before sailing back to New York, had detached the fourteen-gun sloop H.M.S. *Loyalist* under Captain John Plumer Ardesoife to remain in South Carolina with Cornwallis. In his efforts to aid in the subjugation of the inhabitants, Ardesoife cruised along the coast, and near the end of June he dropped anchor in Winyah Bay off Georgetown. There he published Clinton's proclamation and issued a rather pompous demand that the inhabitants come and reaffirm their allegiance to the crown.

In the Williamsburg District, some thirty miles above Georgetown, the population was made up mostly of people of Scotch-

Irish extraction. When the proclamation of June 3 was made known, they grew apprehensive that they might be forced into the British Army to serve against their former friends and neighbors. One of their political and military leaders was Major John James. He had represented the community in the legislature and Provincial Congress, and had been their militia leader. He had distinguished himself when Moultrie was falling back before Prevost and had made a brief stand at Tulifinny. At a mass meeting of his neighbors, James was asked to ride into Georgetown and seek clarification of the proclamation from Ardesoife. Dressed as a country planter James rode into Georgetown.

At headquarters, in answer to the question posed by James, Ardesoife stated that submission to the crown would have to be unconditional. When James next asked if the people would be allowed to live quietly at home, the naval officer began to show signs of irritation, retorting sharply, "Although you have rebelled against his Majesty, he offers you a free pardon, of which you are undeserving, for you all ought to be hanged. . . . But, as he offers you a free pardon, you must take up arms in support of his cause."

James observed that the people he represented would never submit to such terms. Livid with rage, the captain shouted, "You damned rebel, if you speak in such language, I will immediately order you to be hanged up to the yardarm."

James leaped to his feet, and as a protection against the captain's sword, grabbed a chair and thrust it forward, brandishing it in the officer's face. Backing out of the door he leaped upon his horse and sped off toward the village of Kingstree on the Black River.

The word spread, and with each telling there was usually an additional bit of exaggeration. As blood began to boil, men took down and oiled their muskets. Ardesoife's rashly used phrase, "you must take up arms in support of his cause," seemed to many a violation of their paroles, and they no longer felt bound by its terms. This attitude was not helped by the loyalists who had been placed in command of the district: the hard-cursing John Hamilton and Amos Gaskens, who some declared was little more than a petty thief. Ardesoife alienated even the loyalists by sending out two armed sloops, whose crews made little distinction between Whig and Tory, to confiscate property.[12]

Once again the people of the Williamsburg District selected Major James to lead them in their military endeavours. As captains they chose William McCottry, Henry Mouzon, John James (the major's second cousin), and John McCauley. McCottry, whose men proudly took on the name of "McCottry's Rifles," was stationed at Witherspoon's Ferry on Lynche's Creek on the post road running from Philadelphia to Savannah. The movement became something of a general uprising as Lieutenant Colonel Hugh Giles raised a regiment of militia in the area between the Peedee River and Lynche's Creek. Colonel John Ervin issued a call for the men of the Britton's Neck Regiment to come out. Colonel James Cassells and Captain Amos Gaskens and others who held British militia commissions were taken up. About two hundred of the new rebels rendezvoused at Witherspoon's Ferry. Lieutenant Colonel Hugh Horry, Peter's brother, came in from Georgetown. Horry was popular, and it was said that he was offered the command of the Williamsburg group but declined, although he did assume temporary control. It may have been Horry who suggested that they request Marion, for he was termed Marion's "bosom friend." [13]

Cornwallis was soon made aware of the growing spirit of rebellion sweeping through the low country and began to feel some alarm. He noted that "the whole country between Peedee and Santee . . . has been in an absolute state of rebellion, every friend of Government has been carried off and his plantation destroyed. This unfortunate business, if it should have no worse consequence, will shake the confidence of our friends in this province and make our situation very uneasy until we can advance." [14]

To awe the country into a state of tranquility Francis, Lord Rawdon and his Volunteers of Ireland were dispatched into the Waxhaws. Major Archibald McArthur and his battalion of the Seventy-First Highlanders were sent into the Cheraws. But the summer fevers raced through McArthur's men and he was recalled. Yet the return march was too severe for his "miserably sickly" ninety-six soldiers. He sent them down the Peedee on flatboats to Georgetown with a surgeon and under the command of Lieutenant John Nairne of the Seventy-First. They were protected by Colonel Robert Mills, a former doctor, and his loyalist militia of the Cheraw District.

As the boats neared Mars Bluff, they were ambushed by Colonel John Ervin and his men. According to reports later received by Cornwallis, some of the loyalist militia from North Carolina seized their officers and held them for the rebels. Mills and several of his officers escaped by leaping overboard and swimming ashore, but most of his command and the invalids were taken prisoner. This, in turn, concerned Cornwallis because of the importance of maintaining water communications along the river during the "Confusion & terror" in the Cheraw District.[15]

In early July Major James Wemyss and a battalion of the Sixty-Third Regiment had been sent to Georgetown to provide cover for the gathering of loyalist militia. He discovered that smallpox was prevalent in the town and that many feared to come in. He also gained the impression that many of those professing affection for government were instead among the "most Violent & Persecuting Rebelles," and he suggested that things might calm down if the paroles of ten or twelve of the leaders were revoked and they were sent into confinement on one of the islands off the coast. Cornwallis agreed. But the more Wemyss attempted to do, the more he realized "that the longer I remain here, the more I discover the Disaffection of the People. . . ."

There was even dissension among the loyalists, so much so that they delighted in informing upon one another so that it became difficult to determine friend from foe. Reports were that a large number of rebels were marching in to attack Georgetown. Cornwallis concurred with Wemyss's suggestions that it would be wise to evacuate the town, leaving the formation of the militia to Colonels Ball, Mills, and Cassells. Yet Wemyss was not to evacuate the town in too much haste but rather to give out that he was to join a large reinforcement. He was to march up the Black River at a leisurely pace to frustrate any suggestion of flight and take post in the High Hills of the Santee from where he was to protect water communications between Camden and Charleston. Safe passage had become so difficult that one express rider, bringing dispatches to Camden, was forced to slip through the swamps. Wemyss's progress was slower than intended because of the flooded condition of the country.[16]

Banastre Tarleton was ordered out, with the convalescent dragoons in Charleston, to make a diversion in favor of Wemyss. Accompanied by Major George Hanger and slowed by rain and flooded streams, Tarleton led thirty dragoons and forty mounted militia out of Charleston. By August 5 they were no farther along their way than Lenud's Ferry on the Santee, where they were joined by twenty-five loyalist militia under Colonel John Coming Ball. The following day they were encamped on Kingstree green. Messengers galloped off to inform Major James that Tarleton was at Kingstree and his force was relatively weak. At Indian Town the messengers informed Captain McCottry of Tarleton's whereabouts. Without waiting for James, he roused his men and started them toward Kingstree.

But Tarleton had been warned by the wife of the loyalist captain John Hamilton. He had also received word that a force of militia under James was at Indian Town. Hoping to surprise them, he rode off. He and McCottry missed one another along the way. As he bowled along up the west bank of the Black River, he found the loyalists unhappy, constantly harassed by small groups of rebels. To persuade the younger men to join him, he gave out that he would allow them to plunder the possessions of the rebel leaders and said, "If Warfare allows me, I shall give these Disturbers of the Peace no Quarter. . . . I must discriminate with Severity." Before he completed his ride into Camden, he burned the home of Captain Henry Mouzon on Pudding Swamp.[17]

Much of the rebellious spirit was due to the rumor that Benjamin Lincoln's successor, Horatio Gates, was marching with an army toward South Carolina. Already Hugh Giles was collecting cattle and grain to feed the army once it arrived. The Williamsburg men wanted to be a part of any fight against the British. Earlier Major James and the other leaders, meeting in the house of Gilbert Johnston, decided to request General Gates to appoint a Continental officer to lead the rebellious militia of Williamsburg. It seems that most of them expressed a preference for Marion, although the message to Gates apparently did not specifically name him as the choice. On this decision, the future of Francis Marion was hinged.[18]

Hillsborough, in North Carolina, had been designated as the general rendezvous for those Continental troops remaining in the South after the fall of Charleston. By a resolution of the Continental Congress on June 14, 1780, Major General Horatio Gates, the hero of the Battle of Saratoga, had been named to succeed Lincoln as commanding general in the Southern Department. Gates was not General Washington's choice for the command; he would have preferred Nathanael Greene. But Gates had powerful friends in Congress, including many who had grown weary of Washington's leadership because, it was said, he "wore a mantle of defeat." And Greene, who had recently irritated many members of Congress by his resignation as quartermaster general and his caustic remarks, had little support in that body.

Major General Johann de Kalb, the good-natured Bavarian giant, had been marching south with the Maryland and Delaware Continentals when Charleston fell, and he became the ranking general in the south until the arrival of Gates. Because of the shortage of provisions in the Hillsborough area, he had moved down to Coxe's Mill on Deep River.[19]

It was here that Francis Marion had come up with the Southern Army. With him were Major John Vanderhorst, Captains James Theus, Lewis Ogier, and James Melton, the latter from Georgia. In all there were about twenty men, both black and white, in the party; most wore the little leather uniform cap of the South Carolina Continentals. There they also discovered Peter Horry, who had met de Kalb as the army had crossed the Roanoke River and who was now serving as a volunteer aide on the general's staff. They were not at Coxe's Mill when Gates swaggered into camp on July 25, the salute of eight artillery pieces burning badly-needed gunpowder in a show of martial fluff. Some time before July 10 de Kalb had dispatched Marion and his "South Carolina Volunteers" to Cole's Bridge in the area of the Peedee to gather intelligence and supplies.[20]

De Kalb turned over the command of the army to Gates with few regrets. He had been planning to march southward by way of Salisbury and Charlotte through a countryside where the inhabitants were friendly and there was a promise of adequate, though not bountiful, provisions. It had been his intention, should prospects brighten, to possibly attack the British outpost at Camden. Gates dismissed de Kalb's route as too circuitous and decided to drive in a more direct march on Camden, some fifty miles shorter, but through sterile pine barrens and where a majority of the people harbored Tory inclinations. Protests were dismissed with the assertion that "provisions, rum, salt, and every requisite will flow into the camp . . . [and] with a liberal hand be distributed."

Marion and his party rejoined the army sometime after July 27, when Gates confidently marched off at the head of the motley collection of men he termed his "grand army." No provisions flowed into camp; the countryside was stripped clean by the marching army. Foraging in the fields and orchards along the way, the hungry men ate green corn and peaches. When there was no rum available for the daily ration of spirits, molasses was substituted. Officers used hair powder to thicken soup. Men sickened as their bellies twisted in protest.[21]

Unknown to Gates, the British had been concentrating their forces around Camden. When Francis, Lord Rawdon, pulled in his outposts as Gates approached, the American general interpreted this as a sign of fear. But Gates did not know that Lord Cornwallis, alarmed at the exaggerated reports of the size of the American army, had hurried to Camden with reinforcements.

Gates did learn that Thomas Sumter had attacked the British posts at Rocky Mount and Hanging Rock and was following the British forces, seizing the fords and burning boats at ferry sites. Sumter had written Gates on August 12 suggesting that a strong unit be sent across the Wateree to swing in behind Camden. Gates liked the idea, for he was supremely confident of victory. On August 14 he dispatched Colonel Thomas Woolford and a force of Continentals and militia to join Sumter below Camden.

Sumter's exploits and plans excited Marion. In Gates's army he held no command and there was little for him to do. He had been contacted by the messenger from Major James and knew that the militia of the Williamsburg District had requested that a Continental officer be detached to lead them. He requested Gates's permission to leave the army, strike south of Camden, assume command of the Williamsburg militia and hamper the movements of the enemy, perhaps cutting off a retreat by Cornwallis after his defeat at Camden. Gates approved the request. Marion asked Peter Horry, who of late had been acting as something of a volunteer scout, to come with him. It was either August 14 or 15, near Rugeley's Mills, that Marion's little party left the army, his orders "to go Down the Country to Destroy all boats & Craft of any kind, we found on Santee River in Order to prevent Cornwallis & his Troops Escaping him." [22]

Gates was not unhappy to rid himself of this little band of vagrant military men "whose appearance was in fact so burlesque that it was with much difficulty the diversion of the regular soldiery was restrained by the officers; and the general himself was glad of an opportunity of detaching Colonel Marion. . . ." [23]

And so it was that Francis Marion rode off for his great adventure.

Chapter IV

Marion and his party had ridden little more than ten miles when darkness caught up with them. They stopped at the home of a loyalist who was then serving with Cornwallis. His wife so feared the strangers that she fled to her bedroom. Marion posted sentries, wrapped himself in his blanket, and then, with the rest of his men, lay down on the floor of the porch. Sometime during the early morning hours they were awakened by the sounds of distant firing. Guessing that Sumter and his group, on their march to join Gates, had stumbled into a British detachment, Marion roused his men and rode on through the night toward Williamsburg.

Various dates have been given, but it would seem that Marion came up with the militia at Witherspoon's Ferry on Lynche's Creek late in the afternoon of August 17, 1780. He was greeted with happy shouts as the men crowded around to get a look at the man who had been sent to command them. Some must have been disappointed, for Francis Marion was not a particularly imposing military man. He was nearly forty-eight years old, short, and a bit on the frail side, with his ankles and knees obviously malformed. His injured ankle was still tender enough to cause him to limp with every step. Visage hard, his black eyes were steady, while a high forehead sat above a face dominated by a jutting jaw and an aquiline nose. He was dressed in a "close round-bodied crimson jacket, of coarse texture. . . ." On his head he still wore the little leather helmet that bore the silver crescent of the Second Regiment and was inscribed with the words "Liberty or Death." Instead of an officer's sword, a little "cut and thrust" hung at his waist, and it was said that it was to become so rusty that it could not be drawn from its scabbard. He took over from Lieutenant Colonel Hugh Horry, who had assumed temporary command of the group at the insistence of Major James. Among the first orders issued to his new command was one that the men should wear white cockades in their hats as identification.

On a strictly legal basis Marion, as a Continental officer, had no authority to assume command of the Williamsburg militia. Although he did not hesitate in taking over, it could be supposed that he must have felt it to be a somewhat degrading command. Years later Peter Horry was to remember: "Genl. Marion always Said it was a Sculking Position—Their Officers dare not force the Men for fear of Loosing their Commissions . . . no People can war with Success because all are Rulers." [1]

Marion had no sooner surveyed the situation than he ordered Peter Horry to take three companies of militia down to the lower Santee and work up to Lenud's Ferry, gathering as many men as he could, and to forward all available ammunition back to Marion. For those men of the detachment who had no weapons, Horry was to seize the arms of the inhabitants, giving a receipt for each. His primary mission, however, was to destroy all boats, scows, and canoes on the river in addition to placing enough guards on every crossing to prevent anyone from entering or leaving Charleston.

Just as soon as Major James and his captains were able to gather sufficient provisions, they attempted to persuade others to join the group. Marching first to Kingstree, Colonel Marion then struck out across country for the area around Lenud's Ferry on the Santee. On August 19, as he moved down the Santee on his mission of destruction, Marion received incredible information. His informants had talked with him privately, and the colonel refused to divulge their news to his troops lest they become demoralized before the completion of their mission. His informants had reported that Gates, marching against Camden about 2:30 on the morning of August 16, had stumbled into Cornwallis and the British Army, who had also selected the night to move forward to attack the Americans at Rugeley's Mills. The resulting burst of fire had been the noise that had awakened Marion and his companions the night after they had left Gates's camp. The two armies had pulled back after about fifteen minutes of firing wildly into the darkness and on the following morning had come together in full-scale battle. The American Army had been routed, de Kalb had been killed, and Gates had fled the field, borne away, said Otho Williams, in a "torrent of unarmed militia." Tarleton had pursued the survivors as far as Hanging Rock.

Although this seemed enough bad news for one day, there was still more. On August 14 detachments from Thomas Sumter's command had captured Carey's redoubt, guarding the Wateree crossing behind Camden. Sumter should have then fallen down the Wateree to make a junction with Marion, but he was laden with so many prisoners and so much plunder that his movements were ponderous. Cornwallis, after Camden, feared Sumter's force might become a nucleus around which the defeated Southern Army might rally and he sent Tarleton in pursuit. Sumter had not covered forty miles before Tarleton

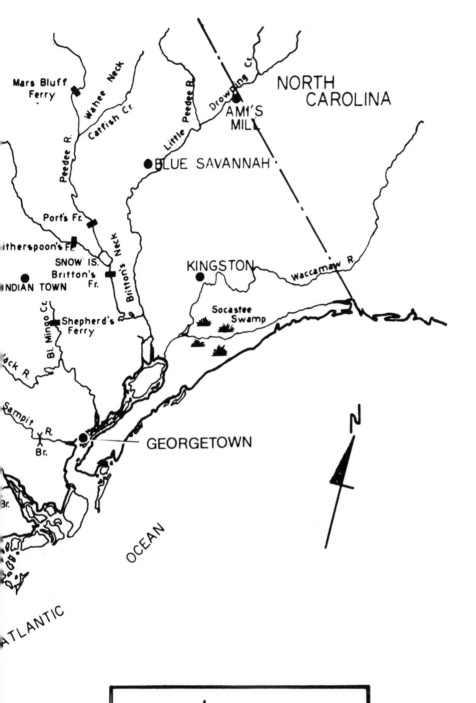

MARION'S CAMPAIGNS

caught up with him. On August 18, feeling so secure that he had neglected to send out patrols, Sumter went into camp on Fishing Creek. Tarleton's dragoons dashed in among them. Some of Sumter's men were cut down before they could reach their weapons; others were taken prisoner without resistance. Sumter had leaped upon the back of an unsaddled horse and made off, riding, it was said, in the direction of Charlotte when last seen. The British claimed to have killed 150 rebels, taken another 300 prisoners and two cannon, "& redeemed our Friends from Captivity." [2]

With Gates's Southern Army shattered, and Sumter's command cut up, Francis Marion found himself an island in a sea of enemies. Fearing their reaction to this chain of disasters, he kept the news from not only his men but also the officers. To keep the men together, and with nothing better to do, he continued destroying boats and canoes. Not only did he continue to operate as though nothing had happened, but he sent Peter Horry down to the lower Santee to try to persuade more militia to turn out.

Marion won few friends among the planters when they discovered their boats were being destroyed by one of their own. Among those destroyed by Horry's detachment were the boats of his uncle, the seventy-three-year-old Elias Horry. When his slaves reported that his boats were being destroyed, the old gentleman took down his fowling piece and rode down to the river. He tongue-lashed his nephew until Horry explained that the boats were being burned to prevent Cornwallis escaping from Gates. Elias stared at his kinsman for a moment before bursting forth with the news that Cornwallis had laid a decisive defeat on the Americans and that Gates and his army had fled South Carolina. Horry was not only astounded but chagrined. Not until August 27 did Marion formally notify Horry that Gates had been decisively defeated, but by that time he could boast of his own victory.[3]

After the battle of Camden, Lord Cornwallis had found himself in possession of a large number of prisoners and was under some apprehension that malaria and smallpox would break out among them if his captives were held too long in close confinement. He sent them marching off toward Charleston, the first division under an escort of thirty-six guards made up of detachments from the Sixty-Third Regiment, the loyalist Prince of Wales Regiment, and loyalist militia. In command was Captain Jonathan Roberts of the Sixty-Third.

Marion at this time was encamped at Nelson's Ferry. An ensign of the loyalist militia was brought into camp. This young officer had deserted and was willing to talk; from him it was learned that about 150 American prisoners and their escort lay encamped at Thomas Sumter's abandoned plantation on Great Savannah, six miles east.

Long before the gray dawn on August 20, the men were routed out. They rode hard toward Sumter's place. Hugh Horry and sixteen men were sent to the ford across Horse Creek to block off that route of retreat. Marion surveyed the situation. The house rested on an elevation above Santee Swamp and the growth of cedars and live oaks was thick enough to provide concealment for an approach march. Circling, Marion led his men around to hit the enemy from the rear.

It was still dark and difficult to find a way through the underbrush. Horry's patrol ran onto a sentinel who fired wildly at their faint shadows among the trees. With the flash of the musket, Horry led his men in a headlong dash down the lane that led to the house. Marion's main party drove in from the rear. Not much of a fight developed. Roberts had allowed his men to stack their arms in a careless fashion outside the front door. Other accouterments, as well as coats, had been cast aside for the night. Later, on orders from Cornwallis, when Major James Wemyss investigated the affair, his conclusion was, "I am afraid negligence will mark the whole of it."

The enemy's weapons were seized with but little opposition. Captain Roberts, a subaltern, two Tory guides, and twenty-two regulars of the Sixty-Third Regiment were either killed or captured. Although Marion reported Josiah Cockfield as the only man killed in his command, Cockfield lived not only to fight again but to receive another wound. Captain Lemuel Benison received a slight wound in the head.

Marion discovered that the 147 prisoners were mostly Maryland Continentals, although there were several from the Delaware Line. Discouraged and disheartened by Gates's defeat at Camden, they were not overly endowed with patriotic ardor. When invited to join his command, eighty-five of the freed Continentals refused outright, perhaps believing that a militia unit was not up to their standards. Two sergeants, McDonald and Davis, were among the three who elected to remain with Marion. Seventy of the freed Continentals actually demanded that they be allowed to continue into Charleston as prisoners of war! Apparently they were granted their wish. Although Cornwallis was to insist that all but twelve of the escort and only forty of the freed Continentals remained with Marion, Colonel James Read reported from Wilmington on September 12 that fifty-seven of the Continentals had been turned over to him. This was Cornwallis's first experience with "a Col. Marian" and he declared that his escort had been overwhelmed by a force of 150 men—actually Marion's band numbered only fifty-two mounted men.[4]

After a ride of over sixty miles to escape possible pursuit, on August 27 Marion and his men went into camp on Britton's Neck, lying between the Peedee and Little Peedee Rivers. The defeat and subsequent flight of Gates led Marion to conclude that he should temporarily curb his operations. It was also near harvest time and many of his men were needed at home to tend their crops. He finally wrote Peter Horry, informing him of Gates's defeat and ordering him to bring in his men. By the time he crossed Lynche's Creek, most of his militia had returned to their homes, with only Major James and a few hardy souls remaining with him. He halted at Port's Ferry to wait for Peter Horry to come up. He found himself in a rebellious neighborhood and as soon as the word got around that he was at the ferry, a number of local people came in to visit and a few decided to remain with him. Among those who joined his band were Francis Goddard and his two half brothers, Samuel and Britton Jenkins, who lived within ten miles of the ferry. Even more important, they were former members of the Second Regiment who had served with Marion at Savannah. The addition of such men added to the military experience of the little band.

The little colonel took time to officially report his recapture of the prisoners to Gates. Lieutenant Keating Simons was sent off with the dispatches to be delivered to the commanding general wherever he could be found. The lieutenant came up with Gates at Hillsborough, who in turn immediately sent the account on to the Continental Congress, perhaps with a view of removing a bit of the tarnish from his own reputation. Newspapers around the country hailed the event as a significant victory, and "Marien," as they spelled his name, was on his way to becoming something of a folk hero.[5]

Marion's exploit and an awareness of the growing spirit of rebellion led General Cornwallis to take harsher measures to force the submission of the inhabitants. He claimed that he had information, prior to the battle of Camden, that a number of the leading rebels who had taken a parole had fanned the flames of insurrection by constantly meeting in Charleston, carrying on a correspondence with other leaders, and spreading propaganda "to encourage the disaffected and intimidate the others." After the decisive victory at Camden, he declared that additional proof of such activities had been discovered in the captured baggage. Many of those, he said, who had enlisted in the British Army had deserted and had joined Gates. They had been joined by others who had taken their parole and supposedly gone home to their plantations. At least five prisoners of war and perhaps more had been hanged on this charge after the battle of Camden, convicted on written evidence or the testimony of slaves.

To hasten the submission of the state, many of the prominent South Carolinians held in Charleston were offered the privilege of exchanging their paroles for oaths of allegiance to the British Crown. Upon their refusal, Cornwallis instructed Lieutenant Colonel Nisbet Balfour, newly appointed commandant of Charleston, to take up the most dangerous members of this "cabal." Accused of corresponding with the enemy, they were supposedly plotting, had Gates been successful, to fire Charleston, and while the garrison was busily fighting the flames, recapture the town. On August 27, 1780, twenty-nine of the group, including Lieutenant Governor Christopher Gadsden, were placed aboard the *Lord Sandwich* and sent into exile at St. Augustine. A short time later thirty others were sent on the same voyage. To all protests Cornwallis answered that these measures had been "adopted from motives of policy."

On September 6, 1780 his Lordship laid on the heavy hand of the conqueror even more with the issuance of a proclamation appointing John Cruden commissioner of sequestered estates and providing for the confiscation of the estates of those who had abandoned their plantations to join the rebels or who were "acting under the authority of the Rebel Congress." Included were those who, by their acts or words, opposed the reestablishment of royal authority in South Carolina. Cornwallis's measures were to receive the full support of the British government, with Lord George Germain calling them "highly judicious" and "extremely prudent and proper."

Despite the burning resentment aroused by such actions, Cornwallis now felt that he could get on with his proposed invasion of North Carolina. A number of southern prisoners in Charleston were transferred to prison hulks in the harbor in order to release troops guarding the prisoners for duty in the countryside to stamp out flarings of rebellion. As a result, the Seventy-First Regiment was able to join Cornwallis. But it also meant that the activities of both Marion and Sumter would appeal to a greater number of people.[6]

Although most of the Scotch-Irish of the Britton's Neck area were rebellious in nature, not all of their lineage were. On Catfish Creek, the Little Peedee, and the tributaries of Drowning Creek, many remained loyal to the crown. Under the leadership of Major Micajah Ganey they had formed themselves into a loyalist regiment of militia; they were joined by a number of Tories from Bladen County, North Carolina. Serving as second in command of this unit was Captain Jesse Barefield, who at one time had served in one of the South Carolina Continental Regiments. He had become disenchanted with the rebel cause when he had received no satisfaction upon appealing what he felt to be an insult from an officer. He had come to the conclusion that the treatment stemmed from the fact that he was a small farmer and something of a backwoodsman, and the officers were low country gentility who would never allow him proper justice. Despite his bruised pride, he had served out his enlistment and then had returned to his home between Drowning Creek and the Little Peedee where, he and his younger brother, Miles, had raised a troop of eighty dragoons.[7]

The news that Marion was on the Neck spread through the settlements. Ganey, a handsome and intelligent man, also had a violent temper which sometimes impaired his intellect, and now he felt compelled to eliminate this new threat to his future. He sent out a call for his loyalist militia. At least 250 came in. Before daylight on September 4, Ganey set out to surprise Marion. He rode out in front with the forty-five men of the vanguard, while Barefield followed with the infantry.

Ganey, and especially Barefield, should have realized that such a large group of undisciplined troops would never succeed in taking Francis Marion, or any other experienced officer, by surprise. Marion always sent out patrols around the clock, and the gathering of the Tory army had been reported to him on September 3. His own command totaled only fifty-three men, but he discounted the odds, reasoning that a surprise attack would throw the enemy into such confusion that their five-to-one superiority in numbers would be neutralized. He mentioned his plan to no one for fear that even a whisper of his intentions might leak to the enemy.

Never a heavy sleeper, Marion was up and about camp before dawn on September 4, rousing his men and attempting to cheer the drowsiness from their eyes. Making sure his men were wearing the white cockades in their hats, he led his little band off in search of the enemy. Out in front rode Major James on his great horse, Thunder; with him were a select group of horsemen as an advance guard. For the first two hours nothing happened as they jogged through the hazy September morning. A scout galloped back; the road ahead was blocked by a company of forty-five armed and mounted men.

Major James, an impetuous fellow, immediately gave forth with a huzza, and shouting for his men to follow him, plunged forward. His men came on behind him in a great rush. James recognized Ganey and selected him as a personal foe. As his men scattered before the sudden charge, Ganey wheeled his horse and fled. James, without looking back to see if his men were following, dashed off in pursuit. Within half a mile Ganey pulled up to join a party of his men who had halted and were preparing to defend themselves from the cover of a thicket. James realized that his men were not following him. His mind working quickly, he drove forward, shouting back over his shoulder, "Come on my boys! Come on! Here they are! Here they are!"

Without waiting to check the size of the group James supposedly was leading, the Tories leaped upon their horses and fled wildly through the forest. So hasty was their flight that no one considered sending a warning to Barefield. James had one man wounded. Of Ganey's advance guard only fifteen men escaped; the rest had all been wounded or killed.

Marion interrogated the prisoners brought in by James and his men. From them it was learned that the main body of the enemy was only about three miles away. He ordered his men forward and came up with the enemy column within ten minutes. But Barefield was no Ganey and was not easily frightened. When informed of the approach of Marion, he calmly wheeled his men into a battle line where his troops stood waiting, muskets at the ready. Marion's prudence overcame any inclination he may have entertained of throwing his fifty men against the two hundred who stood ready to meet his charge. He ordered his men to pull off, feigning fear.

He retreated as far as the Blue Savannah, halting in an open area surrounded by thickets of stunted pine and scrub-oak trees. There he concealed his men in the tangled underbrush and waited for Barefield to march into his ambush.

Perhaps it was because he felt that he had Marion on the run that Barefield ignored proper precautions. His column had lost all semblance of order by the time they came opposite the spot where Marion's men lay hidden. As they charged out from the thickets, Marion's men gave forth with a lusty yell. With cracking pistols and flashing sabers they rode in among the disorganized loyalists. Many of Barefield's men did manage to deliver one scattering volley. With no mounted troops to protect them while they reloaded, the terrified infantry broke for the woods and Little Peedee Swamp, "an Impassable Swamp to all but Toreys."

Marion halted along the skirts of the morass, feeling a pursuit through the underbrush and mire to be too dangerous. His men rode slowly along the edge of the boggy ground, cursing, shouting insults, and daring the fugitives to show themselves.

Occasionally they sent a random shot winging through the trees just to let the Tories know that they were still about. After his men had their fun and their tensions eased, Marion called them off. His casualties had been light; the Tory volley had wounded three men and killed two horses.

After dressing wounds and providing for the prisoners, Marion rode back to Port's Ferry. It had been a most satisfying experience, becoming even more so after a patrol returned from the Blue Savannah reporting that the loyalist army had "disperst." Most of them had crawled out of the swamp and were now in hiding near their homes. At a total cost of four wounded men and two dead horses, Marion had eliminated the threat of a Tory uprising.

There were salutary side effects; the day after the battle, sixty volunteers rode into Marion's camp. With this additional strength the colonel now felt able to hold his own against irregular troops. He began to throw up a small redoubt on the east bank of the Peedee to cover Port's Ferry, as well as to check possible counterattacks by the Tories, and serve as a base from which to disrupt British communications between Charleston and Cheraw Hill. The fortifications were simple, thrown up of logs and clay, but strong enough to stop a musket ball. He even had artillery—two small rusty iron field pieces brought in by the militia. To arm his men he seized the saws from mills and had local blacksmiths hammer them into cavalry sabers.[8]

Marion, by this bold stroke, had endangered future British operations in South Carolina, especially with Lord Cornwallis preparing to move into North Carolina by way of Charlotte. Marion's position threatened the port of Georgetown which anchored the right flank of British posts in the state. Cornwallis was reluctant to make his move until the situation had quieted. Colonel Balfour, commandant at Charleston, ordered the engineer, Major James Moncrieff, and a battalion of the Seventh Regiment to Georgetown, where Moncrieff was to construct a redoubt and other works to protect the harbor. The loyalist militia west of the Santee were called out and stationed in Georgetown under the command of Colonels John Coming Ball and Joseph Wigfall.

And Cornwallis felt that a strong hand should be felt in the country. Major James Wemyss was ordered to march the Sixty-Third Regiment, reinforced by Lieutenant Colonel John Hamilton's loyalist militia, from their post in the High Hills of the Santee to Kingstree. Wemyss's orders from Cornwallis instructed him to organize a stronger loyalist militia and to sweep "the country from Kingstree Bridge to Peedee, and returning by the Cheraws. . . . I would have you Disarm in the most rigid Manner, all Persons who cannot be depended on and punish the Concealment of Arms & Ammunition with a total Demolition of the Plantation." All those who had broken their paroles by an act of hostility were to be hanged without any trial beyond proving the identity of the accused. In addition to Hamilton's men, detachments from the North Carolina loyalists of Colonel Samuel Bryan and Major John Harrison were to lend support to the expedition. Cornwallis outlined a pattern of behavior for Wemyss: he was "to put a good face on things & talk big, threaten the plunderers with the most severe Retaliation . . . & try to give Spirits to our cause. You have only Militia to oppose you, who are often daring & troublesome in attack, always timid and panick struck when attacked." [9]

Wemyss was responsible for augmenting Marion's manpower, albeit unintentionally. Because the men of the Sixty-Third Regiment were sickly, the major decided to mount his foot soldiers before leaving the High Hills of the Santee. He called together all the Whig planters of the High Hills and along the Santee on the pretense of emphasizing the generosity of the British in coming "to rescue you from tyranny and oppression." While he gave forth with these platitudes, his men were roaming around the countryside, rounding up the horses of the absent planters, although most of the animals were later classed as "indifferent." Angry protests had little effect. Although many of those who had attended the meeting were forced to walk home, they saddled the next horse they could come by and joined Marion.

Wemyss and his newly mounted infantry began their march down the Santee. For fear that Wemyss's departure might suggest to the rebels that they cut the Camden-Nelson Ferry road, Captain Frederick De Peyster, with a detachment of George Turnbull's New York Volunteers, was sent into the High Hills. Although De Peyster had been instructed to call out the militia of Major Samuel Tynes, little help was expected of them, mainly on account of their commanding officer, whom Cornwallis had characterized as a "weak, well intentioned Man." At Charleston, Balfour was to employ the militia of Ball and Wigfall on the east side of the Santee.[10]

With all this movement and activity by the enemy, it appeared obvious that the intent was the elimination of Marion. When the houses of three men serving with him were burned, he felt that unless he acted in retaliation his support from the area would be greatly lessened. His scheme was to take the initiative and disrupt British operations by dispersing De Peyster's command. On September 7 Major John James was sent on patrol to reconnoiter the Kingstree area. Leaving fifty men to garrison the redoubt at Port's Ferry, Marion led his remaining one hundred men across the Peedee and Lynche's Creek to encamp at Indian Town, there to prepare to offer opposition to those who were "a Burning all the houses of those men who had Joind me."

Near Kingstree Major James and his detail concealed themselves in a thicket beside the road leading into town. A bright moon was shining. A detachment of Wemyss's command rode by. James and his men leaped from their hiding place and grabbed the last straggler of the weary rear guard. So quickly

74

did they act that their prisoner had no opportunity to sound the alarm. Dragging off their captive, they mounted and rode for the prearranged rendezvous with Marion in the woods near Indian Town.

The prisoner was from Colonel Patrick Ferguson's Rifle Regiment. In response to Marion's questioning, he revealed that around 200 British regulars and a number of Tories were already in Kingstree and that another 200 under Wemyss were to join them that night. An officer's baggage taken at the same time as the prisoner contained an orderly book that suggested that the primary objective of the enemy was the elimination of Marion to be followed by a sweep through the Cheraws. Other intelligence indicated that Moncrieff was already in Georgetown with a garrison of 200 regulars. Marion had come out expecting to fight no more than 150 of the enemy. He had little ambition to attack in the face of such overwhelming odds.

On the following day, September 8, the news was all bad. Intelligence revealed that Wemyss had crossed Lynche's Creek and was approaching on Marion's front. The Georgetown garrison had sallied forth and already were across Black River, while the Tories under Ganey were once more collecting and could come in on his rear. This gathering of enemy forces could surround him in such a fashion as to eliminate any possible avenue of retreat.

Marion and his officers went into council. It was obvious that they were outnumbered and any movement in force by the enemy could crush them. It was no time for a defeat, for such an event coupled with British depredations would so dishearten the militia that they would never turn out again. Many of the men were anxious to return to their homes and look after their families, especially those whose houses had been burned. Marion quickly made up his mind. Many of the men were dismissed, as were a number of their officers. Captain John James, son of

Major James, and ten picked men were left in the area to gather intelligence and offer what aid they could to those harassed by the enemy.

With his remaining sixty men, Marion was unable to engage so large an enemy force in the field. The logical course of action seemed to abandon his operations for the moment and seek safety in flight. Destroying the redoubt at Port's Ferry and dragging along his two rusty field pieces, Marion and his companions rode northward toward North Carolina.

Across the Little Peedee, and out of range from an attack by the loyalists, Marion spiked his artillery pieces and dragged them off into a swamp alongside the road. He had learned a lesson, for never again was he to encumber his mobility by dragging along field pieces. He did not halt for forty miles until he reached Ami's Mill on Drowning Creek, the eastern branch of the Little Peedee near the North Carolina border. Disturbed as to the vengeance that Wemyss might seek upon the families of those with him, Marion suggested that Major James select a few volunteers to return to the Williamsburg District to determine the situation.

Marion knew that Brigadier General Henry William Harrington's brigade of North Carolina militia lay near Cross Creek (present-day Fayetteville) and would afford a measure of protection. He resumed his march toward the Cape Fear in North Carolina, hoping perhaps to drum up a few recruits for his little band. When he reached the southern branch of the Waccamaw River, friends guided him to a hiding place in the Great White Marsh of Bladen County (now Columbus County), North Carolina. There his little command lived a Spartan existence; one meal, for instance, as described by young William James, consisted of boiled hominy, "lean beef, without salt, and sweet potatoes," all washed down by "bad water." [11]

Back in the Williamsburg District, the areas along the Black River, Lynche's Creek, and the Peedee were scenes of almost continuous desolation and destruction. James Wemyss was doing just what Marion had feared. At Kingstree, he had been joined by loyalist militia of Captain Amos Gaskens, an evil man whose soul had been soiled by hatred. Gaskens acted as a guide for Wemyss, pointing out those who had sided with the rebels. At Indian Town, Wemyss had laid the torch to the local Presbyterian Church, declaring it a "sedition shop." Wemyss's general philosophy of subjugation had an economic base. He placed particular emphasis upon the destruction of sheep and looms. Those sheep and cattle not slaughtered as food for his men he ordered bayonetted. Gristmills and blacksmith shops were destroyed. Fortunately much of the corn had not yet been harvested and was overlooked by the marauders. Tory detachments were allowed to plunder at will. Those suspected of rebel tendencies or having broken their paroles were always given a "court-martial" before they were hanged.

In their sweep over the area Wemyss's troops came up on the home of Major James. Wemyss played the role of the gentleman when James's wife, Jean, answered the door. He assured her that if her husband would come in and voluntarily give himself up he would receive a pardon. Mrs. James replied that she had little influence over the conscience of her husband. They argued. Finally, in extreme irritation and exasperation, Wemyss ordered Mrs. James and her children locked in a room in the house, and for the next two and a half days he waited for the major to put in an appearance. The prisoners were fed by Captain David Campbell of Edisto, who slipped food and drink through an unguarded window.

The major's son's experience was more terrifying than that of his mother. Captain John James had been paroled after Charleston, but like so many others he had felt that the outrages committed by the British and loyalists had been a violation of his oath and he was free of its restrictions. Orders went out that he should be taken up, and "If he was found to have broken his parole, he would be hanged in the morning to yonder tree." After his mother and her children had been confined, young James's anger had gotten the best of him and he revealed his presence by firing upon a band of Tories raiding the plantation of one McGill. Shortly afterward, he was captured by one of Wemyss's patrols.

The following morning Captain James was brought before Wemyss in what was declared to be a "court martial." James's relatives remained mute when questions were put to them. Slaves were brought in as witnesses. They either could not, or would not, give evidence, swearing that they knew nothing of illegal activities by the young captain. When he was unable to cull even a shred of evidence from any of his witnesses, Wemyss was forced to release the prisoner and his family. But he had the final word when he put the torch to James's home, refusing to allow any of its contents to be removed.

The case of Adam Cusacks aroused further resentment against British methods among many people of the community. Cusacks, whom Wemyss termed a "notorious villain," had also supposedly been paroled after the fall of Charleston. A quick-tempered man, he had no intention of looking kindly upon his former enemies. Among other things, he had refused to ferry British officers across the Black River, despite a constant flow of threats and curses. Cusacks, in turn, had become angry and fired a shot across the river at the slave of Captain John Brockington, an outspoken loyalist of Kingstree. For this last offense Wemyss had him arrested, taken to Cheraw, and tried by court martial. The chief witness against him was a condemned Negro who may have been promised clemency if he testified properly. Cusacks was convicted of breaking his parole and sentenced to death. On the other hand, there were those who claimed that Cusacks had never taken a parole.

Wemyss was determined to make an example of Cusacks whether he had taken a parole or not. A gibbet was erected beside the road at Long Bluff. As the noose was adjusted about the victim's neck, his wife and children threw themselves before the major's horse, pleading that their husband and father be spared. Wemyss lost his temper and spurred his horse forward as if to ride down the Cusacks family; one of his own officers clutched the bridle and prevented him from doing so. Just before the trap was thrown, Dr. James Wilson of Long Bluff attempted to intercede for the condemned man. He failed, and soon Cusacks's body was swinging from the rope as an example to those who would defy the will of the conqueror. For his temerity in interceding for Cusacks, Dr. Wilson's property was burned by Wemyss. After his wife sought safety in North Carolina, Wilson joined Marion.

Wemyss, on September 20, reported that in his tour through the area he had burned and laid waste over fifty homes and plantations. He boasted that he had slaughtered numerous sheep and cattle and had hanged a number of men adjudged guilty of breaking their paroles. To Lord Cornwallis he explained: "I have done every thing in my Power to get at Mr. Merrion, who with [Hugh] Giles commanded about 150 Men on my Arrival in this Part of the Country. Altho' I never could come up with them, yet I push'd them so hard as in a great Measure to break them up; the few that still continue together, have retreated over Little Peedee." He was forced to admit, however, that his activities had won few friends for Britain, a statement borne out by a Mr. Pugh who noted, "The people [are] in arms against the English."

Wemyss also found himself forced to admit that the area "cannot be kept by militia" but needed the steadiness of regular troops to keep down the insurgents. Marion and other partisans, he claimed, were "burning houses, and distressing the well affected in a most severe manner. Several people from that Country have been with me to represent their distressed Situation. The highlanders in particular who are very numerous here,

79

have been treated with such Cruelty & Oppression as almost exceeds belief."

Cornwallis's laconic reply was that "your account is not so agreeable." To Colonel George Trumbull he complained, "I am much disappointed in the business."

Wemyss's operations had made more friends for Marion in the Williamsburg District than ever before. And now they wanted him to come home.[12]

Chapter V

Back among the moss-laden trees of the Great White Marsh, Marion and his men lay camped. They had no tents, and some did not even have the comfort afforded by a blanket. Marion had only one blanket and that had been badly scorched when it had accidentally caught fire; his little leather cap had been charred in the same mishap. The men were kept busy. Patrols were sent out not only to prevent surprise but to forage for food.

The colonel's first efforts had been bent toward establishing a line of communications with the South Carolina low country. Knowing full well that the British did not have the manpower to keep a force constantly in the area and would have to rely upon loyalist militia should they expand their operations, Marion made plans to operate alone. Gates would not answer his letters, "which has very much Dispirited the friends to America." From Cross Creek he learned from General Harrington of the North Carolina militia that Gates was assembling the remnants of his army at Hillsborough. To arouse some interest on the part of the commanding general, he sent a dispatch to Gates outlining his activities since he had taken leave of the Southern Army.

The hum of the mosquito in the swamp was a constant irritant. It had been a wet summer, and the turgid water ran deeper than usual. The men became sickly; some fell ill of malaria. Among the first to come down with the chills, sweats, and vomiting symptoms of the fever was Captain George Logan, a Continental officer who had chosen to follow Marion. Then came Peter Horry. As others lay shivering under the trees, the camp in the Great White Marsh began to take on the semblance of a primitive hospital.

After they had remained in hiding for about ten days, Major James returned from his scouting mission in the low country of South Carolina. His news was not good. He described the great pall of smoke hanging over the Williamsburg District, along with the sickening odor of dead animals in the air. The cries of women who had lost their men hung in the background. Wemyss had ploughed a row of devastation some seventy miles in length and, in places, fifteen miles wide. According to Peter Horry, Marion would, at such times, observe, " 'Tis a harsh medicine, but it is necessary," feeling that even so dismal a scene would swell his own forces with angry men. In fact, James reported that the men of Williamsburg were now more than willing to take the field.[1]

At Georgetown Major Moncrieff had completed the fortifications, as well as "done all I can to punish the People in the lower parts of this Country." A number of those taken up were sent as prisoners to Charleston, and by September 20 he felt that he had "weeded out the Violent Spirits." Confiscated slaves were sent to work on the fortifications of Charleston. At least 120 horses were seized and sent as remounts for Tarleton's British Legion. He had posted loyalist militia to act as outposts to guard against the surprise of the town. The Tory regiment of Lieutenant Colonel James Cassells had been sent to Britton's Neck to guard against Marion's return, but had later been recalled to act as part of the garrison of Georgetown. Although Cornwallis had warned that the loyalist units of John Coming Ball and Joseph Wigfall should not be sent east of the Santee, Moncrieff had moved them north of the Black River to stifle any uprisings in the Williamsburg District. Neither commanded a large force, but Moncrieff seemed to think there would be no further trouble from Marion and that these small loyalist detachments would be sufficient to maintain order.

Wigfall and fifty men took a position near Black River Church. Ball, with forty-seven men, moved in on Shepherd's Ferry on Black Mingo Creek, twenty miles northeast of Georgetown. He pitched camp near the Red House, a tavern kept by Patrick Dollard, a man respected in the community. Here Ball could control all traffic on the post road, and still remain within striking distance of both Indian Town and Kingstree, should there be an uprising in either of those two places. Along the banks of the Black Mingo trenches were dug and men posted therein to control the water passage on that navigable stream. Lord Cornwallis, who by this time had marched his army up to Charlotte, still continued to feel uneasy about the lower country and expressed a fear that the loyalist units would meet with some serious mishap there.[2]

His fears were well founded. Later in the afternoon of Sunday, September 24, 1780, the men in the camp in the Great White Marsh began to stir about, packing the few possessions they had with them—it required only a short time. Toward the shank of the afternoon, Marion gave the signal and they cantered out of the swamp. It was late the following evening when they rode into Kingston and pitched camp along the Waccamaw River.

Early the next morning they were on the road leading to the

Little Peedee. Some five miles along the way they turned off into Little Peedee Swamp. For three miles they were guided by the Jenkins boys, splashing along beneath the great cypress trees until they emerged on the banks of the river. Marion could not swim, but his horse could. Forcing his horse into the stream, holding tightly to the pommel of his saddle, he was towed along as the animal struggled across the stream. They came out of the water at Woodberry Plantation, and made for Old Neck Church. A horseman suddenly appeared on the path behind them, racing forward as fast as his winded mount could carry him. It was Captain George Logan, who had been left behind at Great White Marsh too sick to travel. That morning, upon hearing that Marion had marched for South Carolina, he bade William James, who had been left behind to nurse him, goodbye and had covered sixty miles that day to catch up with Marion.

The little party reached Port's Ferry late in the afternoon of September 28. There they crossed the Peedee in flatboats and galloped to Witherspoon's Ferry where, in the gathering twilight, they crossed Lynche's Creek. On the far side they were met by Captain John James and ten men. Others came a short time later: Captain Henry Mouzon, Lieutenant John Scott, and a number of volunteer militiamen. They reported that Ball and his Tory militia from St. James, Santee, and St. Stephens were still encamped at Shepherd's Ferry on the Black Mingo. Marion hesitated, feeling that he should perhaps wait for reinforcements, when they reported that the enemy probably outnumbered his sixty men. The men, however, insisted they should strike at once.

Marion wasted no time, and, despite the hard day's ride, he led his men toward the Black Mingo. For twelve miles they rode through the velvet blackness of the night, hoping to surprise the enemy. Shortly before midnight they were slipping across the boggy causeway leading to Willtown Bridge, about a mile above Dollard's house. The bridge was old, with loose flooring.

The horses' hooves, striking the wavering planks, rattled like musketry through the still night air. A sentinel in Ball's camp fired an alarm.

With the shot, Marion led his men forward at a full gallop toward the Red House tavern. When he arrived at the post road, three hundred yards from Shepherd's Ferry, he ordered his men to dismount and fight on foot, with the exception of one small group who were to act as cavalry. He reasoned that an infantry attack would be more effective should Ball have fortified the tavern. He ordered Captain Thomas Waites and several other officers who had no command to make a demonstration in front of the house and, if possible, make a frontal attack upon it. On the right flank Hugh Horry was to lead the dismounted men in a drive on the tavern. The mounted men were to strike from the left, while Marion, with a pitifully small reserve, was to lie back to render aid when needed.

John Ball was no fool; he had no intention of allowing himself to be trapped within the tavern with no route of escape. When the sentinel fired the alarm he had awakened his men and had quickly herded them into the old field that lay near the swamp to the west of the tavern. He deployed them in formation. The men grew nervous and restless as they listened to the sounds of men and horses filtering out of the darkness. Ball wandered among his men, offering words of encouragement and pleading with them to hold their fire until he gave the word. Hugh Horry's infantry came through the field, distinguishable only as dark shadows whose feet made crunching sounds as they trotted forward.

Ball waited, controlling his own tensions until Horry's men were within thirty yards. As he shouted the command to fire, there was a blaze of thunder and lightning in the night. Captain Logan fell dead, Captain Mouzon and Lieutenant Scott sagged to the ground. Brought up short by the blast, Horry's men staggered back. Captain John James refused to panic. He steadied his own men while rallying those who had been under the command of Mouzon. He ordered them forward but at the same time cautioned them to keep under cover as much as possible.

By this time Captain Waites and the supernumerary officers under his command came up on the Tory right flank. With the attack now coming from two sides, Ball's men wavered, their courage melting within them. After delivering a scattering fire, they turned and dashed for the safety promised by Black Mingo Swamp. So hasty was their flight and so great their confusion that there was little chance that they could be rallied, for according to Peter Horry, "They would not halt a moment at Georgetown, though twenty miles from the field of battle; but continued their flight, not thinking themselves safe, until they got the Santee river between him and them."

No more than fifteen minutes had passed since the beginning of the Battle of Black Mingo. Yet the losses were heavy, especially when one considered the length of the fight and the fact that it had been conducted in the middle of the night. But the firing had been done at such close range that Peter Horry said the "wads fell on either side." The dead in Marion's command were one private and Captain Logan, who had ridden so hard from Great White Marsh to get in on the action. Six privates had been wounded in addition to Captain Mouzon and Lieutenant Scott, both of whom suffered such severe injuries that they never again took the field during the remainder of the war. The Tory loss was somewhat greater; three men had been killed, while thirteen had either been wounded or taken prisoner. Several bodies were later discovered in the surrounding woods and the swamp. The wounded were left at Dollard's house, for Marion planned to move swiftly and could not tolerate the encumbrance of wounded men.

The spoils of war were plentiful. Muskets, ammunition, and the baggage of the enemy were taken as well as a number of their horses. The spirited sorrel gelding belonging to Colonel Ball, along with its saddle and bridle, were claimed by Marion. In a moment of rare wit he renamed the animal "Ball." Black Mingo had also taught him a lesson. It was said that henceforth, when there was no ford available and he was forced to cross a bridge at night, he had his men cover the flooring with their blankets.

The colonel next planned to hit Colonel Wigfall at Black River Church before the Tory leader became aware of his return to the low country. But his men had already begun to murmur, and some of those who had been with him at the Great White Marsh were anxious to return to their "wifes & family" to see if their people and property had been among those touched by the vindictiveness of Wemyss. Marion held no legal claim on their services and he was in sympathy with their anxieties. Thanking them for their services and praising them for their fortitude, he told them they could return to their homes, but asked that they rejoin him as quickly as possible.

Marion rode off toward Britton's Ferry; with him were Lieutenant Colonel Hugh Giles, Major Hugh Horry, Major King, and Captains Waites and Milton. Near a dozen other officers and men were escorting the prisoners taken at Black Mingo. Marion and his group rode twenty-six miles before they halted. The following morning they were ferried across the Peedee and were once again among their friends on Britton's Neck. Riding on, they pitched camp that night at Ami's Mill on Drowning Creek.

There Marion delivered up eight loyalist prisoners, along with three soldiers of the Sixty-Third Regiment taken at the Great Savannah and whom he had paroled, to Colonel Thomas Brown, commander of the militia in Bladen County. He had considered paroling those prisoners taken at Black Mingo as they were men of some fortune and had "showed themselves, before this Last Action, to be Good Men." But upon reflection he rejected the thought, "as I thought it would be Acknowledging them to be British Subjects and would give my followers Great Discontent, for the British Imprison all those who are our frie'ds & have hanged one Cusay for Braking his Parole." Yet he did send Major Vanderhorst, under the protection of a flag, into the Santee country to gather clothing and other necessities from the homes of the prisoners so that they might live in some comfort. Five of those taken, shortly after the battle of Black Mingo, were persuaded to take an oath of allegiance and join Marion.[3]

Despite the small group under his command, Marion's reappearance had caused some apprehension among the enemy, especially after exaggerated reports of his strength began to circulate. Wemyss reported to Cornwallis that Marion had at least four hundred men with him on Drowning Creek, and with more coming in every day, "They are burning houses and Distressing the well affected in a most severe Manner."

Upon this occasion Marion received credit for the misdeeds of others. There had been atrocities, but some had been committed by those renegades who always find a way of taking advantage of unsettled conditions and roam about the countryside terrorizing and plundering the inhabitants, always claiming fidelity to the opposite party from that of their victims. Locally these men were termed "outliers," and hated by Whig and Tory alike.

But most of the troubles laid on the loyalists at this time should have been blamed on Captain Maurice Murphy. Patriot though he was, Murphy seems to have been an evil and sadistic man, whose greatest pleasure came from the sufferings of others. After evicting the families of known Tories, he burned their homes. Upon one occasion, after Ganey's defeat at the Blue Savannah, he rode through the country in search of loyalist survivors. On Catfish Creek, when the father of the three Blackman boys refused to reveal the whereabouts of his sons or renounce his allegiance to his king, he was trussed to a gate post and flogged with 150 lashes. When Murphy stopped by at the home of his uncle, Gideon Gibson, the old man had the temerity to criticize him heavily for his ruthless measures. When the argument reached the cursing and shouting stage, Murphy drew his pistol and shot Gibson before his three sons, who were too terrified of their commanding officer to register a protest. Francis Marion had little use for Murphy or others of his ilk and referred to his raids as "that Abominable work." He rightly feared that he would receive the blame for Murphy's depredations.

There was also the problem of Colonel Hugh Ervin. Ervin had left Marion in something of a huff when he had been refused permission to retaliate upon the Tories and had now "adopted the Burning of houses. . . ." In his own defense, Marion wrote Gates, "I assure you, there is not one house Burnt by my Orders, or by any of my People. It is what I detest to Distress poor Women & children." [4]

Yet Marion's return to the area was, in general, salutary insofar as the loyalists were concerned. He reported that "the Toreys are so Affrighted with my Little Excursions that many is moving off to Georgia with their Effects others are rund into Swamps." He was now so confident that he had begun to think of driving down and rescuing those officers taken at Charleston and now held prisoner on Haddrell's Point.

His return had aroused apprehensions among the British. Now that Lord Cornwallis had begun his move into North Carolina, Marion not only constituted a threat to British posts in South Carolina, but his activities, along with those of other partisan units in the state, represented the possible danger of attacks and harassments from the rear, or at the least, the cutting of vital lines of communications. Should the partisans become too active, the loyalists could be awed into inactivity. Because of such possibilities, Nisbet Balfour became obsessed with the idea of "driving off Mr. Marion."

Lord Cornwallis, from Charlotte, ordered Major Wemyss back to Camden from Georgetown, leaving Major John Harrison and his eighty Tory Rangers at Cheraw "to keep some kind of hold of the Country." Major Robert Fraser was sent out to aid in forming the militia, his command made up of eighty mounted men, a number of whom were "old soldiers," and his mission to sweep the rebel forces from the area between the Peedee and Cross Creek. But after receiving information of the rising spirit of rebellion, Cornwallis not only ordered Harrison to join Fraser, but also ordered that all convalescents in Camden be sent to strengthen them. The general's greatest fear was that Ball and Wigfall would suffer some "disaster which will be exceedingly prejudicial to his Majesty's Services."

Wemyss worked through the Cheraws, "Burning & plundering Negroes & every thing in their way." Yet, insofar as the British were concerned, things seemed to be falling apart in the Santee country. Loyalism was fading in the face of the increasing opposition. At Cheraw Colonel Robert Mills resigned his commission in the loyalist regiment and moved southward; he was replaced by Robert Gray, whom Balfour characterized as "by much the best Militia man I have seen." Ball and Wigfall now lay back and refused to entertain suggestions that they take the field. Gray, in attempting to reorganize his new command, discovered that those along the Little Peedee who were well disposed towards government were reluctant to turn out and leave their families and properties exposed to retaliation by the rebels. In the course of the violent little civil war raging in the low country, loyalists were often shot, placed in irons and jail, or were burned out. Many were fleeing to the relative safety of Georgia. So critical had grown the situation that Wemyss was of the opinion that the country could not be held with militia as Lord Cornwallis had hoped, especially after one strong rumor whispered that Marion had driven off the militia garrison at Georgetown. Much of the difficulty, it was felt, was caused by

Marion's band, whom Gray termed a "number of desperadoes who are kept together by the hopes of plunder." Already many British officers were beginning to talk of the "second rebellion."

The general situation had grown so fluid that it was almost impossible to maintain any stable plan of campaign; when Wemyss drove through the country many rebels would fade away before him, some as far as Cross Creek, and would then return when he fell back. Wemyss, accompanied by Gray, had no sooner settled in Camden than Cornwallis ordered him to remount his regiment to return and "guard the Country east of Santee." Once again fate intervened; two days after he had sent off these orders, Cornwallis learned that Lieutenant Colonel Patrick Ferguson had been killed and his loyalist militia had been overwhelmed at King's Mountain in North Carolina. An express clattered off, ordering Wemyss back to Camden.

With Ferguson's defeat, Cornwallis began to feel some apprehensions for his own safety, as his left flank now lay exposed to possible attacks from the over the mountain men of the west. Not only was his army sickly, but the general also fell ill. Thomas Sumter, it was said, was enlisting a brigade to operate south of Charlotte, thereby constituting a threat to the rear of the British invasion army. On October 14, 1780 Cornwallis pulled his army out of Charlotte and fell back on Wynnesborough.[5]

On Drowning Creek Marion was watching these developments while trying to increase his own strength, which on October 4 numbered no more than sixty men. If he could gather as many as 100, "I shou'd certainly pay a visit to Georgetown." But by this time, Georgetown was not so easy a conquest, for the town's garrison had been increased; two howitzers had been added to the heavy armament, while a galley lay offshore to lend additional firepower.

At Hillsborough, where he was attempting to rebuild not only his Southern Army but his shattered reputation, General Horatio

Gates was planning another strike against the British, despite the fact that he was not yet strong enough to mount a major campaign. On October 11, before Cornwallis had pulled out of Charlotte, Gates had set up a harassing action by ordering Brigadier General Henry William Harrington of the North Carolina militia from Cross Creek to make threatening gestures toward Robert Gray and Major Fraser in the Cheraws.

On this same day Gates sent off a dispatch to Marion, congratulating him on his recent success and to "request you earnestly to continue your Hostilities against our Tyrannic & cruel Enemies." It was his hope, he continued, that the enemy would be so diverted by attacks in different areas that he would be forced to weaken himself by splitting off detachments from his own forces. Marion was requested to cooperate with Harrington as much as possible, as well as "create some little diversion below." [6]

Marion was ready for action. As soon as he received the general's communication, he moved over to Britton's Neck to his old post at Port's Ferry. A call went out to the militia. His timing was bad—things were peaceful enough on the Neck at the moment, and for many it was as though the war had briefly laid its heavy hand upon them and had then passed on its way. Then, too, there were homes to rebuild and personal tragedies to mourn.

Francis Marion, himself a compassionate man, was nevertheless unable to comprehend the people's reluctance. He fumed restlessly at the lethargy of the militia, then fell into despair. Finally he called together his field officers and informed them that he no longer intended to continue operations in the low country, and was planning to go to North Carolina to join General Gates, who might be able to find a place for his talents in the Southern Army. Hugh Horry, to whom Marion always felt particularly close, argued that the local men would eventually come in and pleaded with him to change his mind and

Brigadier General Francis Marion in full regalia on the battlefield. Most of his battles were small, hit-and-run skirmishes, and it is unlikely that he appeared very often on the battlefield in the dress uniform shown here.

General William Moultrie. As the colonel commanding the fort on
Sullivan's Island, he led the successful defense of Charleston against
the British fleet in June 1776. Marion, then a major in Moultrie's
regiment, was in charge of the guns on the left.

Charles, Lord Cornwallis, Major General in His Majesty's Army, replaced
Sir Henry Clinton as commanding general in the South in June 1780.
Cornwallis had no difficulty controlling Charleston with his superior
forces, but Marion posed a constant threat to his outposts, preventing
the British from gaining a firm hold on the countryside.

Major General Benjamin Lincoln, left, had an unhappy tour as commander of the rebel forces in the Southern Department. He tried to retake Savannah, was repulsed with heavy losses, and then was forced to surrender at Charleston. In June 1780, Congress named Major General Horatio Gates, below, to replace Lincoln. But an American Army under Gates, the hero of Saratoga, was routed on August 16 at Camden, South Carolina, and two months later Gates, in turn, was replaced.

Major General Nathanael Greene had been Washington's first choice to replace Lincoln as commander of the Southern Department, but Gates had powerful friends in Congress and was appointed. After the disaster at Camden, Congress asked Washington to name a successor to Gates, and Greene finally received the post in which he was to serve most ably. (Emmet Collection, Manuscripts and Archives Division, The New York Public Library, Astor, Lenox and Tilden Foundations.)

General Thomas Sumter, the "Carolina Gamecock." His feuds with Marion over precedence and command reflected in part their opposing temperaments and different military styles. Comparing them, one contemporary said: "Sumter was bold & rash, and run many risks from which his good fortune always extricated them. Marion was timid & cautious & would risk nothing, yet both succeeded in their attempts."

Lieutenant Colonel Henry "Lighthorse Harry" Lee. His green-jacketed legion was the only unit from the Continental Army that Washington could give to Greene when the latter assumed command in the South. Proud and strong-willed, it would not have been surprising if Lee and Marion clashed over who would give orders to whom but, against the expectations, they worked together smoothly on a number of combined operations.

LEFT Lieutenant Colonel Banastre Tarleton, who gave Marion his sobriquet. In November 1780, after leading his legion of dragoons on a seven-hour, twenty-six-mile chase of Marion "through swamps and defiles," Tarleton gave up, saying, "Let us go back, and we will find the Gamecock [Sumter] but as for this damned old fox, the Devil himself could not catch him."

BELOW General Andrew Pickens, of the South Carolina militia. He was a colonel, and his troops were in the front line, when the Americans under General Morgan inflicted a crushing defeat on Tarleton at the Cowpens on January 16, 1781.

RIGHT Pond Bluff, the plantation on the Santee that Marion purchased in 1773. The main house, destroyed during the war and rebuilt afterwards, was no longer standing when this drawing was made in 1849 by Benson Lossing for his *Field Book of The American Revolution*. Lossing based his rendering on the description of one who remembered details of the building.

LEFT Mrs. Rebecca Motte whose strategically located Mount Pleasant Plantation was turned into a fort by the British. Attacking it in May 1781, Marion and Lee decided they would have to set fire to the roof with flaming arrows. When the plan was broached to Mrs. Motte, she quickly produced the necessary bow and arrows, supposedly saying, "If it were a palace, it should go."

Marion, left, entertains a British officer at his camp with a feast of sweet potatoes, in a detail from a painting by G. W. Mark. (Courtesy of The New York Historical Society, New York City.)

remain in South Carolina for just a while longer. Marion listened. He stayed. Shortly afterward the militia began to straggle in. When he convinced himself that the future was not so dark as he had imagined, "he was satisfied, and that one of the enemy detachments should feel his force." [7]

As the numbers of his men increased, Marion's spirits rose. He became his old vigorous self again, spending many of his waking hours on plans to smite the enemy when the opportunity presented itself. At the end of each day patrols of from five to ten men rode out of camp and returned at dawn. Their primary mission was to gather information, but they also lent courage to their friends and caused some fright among their enemies. The sound of hoofbeats in the night became familiar to the people of the community.

On October 24 a patrol came galloping in from their mission in the upper Williamsburg District. Their news was exciting. When Wemyss had been ordered back to Camden, Balfour had ordered Colonel Samuel Tynes, commanding the militia of the High Hills of the Santee, to turn out the militia around Salem and the forks of the Black River. At Camden they had drawn muskets, ammunition, blankets, saddles, and bridles. They had marched over to Tarcoat (also called Tearcoat and Tarcote) Swamp, where they had bivouacked in careless fashion.

This, Marion felt, was an excellent opportunity "to break up the party, before its newly made converts should become confirmed in the principles they had unwillingly adopted." He now had 150 men under his command. He told no one of his plans. He crossed the Peedee at Port's Ferry and marched to Kingstree, letting slip the impression that he was on his way to attack Major John Harrison's Tories at McCallum's Ferry.

Leaving Kingstree on the morning of October 25, Marion led his men toward Salem. Halting only for brief rest periods, they rode on through the afternoon. After dark he swung off the road and forded Black River. As he approached Tarcoat Creek he sent forward a couple of youngsters to spy out the camp of the enemy. They reported that Tynes lay encamped in a large field just off the road. It was a strong position, protected in the rear by Tarcoat Swamp. Good security measures had been taken, but there was an air of laxity about the camp. Men lay sprawled sleeping upon the ground, some sitting around talking and laughing; a couple were scraping away on their fiddles, while still others sat around three large crackling campfires playing cards.

Marion rested his men until midnight, and then roused them so as to make the attack during the early morning hours of October 26. Dividing his men into three parties, he used the same tactics that he had employed at Black Mingo. One detachment was to come in from the right, another from the left, while he led the largest group forward in a frontal strike.

Once his men were in position, Marion signaled the attack by firing his pistol. All three detachments rushed forward, shouting and firing as they dashed into the open field. The Tories leaped to their feet, most of them too surprised or too sleepy to offer resistance. Some dashed for the protection of Tarcoat Swamp, with Colonel Tynes fleeing with them. Those who were able to grab their muskets either were ridden down or fired wildly at the shadows moving swiftly through the camp. It was soon over, and, as young William James noted, "as Tarcote swamp was near, with more dismay than slaughter."

Six of the loyalists lay dead, among them the notorious Captain Amos Gaskens. Fourteen lay groaning with their wounds. Twenty-three men and boys were made prisoners. Among the mortally wounded was one of the cardplayers (some say it was Gaskens) still clutching his last hand—the ace, jack, and deuce of clubs.

The booty was great. There were eighty horses, along with their saddles and bridles. A like number of muskets were found on the field as were a considerable number of blankets. No count was taken of the foodstuff, ammunition, and personal baggage found. Marion's only losses had been two horses killed. An intangible gain was, according to young William James, that "The most of Tyne's men, soon after joined Gen. Marion, and fought bravely."

Yet there was gall mixed with the sweet taste of victory. Tynes had managed to escape, as had Ball at Black Mingo. Marion held to the theory that if the leaders could be put out of the way, the loyalists could be persuaded to lie quiet. He sent Captain William Clay Snipes into the High Hills to run down and bring in Tynes as well as other militia and civil officials of a loyalist bent. After the plunder had been collected and the wounded cared for, Marion led his men back to Kingstree. Snipes soon returned from his hunt, bringing in not only Tynes, but several loyalist militia officers and two Justices of the Peace, "Great plunderers" who had cast their lot with the British.[8]

Marion's activities were aided by the movements of other units. Daniel Morgan was operating in the general neighborhood of Hanging Rock, while William R. Davie, the partisan of North Carolina, was destroying possible food supplies for the British in the Waxhaws.

Brigadier General Harrington had moved down to the Cheraws and had dispersed the forces of Fraser and Gray, establishing himself in that place. When Snipes brought in Tynes, Marion sent him and the other prisoners to Harrington to be delivered into confinement in North Carolina. The presence of Harrington, however, created a problem. Harrington, as a brigadier general of the North Carolina militia, had implied that Marion, a Continental lieutenant colonel, was subordinate to him, and Harrington had, in fact, issued orders to Hugh Horry without Marion's knowledge or approval. In actuality, Harrington held little authority over any Continental officer, and had no right to issue orders to South Carolina militia without the proper authorization. Nevertheless, an angry Marion wrote General Gates that "I cannot think it is your Intention I should be under his Command." A similar protest was sent to Governor Rutledge.

In Harrington's defense, it should be noted that he was not taking such responsibility upon himself by his own initiative. In early August, Gates had appointed Harrington to command all of the militia regiments on both sides of the Peedee River, from the Cheraws down to the mouth of the stream. But Marion considered that this did not apply to him, as he had been given his command subsequent to that date. On October 12, the North Carolina Board of War, apparently with the approval of General Gates, had ordered Harrington to take under his immediate command not only Marion, but other South Carolina partisan groups. And it had been Harrington's understanding that Gates had directed Marion "to apply to me for directions how to act. . . ." [9]

One of these directions may have been a suggestion to Marion that he clear Georgetown of the enemy. Back on August 7 Gates had ordered Harrington to take Georgetown. Despite his having no more than seventy men in camp, Marion was excited by the prospect.

At Grimes Plantation, some sixty miles from Georgetown, he awakened his men early in the morning of October 8 and began riding hard for the coast. He sent ahead an advance guard under the command of Peter Horry and made up of Captain John Baxter, Sergeant McDonald and near thirty horsemen.

As he neared the town, Marion sent in his advance party to draw the attention of the town's defenders. After this diversion had been established, he planned to circle around and hit the redoubt inside the town. About two miles from town the advance party met a group of Tory troopers under Major Ganey and Lieutenant Evans. The two groups came together in a clash of heaving horses, flashing sabers, pistol shots and the shouts and curses of angry men. Shortly after the shock of the first collision, Ganey's men wheeled and fled toward town, Horry's men in hot pursuit.

Sergeant McDonald selected Ganey as the subject of his attention. For two miles they raced along, with neither the pursuer gaining nor the pursued pulling away. As they neared the village, still too far apart for McDonald to effectively use his sword, he lunged forward with his carbine and bayonet. He thrust into Ganey's back with such force that the bayonet penetrated the Tory leader's body, the point coming out through his chest. As the sergeant withdrew his weapon, the bayonet twisted loose from the gun. The bleeding victim still managed to maintain his seat as he fled into Georgetown. Horry broke off the pursuit; he had lost but one man. Among the Tory casualties was Lieutenant Evans, sprawled dead in the road.

Marion, meanwhile, had entered Georgetown. He met with no opposition, but he found the Tory garrison, or at least seventy of them, safely wedged in behind the walls of the redoubt built around the brick jail. He sent in a demand that they surrender. Colonel James Cassells, commander of the garrison, sent out a curt refusal. The redoubt was too strong for a party the size of Marion's to storm, and there was no time for a siege, especially after word was received that a large party of the enemy was crossing over the Santee. An armed galley lay just offshore to furnish added protection to the defenders. Marion paraded his men through the town, collecting six horses and some baggage belonging to the men in the fort. He also took up some of the citizens known to harbor loyalist leanings, paroling them to their homes until General Gates sent for them.

Lest he be caught between the redoubt and the party reported driving on Georgetown, he and his men mounted and rode swiftly for the swamps along the Little Peedee. On October 15 he squatted beneath a tree and recorded his Georgetown venture for Gates. After suggesting a plan for the rescue of the officers held as prisoners of war on Haddrell's Point, he added a postscript, "Please Excuse the Scrawl, having no table to wright in this wild woods." [10]

Francis Marion was not to linger too long in the swamps. Within two weeks he was to be forced to run for his life, but out of the chase he would acquire a new name.

Chapter VI

Francis Marion was beginning to relish the idea of an independent command. Gates seemed to have forgotten him, and he was free to swing back and forth across the low country, striking where his fancy dictated. He liked the mobility of his mounted militia and the absence of a major supply problem. If conditions became such that his men could no longer live off the country, they could always return to their homes. If clothes became worn, they could return for fresh apparel, or have their wives patch up the worn spots. Yet he was worried as to his future operations. Harrington was still hinting that he was going to take over not only Marion's men, but all militia regiments along both sides of the Peedee.

One reason for Marion's concern was that his own force was steadily increasing in numbers and would soon be large enough for an independent command; and he was just vain enough to wish no interference from sources other than the governor or the commanding general of the Southern Department. There were now, in September 1780, at least two hundred men under his command and he expected that number to double within the next few days. Colonel Hugh Giles, who had but recently rejoined him with a considerable body of men, Marion feared would soon be ordered to join Harrington.[1]

The little colonel with the limp had by now become a matter of almost major concern for the British Army, and now that he had numerical superiority over Tory units in South Carolina, he made himself more of a nuisance than ever. The situation was worsened by Cornwallis's feeling for the loyalists, he lamented the "supineness and pusillanimity of our militia, takes off all my compassion for their sufferings. If they will allow themselves to be plundered and their families ruined, by a banditti not one-third of their numbers, there is no possibility of our protecting them." Mounted units led by the British impressed horses from loyalists, giving only receipts in payment. And rather than furnish protection to the king's friends, detachments were sent instead to guard the mills used for grinding grain for the army. The *South Carolina Gazette and American Journal* attempted to discount Marion's popularity by stating that he controlled the people riding with him only by the exercise of a "most despotic and cruel tyranny." Even worse, there were unfavorable rumors "afloat" in New York regarding Cornwallis's operations in South Carolina.

Marion was now strong enough to have patrols ranging along the roads, forcing wagoners hauling supplies from Charleston to Camden to take the long way around, alternately cursing the bad roads and Marion. Colonel Balfour sent fifty men out to Monck's Corner to act as a buffer against Marion crossing the Santee and operating in the vicinity of Charleston. To Cornwallis he urged the necessity of the establishment of posts in the High Hills and at Kingstree Bridge, "otherwise communication is at an end betwixt the Army and this Town." [2]

Lieutenant Colonel George Turnbull, commanding at Camden, wrote Banastre Tarleton at Wynnesborough on November 1, 1780, urging him to bring down his British legion and eliminate this menace to the supply line to Charleston. As an extra inducement, he suggested that cattle and corn could be collected for the army at the same time. He also offered Major John Harrison and his Provincials as guides. Tarleton, just recovering from an attack of yellow fever, was anxious to get back into action, although he did seem to feel that chasing a group of partisans around the countryside was beneath the dignity of his dragoons. Nevertheless, he requested the mission, and Cornwallis gave his permission with "I . . . most sincerely hope you will get at Mr. Marion."

From their camp at Brierly's Ferry on Broad River, Tarleton's legion and Harrison's loyalists marched, crossing the Wateree at Camden on November 3. After a briefing by Turnbull, they set out after Marion on November 5. A number of horses were taken from their owners so that the infantry of the legion could be mounted and the mobility of the unit increased. Turnbull had passed on to Tarleton the information that both Marion and Snipes had their headquarters at Singleton's Mills in the High Hills and that perhaps four thousand rebels had gathered there. Turnbull should have known better than to believe such a story. Marion was never content to adopt a strategy so static as to require the establishment of a "headquarters"; his primary concern was the disruption of British supply trains, both to Camden and Cornwallis's army at Wynnesborough. On November 5 he camped at Jack's Creek on his way to attack the guard at Nelson's Ferry.

When Marion learned that Tarleton was out he guessed that he would cross at Nelson's Ferry and planned a warm reception. By cutting leafy branches and planting them along the edge of the swamp he laid an ambush. His two hundred men lay waiting for the better part of two days before the colonel received word that Tarleton had already passed on his way to Camden. Marion bent his path in that direction, hoping for another opportunity to surprise the green-coated dragoons.

But Tarleton too could play the game of ambush. He had stopped and questioned all travelers, most of whom were "dark & mysterious." He became so frustrated by their evasive answers that he convinced himself that "Nothing will serve these People but Fire & Sword." Finally a black man told him that a sizable body of men were bivouacked on Jack's Creek. Realizing that this party was probably Marion's, Tarleton led his men to the plantation of the widow of the late Brigadier General Richard Richardson who had died some six weeks earlier. He arrived at the plantation on November 7. He positioned the two small artillery pieces, or "grasshoppers," and stationed his men in concealment. Spreading the rumor that his main body had returned to Camden, he sent out patrols in an effort to entice Marion into the ambush. He hoped to do this by showing "Tokens of Fear," erratic movements, and by having his decoys leave campsites with provisions still cooking over the fires.

Marion saw the campfires of Tarleton's camp reflected against the sky from some distance away and felt that Tarleton must be burning the Richardson home. If it wasn't Tarleton, it might be the patrols that had been reported working through the neighborhood that day. He began to work his way toward the flames.

Mrs. Mary Richardson feared that the partisans would be drawn into Tarleton's trap. Her son, Captain Richard Richardson, had been a Continental officer who had been confined to Haddrell's Point after Charleston and had caught smallpox. He had been paroled and was now hiding on the plantation. The widow Richardson sent him to warn Marion. He found Marion within two miles of Tarleton's camp, creeping up to deliver a surprise attack. Young Richardson reported that Tarleton's main body of two artillery pieces, one hundred cavalry, and three hundred infantry were ahead waiting for him to make his move.

Marion wheeled and rode down the road to Jack's Creek and did not rein up until his men were on the far side of Richbourg's Mill Dam, six miles away.[3]

Somehow a prisoner escaped from Marion that night. He was brought into Tarleton's camp sometime before daylight. He reported that Marion would have attacked the night before had he not obtained intelligence from a "treacherous Woman." The men of the legion were routed out of their blankets, horses were saddled, and the dragoons rode hard for Richbourg's Mill.

After the escape of the prisoner, Marion expected as much. He likewise had his men in the saddle before daybreak. Local men who knew every animal track were chosen as guides. Major James was given the rear guard. And then Marion led Tarleton a merry chase over a thirty-five-mile route; to the head of Jack's Creek, around to the Pocotaligo River, back to Black River, and finally halting at Benbow's Ferry, much of his flight through trackless swamps. At Benbow's he waited, for it was an excellent defensive position.

Tarleton kept up the pursuit "through swamps and defiles" for seven hours and twenty-six miles. When he came to Ox Swamp on Pocotaligo River, both his troopers and their mounts were too weary to attempt the foreboding wastes of the swamp. It is said that Tarleton, as he pulled up his jaded men, cried out, "Come my Boys! Let us go back, and we will find the Game-cock [Sumter], But as for this damned old fox, the Devil himself could not catch him." The story spread and grew with each telling until the people along the Santee began to refer to the gimpy little colonel as the "Swamp Fox." [4]

At Benbow's Ferry on the Black River, Tarleton's quarry had begun to fell trees in the narrow passageway leading down to the ferry. Pickets were thrown out for some distance. Then he gathered his men and told them that if Tarleton should come up and succeed in scattering them (which was possible because of the shortage of ammunition), they should rendezvous at the passes between Pudding, Claps, or Flat swamps between Benbow's and Kingstree.

Even though Tarleton had given up the chase, he punished the community, as one observer reported, "after the manner of the East, and the coast of Barbary." From Jack's Creek to the High Hills, thirty plantation owners felt the heavy hand of retribution as they saw their homes and grain go up in flames. These "violent Rebels," said Tarleton, "now seems convinced of the Error of Insurrection." "It is distressing," wrote Marion to Gates, "to see the Women and Children, sitting in the open Air, round a Fire, without a Blanket, or any Cloathing but what they had on, and Women of family, and of ample fortunes; for he spares neither Whig nor Tory."

As the smoke rose above the trees, many of those who had fled at Tarleton's approach crept out of their hiding places in the swamps. The torch was laid aside, and on November 11, Tarleton published a proclamation offering pardon to "delinquents" and concluding with the smug statement, "It is not the Wish of Britons to be cruel or to destroy, but it is now obvious to all Carolina that Treachery Perfidy & Perjury will be punished with Instant Fire & Sword." He also claimed that the flight of Marion had a salutary effect, in that the militia now flocked into his camp, assuring him of their friendliness, "which they durst not manifest before Marion's retreat."

For the widow Richardson, Tarleton's punishment seemed the product of a cruel and ingenious mind. Not only did he order the body of General Richardson exhumed so that he could "look upon the face of a brave man," but he allowed his men to plunder the household goods. In fact it was later stated that the grave was opened because it was suspected that the family plate was hidden therein. After forcing the household servants to serve him dinner, Tarleton had his men herd the plantation's cattle, swine, and poultry into the barn where, along with the corn stored in the building, they were consumed by flames. Marion himself reported that Mrs. Richardson had been flogged to force her to reveal where Marion was hiding.

A suggestion that Tarleton's foray was a success lay in the report of a Negro who had come in with the story that Marion had planned to join William Washington and Daniel Morgan at Hanging Rock to make a joint attack on Camden. The dispersion of Marion's forces had frustrated that scheme. So anxious were the British to eliminate the partisan that they seemed quite willing to accept the story, and Cornwallis declared that Marion was now "cautious and vigilant."[5]

So convincing were Tarleton's brags that Lord Cornwallis wrote Sir Henry Clinton a puffed version of the dragoon's report:

Col. Marion had so wrought on the minds of the People, partly by the terror of his threats & cruelty of his punishments, and partly by the Promise of Plunder, that there was scarce an Inhabitant between the Santee and Peedee that was not in Arms against us, some parties had been crossed the Santee, and carried terror to the Gates of Charles-town. My first object was to reinstate matters in that quarter without which Camden could receive no supplies. I therefore sent Tarleton, who pursued Marion for several days, obliged his Corps to take to the Swamps, and by convincing the Inhabitants that there was a power superior to Marion who could likewise reward & Punish, so far checked the Insurrection, that the greatest part of them have not dared openly to appear in Arms against us since his expedition.[6]

Tarleton was shortly to leave the area, only to discover that his efforts had not been so effective as he had stated. Major James Wemyss had been patrolling along both sides of the Broad River to protect the mills that were grinding corn for the British Army. On November 7 he had come to Cornwallis and asked permission to surprise Sumter who then lay twenty-five miles below his own position. And so it was that on November 7 Cornwallis sent out Wemyss with part of the Sixty-Third Regiment and forty dragoons of the British Legion. However, Sumter was not at Moore's Plantation, thirty miles above Camden, as had originally been reported.

Before dawn on November 9 Wemyss's command stumbled into Sumter's new camp at Fishdam Ford on Broad River. Wemyss chose not to wait for daylight but attacked while it was still dark. And rather than dismounting his men to take Sumter's sleeping troops, Wemyss led his men in a headlong dash among the campfires. It was, as Cornwallis was later to note, the action of a "Mad Trooper." After the initial charge, Sumter's men recovered both their wits and their arms and not until then did the Sixty-Third dismount and drive them from the field. Although Sumter had been forced from the camp, Wemyss had been wounded in both his arm and his knee. Rather than remain to secure the ground, Wemyss's lieutenant put the major and twenty-two other wounded in a nearby house, where on the following morning they were discovered by "skulking parties" of the enemy. Two hours after sunup, Sumter came in and paroled them. In Wemyss's pocket was a list of those whom he had hanged and of the houses that he had burned. Sumter had thrown the paper into a nearby fire for fear that if his men found out about it they would surely kill the prisoner. And Sumter did treat the captives with every courtesy.[7]

Cornwallis immediately recalled Tarleton and his legion. On November 14 they saddled up and rode out of Singleton's Mill on their way to join the main army at Wynnesborough. To divert attention, Marion pretended to follow the green-coated legion as far as Nelson's Ferry, but he also had hopes of intercepting those boats in the Santee that might be carrying supplies for Camden. There were none.

Georgetown still preyed on his mind. He decided to make another try when intelligence was received suggesting that there were only fifty British regulars, mostly invalids, now making up the garrison at Georgetown. Making sure that Tarleton's destination was Wynnesborough, Marion wheeled and galloped at a steady gait through the Williamsburg District. Keeping his plans to himself for fear of a leak, he stayed away from settled areas as much as possible, swinging around Kingstree, crossing the Black River at Potato Ferry, and splashing his way through Gapway Swamp.

But he had not reckoned on British defensive maneuvers. After Tynes's defeat Nisbet Balfour had ordered Jesse Barefield to reinforce Georgetown with his mounted Tories from the Little Peedee. While Marion was being chased about the countryside by Tarleton, Barefield had marched for Georgetown. There he had a brief encounter with the men of Maurice Murphy, after which Barefield led his two hundred followers, along with the men of Captain James "Otterskin" Lewis, into Georgetown.

Marion had been too occupied dancing away before Tarleton to have received news of this latest development. On November 15 his men lay hidden two miles above Georgetown in "the Camp" behind White Bay Swamp. At dawn two parties were sent out. First, Peter Horry rode toward the Black River and the road leading into Georgetown. A little later, when he received word that a number of Tories had pitched camp at the "Pens," the plantation of Colonel William Alston, Marion sent Captain John Melton to investigate as well as to spy out the Sampit Road leading into town. Although he had no command of his own, the colonel's nephew, Lieutenant Gabriel Marion, rode along with Melton as a volunteer.

As they cantered through a rather dense swamp, they came suddenly upon Captain Barefield and his troops. There was a burst of fire from both sides. Blood streamed down Barefield's face as a load of buckshot caught him in the face and shoulder. As Melton's men turned to fly, the Tories fired at the horses. Several went down, including the mounts of Francis Goddard and young Marion. As his horse collapsed beneath him, young Goddard ran. He caught a riderless horse and sped back to camp. But Gabriel was not so fortunate. Once the enemy had ridden him down, they began to club him unmercifully. Among his captors was one whom young Marion recognized as having been a guest in the home of Francis Marion. In desperation, Gabriel called out his name to plead for mercy; as he did, one of the Tories yelled, "He is one of the breed of that damned old rebel."

As the angry cries increased, Gabriel reached out and clung to the saddle of the man whom he had recognized. Milling around the two, the angry loyalists shouted to Marion's protector that if he did not thrust the prisoner from him that he too would be shot down. As he was pulled away, a musket was thrust against Gabriel's chest and fired, so close that the linen was scorched. Young Marion's death was the second resulting from the skirmish; all but one of the four wounded died soon afterward. At least four of Melton's men had been captured.

In the meantime, at White's Plantation near Georgetown, Peter Horry's detachment came up on a number of "Otterskin" Lewis's company busily slaughtering cattle. They fled as Horry came in sight, firing a few wild shots as they ran. Their comrades and a number of Barefield's men came to their aid and a fight soon developed, which Horry described as "some flying, others pursuing; and with muskets and pistols, and swords, shooting and cutting down as fast as they could."

As the fight moved away, Horry found himself left only with a boy of fourteen named Gwynn, who was armed with a musket and had something of a reputation as a marksman. Between eight and ten enemy horsemen led by Captain Lewis suddenly galloped up to surround them. In answer to Horry's challenge if they were friends, the answer came back loud and clear, "Friends to King George!"

As Lewis raised his musket to bear on Horry, young Gwynn quickly raised and fired his own gun loaded with buckshot. Lewis toppled from his horse, dying, but he still had enough strength to force himself to lift his pistol and pull the trigger. Horry's horse crashed to the ground. Hearing the shots, Horry's men came back, shouting as they advanced. The loyalists rushed from the scene, leaving behind four of Melton's men whom they had captured and, said Horry, "beaten very barbarously with the butts of their muskets."

A number of the enemy took to the swamps. As Marion came up with his entire force, the survivors fled toward the protection of Georgetown. Within a quarter mile of their redoubt, and within the range of its guns, they drew up as if to make a stand. Marion detached a group to try to cut them off from the fort. Seeing this maneuver, the Tories hurriedly made their way to safety within the walls of the redoubt. The sight of the cohorns (small mortars) and swivel guns on the walls was enough to discourage Marion from attempting to storm the redoubt. His men were too short on ammunition, with only four rounds to a man, to make even a pretense at siege warfare. He drew off. He had killed three of the enemy and had taken twelve prisoners.

For the next two days he lay within three miles of the town, watching the enemy and gathering information. His men began to steal away, frightened when they heard of Tarleton's manifesto, "Threatening Fire & Sword."

Francis Marion, usually a taciturn soul, mourned his nephew, although to his companions he had changed little other than having a worn cast to his face. The day after Gabriel's death, a mulatto called Sweat was brought into camp. Somehow the rumor began to float around the campfires that Sweat was responsible for the death of young Marion. All that afternoon and the next angry glances were cast in the direction of the prisoner. One officer, ran the whisper, had offered a bottle of rum to the man who would kill the mulatto.

That night, on the ride back to Williamsburg, Sweat was among the prisoners who were marched along under guard. As they were wading the swamps, a militia captain rode up to Sweat, placed his pistol against the prisoner's head and calmly blew his brains out. Marion was furious and dressed down the officer in command of the prisoners' guard, although there is no indication that the captain who actually did the shooting was ever punished.

Marion and his band went into camp at Shepherd's Ferry on the Black Mingo. The following morning, in a bit of martial fluff, he called the men together in a large circle. After he told them that his nephew "was a virtuous young man—that he had fallen in the cause of his country, and he would mourn him no more," he called young Gwynn out and presented "Otterskin" Lewis's fine charger to the lad as a reward for his action as a "brave little man," and sent his congratulations to the boy's mother.[8]

Although intelligence suggested that many Tories had gone home after their scrimmage with Marion, and that there were no more than eighty men comprising the entire Georgetown garrison, Marion felt that he should abandon all ideas of attacking that post until he could once again have surprise as an element in his favor. Not only was his own ammunition low, but he was not equipped to assault a fortified post with artillery.

Five of the prisoners he had taken at Georgetown experienced a change of heart and took an oath of allegiance to the United States and joined his band. On November 17 Captain Thomas Potts escorted the remaining captives to General Harrington's camp on the Peedee. Marion also requested that the general replenish his ammunition supply. He made a futile effort to convince Harrington that if he would lend him his mounted troops he could remove the enemy post at Kingstree. Yet his greatest concern was his own rapidly diminishing force. He placed the blame on Gates. On November 21, in a letter almost pathetic in its melancholia, he wrote, "Many of my people has Left me & gone over to the Enemy, for they think that we have no Army coming on, & have been Deceived. As we hear nothing from you a Great while, I hope to have a line from you in what Manner to Act, & some Assurance to the people of Support." There was a possibility of some cooperative action, or support, for rumors had it that Colonel William Washington and his mounted troops were at Rugeley's Mills, twelve miles north of Camden.[9]

Tarleton had returned to Camden and had then gone on to Wynnesborough to join Cornwallis, boasting of his pursuit of, and the flight of, Marion. Feeling that he had eliminated the Swamp Fox, Tarleton was eager to add to his laurels by disposing of the Gamecock and wished to "put a stop to Mr. Sumpter's Braggins." Sumter had become an irritant, so flourishing his victory over Wemyss that many were beginning to flock to his brigade, while many loyalists, said Tarleton, "are in the utmost terror and running down to the Congarees as far as possible."

On November 20, 1780 Tarleton came up on Sumter and Colonel Elijah Clarke at Blackstock's Plantation on Tyger River and attacked with 194 of the legion cavalry and eighty mounted troops from the Sixty-Third Regiment. Sumter took a position on an eminence with his back to the river. In the ensuing fight, both sides claimed victory, but upon examination, it seems to have ended in a draw rather than a clearly defined decision, although Sumter was badly wounded through both shoulders and was carried from the field in an oxhide used as a litter. Despite casualties of over fifty-one killed and wounded, Tarleton's claim to victory was supported by the fact that it had been his dragoons who pursued Sumter's after the battle; there was even a report that the Gamecock had been killed. Shortly afterward there was an erroneous report that Elijah Clarke had also suffered a mortal wound, leading Cornwallis to write to Balfour, "We have lost two great plagues in Sumpter and Clarke, I wish your friend Marion was as quiet." [10]

Marion, however, had no intention of lying quiet just to give his Lordship peace of mind. According to one exaggerated British account he was leading some 406 men in wide swings through the Williamsburg District, advancing to Gaillard's, falling back across Black River, and then sweeping in toward Kingstree. Always on the move, and usually marching at night, he seldom gave any indication of his next move. Yet Cornwallis felt that Marion had suffered because of Tarleton's blow against Sumter in that men would be reluctant to join him in the face of the defeat of that bold partisan.

Yet the very presence of Marion constituted an almost constant threat to his flank, and Cornwallis came to the conclusion that Kingstree should be occupied as a means of discouraging sudden rampages. He ordered Balfour to station a regiment in that community. In executing this directive, Balfour had American prisoners of war transferred from camps on shore to prison hulks in the harbor, thereby releasing their guards for duty in the field. The detachment as assembled was made up of these guards, Hessians, and loyalists; it was attached to the battalion of the Sixty-Fourth Regiment commanded by Major Robert McLeroth. In all, there were 275 men, supported by two three-pounder field pieces.

McLeroth seems to have been given the command because neither Cornwallis nor Balfour wanted him around. He had no more than left when Balfour began to complain to Cornwallis, "how I am disappointed in my man, I will not now explain . . . he now stands in a situation where he can scarcely go wrong," but "he is by no means to be trusted, to act for himself." McLeroth was to give some support to Colonel James Cassells, the Tory leader on the lower Peedee, who had been begging to be given only an "opening" and the loyalists would flock in to man the posts along the rivers. Balfour had added weight to his arguments by declaring that many people wished to desert Marion, "whom they all look upon only as a plunderer. . . ." [11]

By November 20 McLeroth had pitched camp in Kingstree; a messenger was sent hustling off to Marion with the news.

Marion was not fool enough to make a blind attack on Kingstree, especially after an intercepted letter from Lord Rawdon revealed that the New York Volunteers had been mounted and alerted to ride through the country with a view toward destroying crops and driving off cattle. Marion moved down and took a post on the Peedee. His patrols constantly worked over the area not only near the camp but at some distance. A dispatch to General Harrington urged him to detach his mounted troops to aid in driving out McLeroth.

By this time Francis Marion had become aware that patriotism was a fluid emotion. A pattern had been established: after the Tories had been temporarily subdued, his men would spin off to return to their homes. As volunteers, they could come and go as they pleased, and Marion held little power, especially with no civil authority active within the state. He seldom had the same people under his command for as long as two weeks, which meant there was almost continuous instruction, along with some superficial training in the tactics of partisan warfare. He had no ready source of military supplies, and he begged Gates to send him clothing, ammunition, and medicine, "for we are all poor Continentals without money." Medical care was a critical item as "I am Greatly in want of a Surgeon; one of my wounded Bleed to Death for want of one, & many is Oblige to retreat for want of Medicines, for I have not any whatever."

He was disgusted with Harrington, who seemed to do nothing more than sit and wait and issue orders. A letter to Gates requested that the general order Harrington to detach his cavalry to aid in driving the enemy out of Kingstree before they gained control of the country.[12]

At Kingstree McLeroth fretted when there was no sign of Marion. Nor would the loyalists, either out of fear or ignorance, give information as to where the Fox was hiding. Unaware that Jesse Barefield had been wounded in the Georgetown skirmish,

McLeroth waited for the Tories to come in. Fearing that he might become cooped up within the town by the enemy, he moved down to a better position at Murray's Ferry on the Santee.

He had little to fear from Marion. The steadily decreasing number of men under his command left him no alternative but to go to cover. It was counter to his philosophy to go deliberately into action unless he held advantages that carried some promise of victory. He lost himself in the swamps on Britton's Neck.

With Marion out of the way and Sumter wounded, the British hold on the Santee was firm. It was with some relief that Balfour wrote Cornwallis: "Marrion has crossed the Pedee and has been rapid in his movements since the appearance of the 64th." Although he felt this retreat would spirit up the Tories, Balfour doubted whether Marion's withdrawal was permanent. When a magazine of stores was established at Monck's Corner, he not only stationed a galley in the river, but he garrisoned the post with a detachment of Hessians and convalescents, for "Marrion is to formidable to trust so near the boats, and stores, without something better than militia."

The disappearance of Marion, on the other hand, only heightened the apprehensions of McLeroth, who suspected the Fox was off somewhere raising troops to attack him. His concerns were not lessened by Cornwallis's speculations that Marion would next attempt to interrupt communications between Georgetown and Camden. McLeroth moved up to the Great Savannah where his men pitched camp near the home of Thomas Sumter, and where he was joined by reinforcements bringing the number under his command from 275 to 400 men. Yet he was made to look worse by the continuous boastings of James Cassells, and Cornwallis was fearful that the fervor of the Tory commander would lead McLeroth into rash moves. He cautioned Rawdon: "I tremble for McLeroth & hope Cassels will not tempt him too far."

Marion's departure, however, had lessened some of the fears of the British commanding general. His preparations for an invasion of North Carolina were speeded. He was happy when Colonel Samuel Tynes escaped from Harrington, for he had been attempting to arrange an exchange for the Tory leader so that he might organize the militia and secure the country once the main army had marched northward.

Captain John Coffin of the New York Volunteers was ordered to seek out a suitable site for a strongpoint in the High Hills of the Santee so that the countryside might be kept under tighter control. Coffin selected the rising ground near the Wateree known as Upton Hill. With the aid of slaves commandeered from nearby plantations he constructed a redoubt, mounting two small artillery pieces on its walls. He and his men garrisoned the post until Tynes could collect his men and move in.

Major McLeroth was cut from a different bolt of cloth from Tarleton, Wemyss, or the other British officers who had blazed their fiery trails through the Santee country. He took no delight in seeing a home go up in flames. In fact, it might be said that he was something of an anachronism, for he possessed none of that streak of brutality that seemed to characterize the professional soldier of the eighteenth century. He held no favor in the eyes of Balfour, who suggested that McLeroth be placed under Rawdon's direction as "I can spare him very well. . . . I think the sooner he can be put in a situation where he has not to act for himself the better—otherwise I fear some accident to him." Cornwallis was likewise unhappy with McLeroth's detaching small units to roam the countryside rather than making a push with his full strength. Rawdon was as unhappy as Balfour with the prospect of commanding McLeroth, and in reply to his complaints, Lord Cornwallis cautioned, "I trust, my Dear Lord, that you will have a constant eye to McLeroth who by his letters requires much looking after. A blow to any British Regiment cuts deep." Ultimately Cornwallis decided to take

McLeroth into North Carolina with him, replacing him with Lieutenant Colonel John T. Watson and his Third Regiment of guards. But Rawdon would have to put up with McLeroth until the exchange could take place. No one felt that the trade improved matters too much, but the general ordered the shift because of a possible command conflict between Watson and Tarleton.[13]

The game of military chess required time, and Francis Marion had made use of this interval of British indecision to better his own situation. When he had withdrawn earlier, the Jenkins boys, Samuel and Britton, had informed him of a spot that sounded as though it would be an ideal hiding place. They led him to Snow Island, named for William Snow, an early settler of the Williamsburg District.

The low ridge that formed Snow Island was some five miles long and two miles wide, rising out of the water and boggy ground that formed its boundaries. On the east was the Peedee River, while Lynche's Creek lapped its skirts on the north before it emptied into the Peedee. Here the creek was wide and deep and well nigh choked with a great raft of a logjam. Clark's Creek, a deep stream, ran along the south and west. Snow's Lake also lay to the west, along with the turgid waters and marshy lands of Muddy Creek and Sockee Swamp.

On the highest part of the ridge near the middle of the island William Goddard had built his home, little more than a cabin in the wilderness. Except for the fields that Goddard had cleared, the area was heavily wooded by gum, oak, and pine trees, while giant cypresses loomed against the horizon in the marshes. Underbrush tangled itself to form natural barricades, while canebrakes rambled along some of the watercourses. The site was also near enough to Ganey's Tory country that frequent parties could be sent across the river to awe the Tories and take the edge off their military ambitions. And it was better to forage in enemy country than among friends.

The partisan camp was pitched in the forests and fields near Goddard's house, where the men screened themselves from the elements as best they could by throwing up brush and log shelters. Crude storage bins were constructed to store those provisions they might accumulate. Goddard's barn was strengthened to be used as a prison; so proud of their work were the men that they christened the barn the "Bull Pen."

Boats were collected and tied up on the island side of the streams. Trees were felled across many of the approaches and bridges were destroyed to further isolate the hideout. Those boats that were not needed were ordered sunk. To provide a fortified outpost, Colonel John Ervin threw up a redoubt on the lower side of Dunham's Bluff on the far side of the Peedee and garrisoned it with Captain John Dozier's company of Britton's Neck militia.[14]

Marion was now ready to take to the field again. A call went out to his men. The response was good; as his numbers grew, Marion sent out patrols to guide them in, to gather supplies, and to guard against surprise. Knowing the value of good public relations in the midst of a civil war, he always cautioned against the use of violence by the patrols and foragers.

Yet, once away from the camp, the men found it difficult to stifle the strong urge for vengeance and often satisfied their blood lust on those loyalists who were so unfortunate as to meet up with them. They ranged far from camp. A few weeks later an officer new to the South was to comment that the Tories "are chased from their homes, hunted thro' the woods and shot with as much indifference as you would a buck—even the enemy treat them with the greatest contempt and deny them the common necessaries of life."

According to Rawdon, two brothers of Major Samuel Harrison, who lay ill with smallpox within eight miles of Camden, were slaughtered in their beds when a "Scouting party of Rebels" burst into their rooms on the night of December 4, 1780. They then shot the father of the victims. The following day a British officer on patrol came across a house which had just been stripped by the rebels, while "the Woman was left standing in her Shift, even her Stockings & Shoes having been pulled off of her; & her four Children were stripped stark naked. These are the Enemies, who talk of the laws & usages of war." [15]

With every passing day Marion was nearer to taking the field again. Opportunity presented itself earlier than he had anticipated. Intelligence revealed that McLeroth, reinforced by 150 men under John Coffin, was moving from Nelson's Ferry back to Kingstree. News also came that Tynes had made his escape and was even now calling out his Tories, and rumor had it that he would soon join McLeroth with a large force. Now, Marion felt, was the time to strike lest the enemy at Kingstree grow strong enough to dominate the country. He alerted his men.

Crossing Clark's Creek, he moved over to Indian Town. There he halted long enough to gather enough information to plan his strategy and the proper precautions against surprise. Peter Horry's troop was detached to take a swing through the High Hills and to take a good look at Colonel Tynes's new post at Fort Upton.

Horry and his men rode that night, taking the road that ran east of Black River. At noon of the following day they pulled up at a tavern kept by one whose loyalist sympathies were common knowledge. They treated him with the rough attention they felt one of his political persuasion deserved. After lunch, while Horry was questioning the tavernkeeper, the man's wife was shrewd enough to lead one of Horry's troopers to a storehouse; she said not a word but merely pointed to a barrel of apple brandy. As soon as the trooper had slaked his rather powerful thirst, he called for his companions. They drank heartily and then drank again before filling their canteens.

As they rode through the chill December afternoon after leaving the tavern, Horry noticed that his men were uncommonly gay, and they were turning up their canteens frequently. When he asked what they were drinking, they smirked in witless fashion as they answered, "Water, sir, water! Nothing but water." The lie was obvious, "For some grinned in my face like monkeys; others looked as stupid as asses; while the others chattered like magpies." With the exception of Captain Neilson and Horry, the entire troop was silly drunk.

Their guide, a "jolter-headed fellow," who was possessed of a great belly, lurched back and forth in such magnificent sweeps that he finally lost his balance and toppled to the ground, a limp and sodden mass of drunken blubber. There was no need for going on to complete the mission—the sound of the troop's revelry was already ringing through the forest and they were too drunk to fight if forced into an action.

Horry ordered a retreat. The movement, he said, was executed "with all the noise and irregularity that might have been expected from a troop of drunkards, each of whom mistaking himself for commander-in-chief, gave orders according to his own mad humour; and whooped and hallooed at such a rate, that I verily believe no bull drivers ever made half the racket."

Back at camp, when the crestfallen Horry made his report, Marion allowed a rare chuckle to escape his lips. He agreed that Horry had done the proper thing in withdrawing, but slyly added, "But pray keep a careful eye on the apple water next time." [16]

Although Horry's adventure bore all the hallmarks of a comic opera, it was possibly more effective than had he launched an attack against newly built Fort Upton. Certainly the casualties, aside from monumental hangovers, were fewer. The results came about through one of the strange quirks of fate on which history is so often hinged.

Horry's drunken troopers, reeling and whooping their way along the roads, had created considerable alarm among the Black River loyalists. They spread the word, and by the time it reached the fort on Upton Hill, the story had become so over-

blown that now it was General Harrington and his entire command marching against the post. All but twenty of Tynes's
militia immediately walked off. Tynes, feeling this number too
small, rode off to Camden on December 8, as Rawdon noted,
"exceedingly frightened." He told Lord Rawdon that he was now
convinced that he could not control militia and begged that he
be allowed to tender his resignation. It was accepted. With the
legend of Tynes's ability to handle militia now dissolved, Lord
Cornwallis wrote, "I find Tyne's Militia has again squandered."

Some time earlier a number of recruits for the Seventh Regiment had arrived in Charleston, but two-thirds of them had
been such poor specimens that they had been listed as "bad."
Balfour had been anxious to get them off his hands and to
their regiments. He planned to march them down to the Great
Savannah to McLeroth, who was to then escort them to the
High Hills of the Santee where a cavalry unit from Camden
would meet them, although Cornwallis did not want this to take
place until "Mr. Marion is disposed of." [17]

Marion received word that the recruits had left Charleston. A
call went out to the militia. It was the off season, the crops
were in the barn, and the militia came trooping into camp.
When he had assembled seven hundred mounted men, Marion
led them across the Williamsburg District and up the Santee
road. He had passed Halfway Swamp, twenty miles above Nelson's Ferry, when he overtook McLeroth escorting his recruits
in a leisurely fashion.

A sudden charge drove in the British pickets. Riflemen were
sent forward to harass the rear guard. Marion circled around
McLeroth's flanks and led his mounted troops forward in a frontal attack. McLeroth was under a distinct disadvantage in not
having mounted troops to protect his infantry against cavalry
charges. The Sixty-Fourth Regiment retreated slowly, firing as
they fell back on a field enclosed by a rail fence. They quickly
sought what protection the rails had to offer, herding the

frightened recruits in behind them. Thus protected, they had a chance to inflict some damage upon charging horsemen.

As the fight developed, McLeroth sent out swift riders carrying pleas for assistance. They met up with Captain John Coffin and 140 mounted infantrymen riding forward to pick up and escort the recruits into Camden. Coffin, rather than rushing forward to add his strength to McLeroth, turned off and posted his men in a secure position behind Swift Creek. Later it was revealed that Coffin felt that McLeroth was holding his own or else the messenger would not have been able to escape. Coffin also claimed that he had received intelligence that he was to be attacked that night.

Back at the battlefield, Marion had pulled up his men along the half-pond, half-swamp that lay just east of the Santee road. He waited. A British officer appeared, walking towards them under the protection of a flag. He no sooner reached Marion than he began to vehemently protest the shooting of the British pickets by Marion's men as against all the rules of warfare between civilized nations. In his wrath, he threw out the challenge to the Americans that they come out into the open and fight like soldiers.

Indignation welled up within Marion. He answered the charge of shooting pickets with indictments of Wemyss and Tarleton burning the houses of helpless civilians. If the British continued to burn houses, then he would continue to shoot pickets. As for the rash dare to come out into the open and fight, it appeared to him as the last resort "of a man in desperate circumstances," but if Major McLeroth "wished to witness a combat between picked men on each side, he was ready to gratify him." McLeroth picked up the gauntlet as flung down by Marion.

The area south of an old oak tree that stood in the middle of the field was selected as the dueling ground. McLeroth chose twenty of his best marksmen to represent the redcoats. Marion held an advantage in that many of his men were equipped with rifles whose range was much greater than the heavy muskets of the enemy.

To command the Americans, Marion selected Major John Vanderhorst with Captain Samuel Price as second in command. As Marion thought of a man who would perform well for his team, he put his name on a slip of paper and handed it to Gavin Witherspoon, who held a reputation as an excellent sharpshooter. When his name was called, not one man held back. Calling his twenty men together, Marion gave them a spirited talk:

My brave soldiers! You are twenty men picked this day out of my whole regiment. I know all of you, and I have often witnessed your bravery. In the name of your country, I call upon you once more to shew it! My confidence in you is great, and I am sure it will not be disappointed. Fight like men, fight as you have always done, and you are sure of the victory.

As the men readied themselves for combat, Vanderhorst asked Witherspoon at what distance buckshot would be most effective; the reply was that the first fire should be delivered at fifty yards. Vanderhorst, who admitted to being a poor judge of distance, asked Witherspoon to tap him on the shoulder when they reached the proper spot. Then, he said, he would give the word and the marksmen were to form on his left. As each man found his place, each was to aim and fire at the redcoat directly opposite him, and then, "on my word for it, few will be left for a second shot."

Vanderhorst led his party out to within one hundred yards of the British line. As he continued to press forward, an officer walked quickly along the front of the enemy team, drawn up near the great oak. A command rang out. With this, the redcoated line shouldered their muskets and quick-stepped briskly back to their own lines. McLeroth had agreed to the combat and had staged the little farce only as a means of gaining time.

The day ended with the troops of both sides engaging in little more than a staring match. After dark, McLeroth's camp bristled with great campfires as his men piled fence rails and logs on the flames. They were noisy, engaging in loud and boisterous conversation until near midnight. It was all a ruse to divert the enemy from their real intentions. Leaving their heavy baggage, they slipped quietly out of camp, taking the road to Singleton's Mill, ten miles away.

It was not until dawn that Marion discovered he had been deceived by blazing bonfires and loud talk. He immediately detached Major Hugh Horry with a hundred men to overtake McLeroth. There was some rear guard action, skirmishes in which some on both sides were wounded. These little fire fights did not last long, but each time one developed Horry had to dismount his men to fight on foot. Realizing that these delays would make it impossible to move fast enough with so large a force as his, Horry ordered Major James to choose those men with the swiftest horses and ride around the mill pond and occupy the houses at Singleton's Mill. Singleton's house stood on a rather high eminence and commanded the defile between the hill and Wateree Swamp. If James could take possession of the houses he could retard McLeroth until Horry, and then Marion, came up to engage the British column.

James raced ahead. The vanguard of the British column was just coming into view as James and his party sped up the hill. They dashed into the house in time to deliver one fire and see a British captain fall. And then the enemy could only stare open-mouthed as James and his men fled the protection of the buildings, leaped upon their horses and galloped away. They had discovered that the Singleton family had smallpox!

Coffin finally abandoned the safety of his position at Swift Creek and had ridden on to meet McLeroth. Deciding that it would be imprudent to turn and make a stand, Coffin and McLeroth marched rapidly for Camden. Rawdon was furious that McLeroth had not made a better showing in this "scram-

ble." "I must immediately dislodge Marion," he wrote Cornwallis, "But as McLeroth has not quite enterprise enough, I shall
let him go to Charleston (which he wishes)." Major John
Campbell was assigned the command of the Sixty-Fourth,
which was stationed sixteen miles from Nelson's Ferry.

Perhaps the British, in pulling McLeroth out of the area,
did not fully understand his importance to their cause, for he had
been more popular than his predecessors along the Santee.
Although one of the supposed reasons for his removal was his
refusal to burn houses as ordered, even Rawdon was forced to
admit "that his Mild and equitable Behaviour to the Inhabitants of that Country has been of great Service."

During McLeroth's retreat those wounded on both sides
(nearly half of whom were Marion's) had been gathered up and
left at a tavern under a flag. Leaving his own surgeon to attend
them, McLeroth also did something almost unheard of—he left
money with the tavernkeeper to pay for their subsistence. When
Marion stopped by, the old woman who kept the place prattled
on about McLeroth as the "sweetest-spoken, mildest-looking,
noble-spirited Englishman I ever saw in all my born days." And,
she went on to demand of Marion, "would it not be a burning
shame to go kill such a dear good gentleman as that?"

But whatever his good qualities, McLeroth's withdrawal had
left Marion in command of the river and the Santee road, leading Rawdon to declare, "I must drive Marion out of that Country; but I cannot yet say what steps I shall take to effect it." [18]

Chapter VII

With Marion in control of the routes along the Santee, British supply trains were once again forced to take the longer, more circuitous route from Monck's Corner to Friday's Ferry on the Congaree. Balfour issued orders that no supply boats were to go upstream beyond Murray's Ferry. One boat coming down from Camden, whose captain had not been informed of this directive, swung confidently into the dock at Nelson's Ferry on December 14, 1780. After removing the cargo and all equipment thought useful, Marion's men set fire to the vessel. Marion lay back in wait, hoping to capture other boats with cargoes of arms and ammunition, but all were stopped before they reached the ferry.

On the far side of the river, the British maintained a post, originally composed of eighty Hessians, at the ferry. When they took up a number of Negroes to repair the causeway leading to the ferry, Marion's men so harassed these working parties that on December 18 a reinforcement of 150 troops had been sent out from Charleston. Earlier in the month the enemy had attempted to cross over the river to establish a bridgehead, but they had turned back when Marion's men rode down to the ferry landing.

Major John Campbell and the Sixty-Fourth Regiment kept a close watch over the activities of the partisan leader but felt it unwise to attack, for the partisan camp at Nelson's Ferry appeared too strong. Marion was equally vigilant with regard to Campbell; his patrols and those of the enemy exchanged an occasional passing shot as their paths crossed while making their rounds. As the enemy began to show more interest in him, Marion moved over to Benbow's Ferry on Black River.[1]

But far to the north, in Philadelphia, changes had been taking place that not only would affect the character of the war in the Southern Department, but would make it possible for Marion's operations to become coordinated with the movements of the Southern Army. Gates had neglected Marion, answering few of his letters and making little use of his talents. Other than the brief period when he was with the army, Marion had seldom known where the Southern Army was located or what he could do to further its success.

Ever since the disaster at Camden, many of those in the Continental Congress, including members who, in July 1780, had insisted on Gates's being sent southward to "Burgoyne" Cornwallis, were now clamoring for the recall of the unfortunate general. On October 5, 1780, as a result of almost constant prodding, Congress passed a resolution requesting General Washington to name a successor as commanding general in the Southern Department. John Matthews, of the South Carolina delegation in Congress, wrote to the General, suggesting Nathanael Greene, "if it would not be incompatible with the rules of the army." Greene now stood higher in the favor of Congress than when Gates was selected, and in general it was a popular appointment, with Major General Robert Howe declaring: "General Greene will deserve success whether he obtains it or not."

Baron von Steuben, the fabulous Prussian who had done so much to whip the American army from an armed mob into the semblance of a fighting machine, was detached to Greene as was the Legion of Lieutenant Colonel "Lighthorse Harry" Lee. But this was all the active support that Washington could give, and he could promise little for the future. On his way south, Greene stopped by the Continental Congress in Philadelphia and the Pennsylvania and Maryland legislatures, and in Richmond he discussed the situation with Governor Thomas Jefferson. His wry comment as to the attitude of the Continental Congress could be applied equally well to the others, in that "poverty was urged as a plea, in bar to every application. They all promised fair, but I fear will do little: ability is wanting with some, and inclination with others."

Steuben was left in Virginia to further recruiting and forward supplies to the Southern Army. Greene had first stopped by Hillsborough in North Carolina, where Gates was believed to be, but discovered that his predecessor had moved on down to Charlotte where the supply situation was supposed to be more favorable. On December 2, 1780 Greene arrived in Charlotte and assumed command. Prospects were less than dismal, and one of the first observations he made was to the effect that his new command was nothing "but the shadow of an army in the midst of distress." [2]

Captain John Melton had served as Marion's courier to Gates and was in camp when Greene arrived. After the general had spent some time in reorganization, he took time to have a talk with Melton, who reported Marion's methods of operations and his desperate need of supplies and ammunition. On December 4 Greene wrote to Marion promising nothing in the way of supplies or aid from the army in the near future, although he was "fully sensible your service is hard & sufferings great, but how great the prize for which we contend." His initial task for Marion was relatively simple, for "Spies are the eye of an Army.

137

. . . At present, I am badly off for intelligence. It is the highest importance that I get the earliest intelligence of any reinforcement which may arrive at Charleston."

Melton caught up with Marion at the camp at Benbow's Ferry, where he was feeding his men through the efforts of the foraging parties working along the Black River. Greene's letter suddenly made him and the work he was doing seem important. It was vastly different from the situation under Gates, when both he and Thomas Sumter had been forced to wage their own isolated campaigns. Such operations appeared to please Sumter, but Marion seemed to need being part of a larger operation.

He was not sure just how much intelligence he could furnish Greene, "as nothing but gold and silver passes here and I am Destitute of Either. The Enemy is so Suspicious they will not permit any man to pass on the South of Santee without the Strictest Examination and they have patroles along the river & guards at several Passes." He was able to report that Major General Alexander Leslie had disembarked at Charleston with a number of reinforcements for Cornwallis, and he gave careful details of the disposition of various enemy detachments. Then he added, a bit wistfully, "If I had a few Continental Troops I should be able to do more than I am at present by them awing the militia who act with diffidence, 100 would be sufficient for this purpose."

But he knew that this was but a daydream, for Greene was crying for more Continentals to bolster his own forces and he, too, nurtured a dream, a grand scheme for the creation of a "flying army," an elite, mobile striking force with which he could carry through all the basic patterns of warfare. The majority of the Southern Army was militia, and Nathanael Greene despised these citizen soldiers, for "with the militia everybody is a general."

It is to be suspected that Marion wished to have the loan of the hundred Continentals to make a strike at Georgetown. His

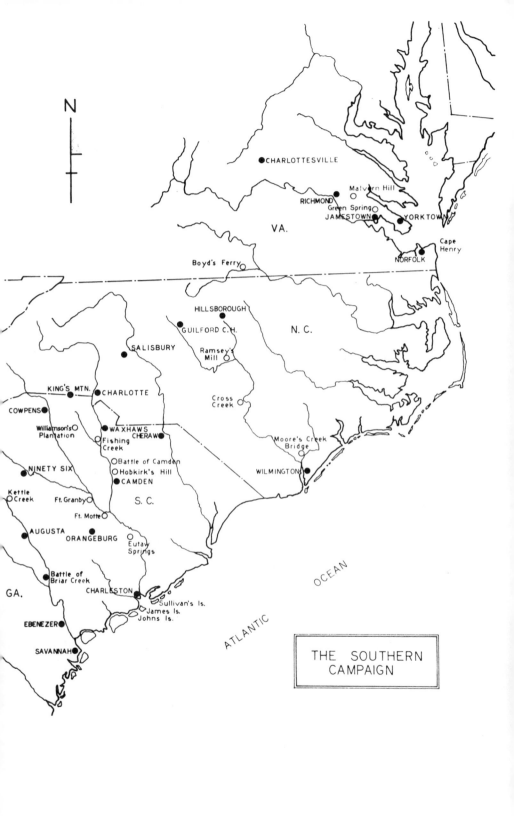

N

CHARLOTTESVILLE

Malvern Hill

RICHMOND
Green Spring
JAMESTOWN
YORKTOWN

VA.

Cape
Henry

Boyd's Ferry

NORFOLK

HILLSBOROUGH

GUILFORD C.H.

N. C.

SALISBURY

Ramsey's
Mill

KING'S MTN.
CHARLOTTE

Cross
Creek

COWPENS

Williamson's
Plantation

WAXHAWS
CHERAW

Fishing
Creek

Moore's Creek
Bridge

NINETY SIX

Battle of Camden

Hobkirk's Hill

CAMDEN

WILMINGTON

Kettle
Creek

Ft. Granby

S. C.

Ft. Motte

AUGUSTA
ORANGEBURG

Eutaw
Springs

Battle of
Briar Creek

CHARLESTON

OCEAN

GA.

Sullivan's Is.
James Is.
Johns Is.

EBENEZER

ATLANTIC

THE   SOUTHERN
CAMPAIGN

SAVANNAH

two failures before that town plagued him. On December 6 he had written Gates that the garrison in the town amounted to no more than eighty regulars, implying that he should be allowed to go against it. But before an answer was received, reinforcements had swelled the size of the garrison and additional and heavier guns had been mounted in the redoubts. Marion then shied away from his plan, but he did keep small parties ranging through the area, harassing and driving in their foraging parties.

He was too weak to stay long in one place. Following practices that had now become routine, Marion kept on the move, leaving Benbow's Ferry on Christmas Eve and trotting back to the Santee. After Leslie had landed in Charleston on December 20, Marion had kept him under constant observation, and as the long British column crawled its way through the swamps to make a junction with Cornwallis, he fell away before it. He went into camp at Snow Island.[3]

Marion's withdrawal seemingly cleared the way for the British to consolidate their hold on South Carolina before Cornwallis began his delayed invasion of North Carolina. When Rawdon reported that Marion had crossed the Black River, Cornwallis replied that he was "glad to find that Marion has left the Coast clear." There was, however, a lingering suspicion that it was all a ruse, and no definite moves were made until patrols reported that there were no ambushes or traps. Cornwallis gave orders for the Sixty-Fourth Regiment to remain in South Carolina rather than take them on campaign as he had planned.

Even then the Sixty-Fourth was not adequate to protect the supply routes between Camden and Charleston, but Cornwallis had concluded that additional regulars had to be left behind to aid the loyalists against the partisans. Lieutenant Colonel John W. T. Watson, whom Cornwallis termed "that Plague," was detached from Leslie's force and assigned to the Camden command, although Rawdon was not particularly happy to have him. Watson and his Third Regiment of Foot, or the "Buffs," joined Campbell and the Sixty-Fourth who had taken a position at Sumter's house at the Great Savannah on the Santee.

Looking over the ground, Watson came to the conclusion that Sumter's house could never be made into a proper strongpoint. He then marched to Wright's Bluff, on Scott's Lake, ten miles above Nelson's Ferry. Here was an old Indian burial mound some thirty or forty feet in height rising out of a great open plain. On its slope Watson constructed a strong redoubt, complete with three rows of abatis. Two artillery pieces were positioned within its walls. In a puff of self-satisfaction, he named the post Fort Watson.

This display of might, the injury to Sumter, and Marion's seeming inactivity led one army surgeon in Charleston to note: "This Province has been greatly teazed by some Partisan militia headed by Sumpter, Marrion, & Clarke, and the Progress of the Army has been much retarded by their depredations. They are now pretty well cut up, and I sh^d hope a perfect tranquility w^d take place." [4]

About December 6 Marion had dispatched Captains Thomas Mitchell and Thomas Waites to Greene's camp at Charlotte. When they arrived they discovered the Southern Army had been reorganized and was now on the move. The general had found the supply situation at Charlotte intolerable. On December 16 he had given the command of a select group to Brigadier General Daniel Morgan and had ordered him to move in the general direction of Ninety Six, there to take a position to the Broad River to harass the enemy and "spirit up the people." Greene was taking the major portion of the army and moving down to the Peedee where provisions were reported in more plentiful supply. These two stations placed the two divisions of the army in positions that would enable them to hammer at the flanks of the British Army should Cornwallis begin his march into North Carolina. Because of a heavy downpour the two armies did not move out of Charlotte until December

20, and Greene's army did not reach their "camp of repose" on Hicks Creek and the Peedee until the day after Christmas.

Now that he had been able to evaluate the situation, the general had definite plans of operations for both Marion and Sumter, for with his fading hopes of additional Continental support, he was forced to build a more effective force from the irregulars already in the field. By the first of January 1781 he had come to the conclusion that the enemy must be so harassed and annoyed that every movement of the Southern Army would add to their confusion. A fundamental feature of his scheme was the utilization of guerilla tactics, and in this he was fortunate in having the support of Francis Marion, who appeared eager to cooperate with the Southern Army.

Greene suggested that Marion continue his "clever," shifting type of warfare as one means of bolstering the allegiance of those who held some attachment for the American cause, keeping the loyalists under control, and putting down those who seemed to be "in pursuit of private gain or personal glory." He wanted the forest-wise men of Marion's command not only to observe the motions of the enemy but to detain all messengers from the enemy traveling under the protection of a flag until a release order could be received from Greene. The general was fearful that if such messengers came into his camp they would observe the miserable condition of his army and report his weaknesses to the enemy.

Greene wanted Marion's outfit to act as something of a service organization, gathering and forwarding supplies to the army, a role that Marion did not particularly relish. Yet Marion was to continue his raiding tactics as a means of keeping the enemy off balance, for if Marion could cause apprehension among the British for the safety of their posts, Cornwallis would be forced to weaken himself by detaching units for their protection. If the British should move in his direction, Marion was to fade away before them, removing all horses from the path of the enemy.

The only positive tone in the general's letters was that he did promise to send some ammunition.

Among the first tasks he assigned the partisan band was the collection of horses, while all boats suitable for the transportation of men and supplies were to be collected from as far downriver as Georgetown. Shortly afterward he asked Marion to send him a number of Negroes to aid in the housekeeping chores of the army. All boats, cattle, and rice were taken up and moved across the Peedee out of reach of enemy foraging parties. The collection of horses proved to be a different story. The British had long since seized the better ones; the Tory press had boasted: "Colonel Tarleton took so great a number of exceeding fine horses as enabled him to produce four hundred as well mounted and well appointed cavalry as would do him credit *en revue* at Wimbleton." The best animals still in the low country belonged to Marion's men and they were not about to give them up. He did manage to round up fifty "very Ordinary" mounts to send on to the army. If Marion ever resented the implication that Greene planned to use his force primarily as a utility group he never publicly voiced his displeasure.

With Thomas Sumter it was a different story, for his was a temperament in direct contrast to Marion's. Sumter was a superb leader of militia and was extremely popular with those who served under him. Greene wished to benefit from his talents and invited him, "as soon as your sword is heated," to join the Southern Army with his brigade. He emphasized the role of the Southern Army, explaining that skirmishes on the fringe of war had their importance, but

The salvation of this country don't depend upon little strokes, nor should the great business of establishing a permanent army be neglected to pursue them. Partizan strokes in war are like the garnish of a table, they give splendor to the Army and reputation to the Officers, but they afford no national security. They are most necessary and should not be neglected, and yet, they should not be pursued to the prejudice of more important concerns. You may strike a hundred strokes, and reap little benefit from them, unless you have a good Army to take advantage of your success. . . . It is not a war of posts but a contest for States.

But Thomas Sumter, whom Greene knew as a man whose soul was full of enterprise, could not see himself as anyone's subordinate. He liked to operate, insofar as his own maneuvers were concerned, in a military vacuum. As one example, Sumter's anger had bordered on the violent when Governor Rutledge had placed his troops under Daniel Morgan until the Gamecock had recovered from his wounds enough to take the field again. When Morgan had issued orders to South Carolina militia officers without first clearing them through Sumter, he became so inflamed with anger that it required all of Greene's tact and persuasiveness to placate his smoldering indignation.[5]

All these movements by the components of the American Army annoyed Cornwallis, and a glance at the map revealed the dangers that could arise from Greene's disposition of troops. Marion was a factor in his planning. According to inflated intelligence from one "filinghausen" Marion now had three to four hundred mounted militia, and orders had gone out that when the British Army moved up to Charlotte, he was to close in behind to harass the rear guard. Then there was always the possibility that once Cornwallis moved, Greene would move down from the Peedee to make a junction with Marion and between them completely isolate Camden. The British general began to make some troop dispositions of his own. He ordered that the Indians be stirred up against the whites so that the mountain men could not come to the aid of the east. On January 1 he had ordered Tarleton and his legion, along with the first battalion of the Seventy-First Regiment, and one three-pounder to move out, close with Morgan and force him to give battle, thereby eliminating this menace to the flank of the British Army and communications with the garrison at Ninety Six. Balfour was ordered to find some "enterprizing Man" to take care of Marion.

Balfour reacted by sending Lieutenant Colonel George Campbell with the King's American Regiment, along with some regulars whose regiments were elsewhere, to Georgetown, his primary mission to clear the roads of "such Lurking parties of the Enemy as may invest them." Major Ganey, now on the mend from McDonald's bayonet, was told to embody his loyalists and join Campbell. Mobility was added when Captain John Saunders's company of John Graves Simcoe's Queen's Rangers was stationed at Georgetown. Saunders had but recently arrived in South Carolina with Leslie and was not particularly happy with his new assignment, wishing to return to Simcoe and his native Virginia. Sending his men into Georgetown under Cornet Thomas Merritt, Saunders rode off to Wynnesborough to attempt to persuade Cornwallis to order him back to Virginia.

To keep the supply line open, Colonel Campbell was ordered to push up the Peedee and seize Kingstree. Colonel Watson was alerted to move against Marion. The scheme looked good on paper—so good, in fact, that Lord Rawdon felt that "Marion may be in a scrape." [6]

By December 27, 1780 Marion had moved over to Indian Town, feeling that he should, in compliance with Greene's directive, determine the strength of the Georgetown garrison. He detached Colonel Peter Horry, Captain John Baxter, Sergeant McDonald, and thirty horsemen to gain information of the situation in Georgetown. Crossing the Black River to Winyah Bay, they sought concealment in the thickets near the road. It was near breakfast time when a carriage containing two young girls came from the direction of Georgetown under the escort of Cornet Thomas Merritt and another officer both dressed in the green tunics of the Queen's Rangers. As they got farther from town, it was decided that additional protection was needed, and the officers galloped back to town to fetch a squad of troopers, leaving the young girls to go to the nearby house of a prominent Whig to await their return.

By chance Horry and his men stopped by the same house to beg a breakfast. When he came into the house he was startled to recognize the same two girls who had passed in the carriage; one was so bold as to challenge his right to be there, declaring that the man of the house was away, there were no provisions to be had, and that she was "sure you are too much of a gentleman to think of frightening a family of poor helpless women."

Not until she got Horry off to one side did the lady of the house attempt to speak with him, implying that she was fearful of what the friends of her uninvited guests might do if she willingly supplied them with food. She suggested that they return to the house demanding provisions and, when she refused, the colonel was to threaten to put her home to the torch.

As Horry carried through these directions, the wife of his friend, in all of her pretended anger, threw her keys to the floor. Horry picked them up and helped himself to those things he needed to feed his men and horses. Just as they finished eating there was a warning shot from the vedettes, the mounted sentinels out beyond the pickets. They were just mounting when the outpost guards came in, riding hard and with Merritt and his men close on their heels. As they neared the house, Horry bellowed the order to charge. They rode down the outnumbered Rangers, with the survivors racing down the road to Georgetown. Merritt escaped into a nearby swamp; he was to later state "that he turned as gray as a badger before he crawled out of the swamp and reached Georgetown that night." [7]

When Horry returned Marion left Indian Town and moved back to Snow Island, for there was some evidence that the British might be planning a strike against him. He reported to Greene that enemy strength in Georgetown was now near three hundred, that three nine-pounders had been added to the firepower on the walls, and that there were two row galleys to afford covering fire. This information was something of a deterrent to Marion's own ambitions toward another try at that town.

In retaliation for Horry's humiliation of Merritt, Colonel Campbell sent out the young cornet and his Queen's Rangers through the southern part of the Williamsburg District. When, on the morning of December 30, Marion received this information, he led his men out in pursuit. He never caught up with the raiders, as he noted they "made so much haste in returning. . . ."

To carry out Greene's orders to collect boats, Marion called in Captain John Postell, who knew the people and was familiar with the terrain along the lower Peedee. Postell was told to patrol along the Black Mingo to the mouth of the Peedee, then back up to Snow Island, taking up boats, canoes, and Negroes. The boats were to be hidden along the river banks until needed; heavy, flat scows were to be destroyed. Every horse, whether belonging to friend or foe, was to be brought in, as well as all arms, ammunition, grain, and rice. All inhabitants were to be forbidden to "thresh their grain until further notice." Postell was to prevent anyone from carrying provisions into Georgetown "on pain of being held as traitors and enemies to the Americans." All persons who would not support him, or even acted unfriendly, were to be brought in to Marion. When Postell sent back word that there were 150 bushels of salt on the Waccamaw to be used by the British in preserving beef, Marion sent a party to bring it off; he distributed much of it among Whig families in the area. In effect, the Swamp Fox was declaring something akin to martial law over those areas he could control.[8]

Now Francis Marion held greater authority to implement his dictates. At the end of 1780 Governor Rutledge had appointed him a brigadier general of South Carolina militia, placing all regiments east of the Santee, Wateree, and Catawba Rivers under his command. West of that line was to be the territory of Thomas Sumter; in other words, Marion was to have the low country, Sumter the upper. The courier bringing the commission had arrived in camp about New Year's Day 1781. The appointment met with the hearty approval of both the officers and men. Peter Horry reported his own emotions as "I snatched his hand and exclaimed 'Huzza! God save my friend! My noble GENERAL MARION!'"

Marion, now that he had wider authority over the militia, began to organize his brigade. Captain John Melton became his chief aide, with Captains Lewis Ogier and Thomas Elliot as junior aides; Elliot's prime duty was to act as military secretary. Colonel Hugh Ervin, as senior militia officer, became second in command. Peter Horry was given the command of the cavalry, with the other officers in his regiment Major Lemuel Benison, Captains John Baxter, John Postell, Daniel Conyers, and James McCauley.

The regiment that under ordinary circumstances would have been under the command of Colonel Adam McDonald was assigned to Hugh Horry, since McDonald at this time was a paroled prisoner of war. Horry's subordinate officers were Major John James, Captains James Postell, John James, and James Witherspoon. Captain McCottry retained command of his independent company of crack riflemen.

For his personal mess, the general selected Hugh Horry and James Postell. Sergeant Davies was cook, while Oscar still looked after his master.

The greatest deficiency of the brigade was arms and ammunition. Greene, who had sent him some ammunition, was unable to supply Marion with weapons, for he could not properly arm the men of his own command. Marion's solution was to designate a large number of those without muskets as cavalry. Every saw that could be confiscated was hammered into a sword.

The increasing size of Marion's command had a salutary effect upon many of those whose former inclinations had been toward the side of royal authority. Those of wavering allegiance,

148

who had been active on both sides, now felt it expedient to follow Marion, "confirmed in their views, by his apparent abilities and successes." Several of those who had been caught marauding were tried by court martial.[9]

An increase in command meant an inflation of the supply problem. Marion's solution was to gather up all provisions when available and stockpile them against future needs. Reports indicated that the plantations in All Saints Parish on Waccamaw Neck, relatively untouched by maneuvering military forces, had a great surplus of food. Peter Horry and John Postell were sent off to collect cattle and drive them in to Snow Island where they were to be penned until slaughtered.

Horry, with Captain Clarke and Sergeant McDonald, rode out early in the morning and by noon had crossed the Waccamaw below Kingston. As they rode down Waccamaw Neck, a Negro slave belonging to Captain Joseph Alston was captured and taken along as a prisoner lest he give information about them to the enemy. That night they encamped near the Alston Plantation. Captain Clarke, who knew the slave, cut the ropes that bound him and bade him go home. The next morning an angry Horry reprimanded the captain and was even more unhappy when he became aware of the consequences of Clarke's charitable act.

Because of the recent salt raid, Campbell had led some sixty of the Queen's Rangers out from Georgetown to patrol the area. He also entertained the notion of establishing a post in All Saints Parish as a means of controlling the area between the Waccamaw and Little Peedee Rivers. It was near sunrise when the patrol found the slave who was making his way back to the Alston Plantation. Under harsh questioning, the unhappy black revealed the whereabouts of Horry's detachment. Remounting, the Rangers rode at a fast trot toward the American encampment some three miles away.

But Horry had left his camp and was on the road with

Clarke and five men out in front acting as a vanguard. Near Alston Plantation, the officer leading the Rangers caught a glimpse of Clarke's group through the trees. He had the bugle sounded to call in his outriders. Clarke, however, was a naive soul, and thinking it to be a huntsman's horn, called out to his men to hold up and look for the deer as it crossed the road. To his surprise, the huntsmen turned out to be twenty of the Queen's Rangers and he was their quarry. As they rushed forward, swinging their sabers, Clarke surrendered. Rather than encumber himself with a prisoner who would require a guard, Campbell paroled him on the spot, with the captain giving his word that he would go into Georgetown and turn himself over to the British. Clarke, thoroughly frightened, fled to the safety of the tangled thickets of Waccamaw Swamp.

With the sounds of action ahead, Horry and his men spurred forward. As they came in sight of the Rangers, they loosed a peppering volley of swan shot. Horry's mount was a magnificent charger that had been discovered hidden in the swamp the day before. With the sudden burst of noise, the animal, unused to the blast of guns, bolted, throwing the colonel to the ground. He was a tempting target; a British sergeant with drawn saber turned toward him. Horry was saved from death or capture by one of the quirks of fate that so often occur in the heat of battle. The sergeant appeared to be riding him down but then pulled up short, gave him a puzzled look, and turned away. The only explanation Horry could give was that his uniform closely resembled that of a British officer and the trooper had not taken the time to take a good look at him. Suddenly the Rangers, supposedly beaten, drew off.

Thinking he had whipped the entire group, Horry sent off under guard the two Rangers taken prisoner. He had no sooner ordered the pursuit than Campbell dashed up with his entire command. Horry had not yet been able to catch his horse and, with the approach of the enemy, his outnumbered men had fled. Sergeant McDonald, seeing the plight of his commanding officer, leaped from his own mount, threw the reins to Horry, and, as the general galloped to safety, ran for the dank but friendly bogs of the swamp.

Casualties among the Queen's Rangers were one officer and four privates killed, six wounded, two taken prisoner, and several horses lost. Horry had one man wounded and two horses killed. Upon receiving Horry's report, Marion sent reinforcements. Campbell retired into Georgetown without establishing his outpost. Horry followed at a distance as far as Sand Hill Plantation. In friendly country, with an abundance of provisions, Horry proposed building a redoubt as a means of controlling and protecting the neighborhood. In recalling him, Marion explained his basic philosophy of warfare: "the open field was our play, that the enemy knew better how to defend forts and entrenched places than we did, and that if we attempted it, we should fall into their hands." [10]

To Marion Georgetown seemed to be the key to the low country; still he did not have the strength to launch an attack in force. He was soon to get some aid. When Greene had come south, the only Continental unit that Washington could spare from the Northern Army was Henry Lee's legion, but this had given the Southern Army a well-drilled and well-disciplined mobile striking force. Although a Virginian, Lee had been in no great hurry to come south. A conceited and persistent individual, he had refused to leave Philadelphia until the Continental Congress had supplied him with enough specie to cover fully the expenses of the journey. In Richmond he had paused long enough to recruit an additional twenty-five men for his green-coated legion. He was in Greene's camp by January 9, and had made such a favorable impression on Governor Rutledge that he agreed to aid in enlisting an additional 150 men for the legion, which already numbered between 260 and 280 men.

Although Greene was pleased to have the legion with him,

their arrival meant an added strain on already sparse provisions and forage. The general also saw the possibility of granting Marion's request for Continentals to bolster his militia—at least for the time being. He had also received intelligence that Watson lay at Nelson's Ferry and he hoped that Lee and Marion, acting together, could cut him off from all aid. He ordered the legion to the Peedee "to support Brigadier Marion." There was some difficulty in locating Marion, for the natty green jackets of Lee's men so nearly resembled the tunics of Tarleton's legion that the local inhabitants refused to give him information. Lee went into bivouac at Bass's Mill on Catfish Creek and sent Major John Rudulph to seek out the partisan hideout. He rode into Marion's camp on January 20.

One would suspect that when these two men tried to cooperate on any venture there would be a clash of personalities, for one question that was certain to come up was that of command. Marion had no intention of taking orders from Lee, and it was to be assumed that Lee would balk at direction by a militia general, especially after he had arrived in Marion's camp speaking rather grandly of "my designs" and claiming that Marion did not have the imagination to carry them through. Marion, on the other hand, set forth his position in a blunt statement to Greene, "I expect to command, not from the Militia Commission I hold, but from an elder Continental Commission."

But, surprisingly, there was no trouble between the two, and apparently both were in accord from the moment they first met. Each was an advocate of the slashing, flashy type of warfare that depended upon surprise and a quick withdrawal once they had inflicted damage. Although Marion seemed to hold some reservations, within a short while the two had drafted a scheme for an attack on Georgetown, subject to the approval of the commanding general.

Greene was reticent about so daring a venture, but as time

went on he seems to have become intrigued by the idea and on January 25 he wrote Marion, "I cannot give up the idea of an attack upon them. . . ." Not only would a successful raid open up a supply route to his camp in the High Hills, but if the port fell, it was probable that Cornwallis would be delayed in his push northward, which, in turn, would allow Greene an opportunity to enlarge and properly reorganize his army. And a victory, large or small, always carried a salutary byproduct because it bolstered the spirits of lukewarm Whigs and awed nervous Tories into quiescence. There was always the possibility that such a raid would draw off any concentration of troops against Daniel Morgan. The loss of Georgetown would certainly give the British cause for general alarm; yet a failure could develop into a critical situation for the Southern Army. If Lee and Marion were cut off and penned up within the town, Greene's entire force might be needed to extricate them, for both corps were too valuable to be wasted. Cautioning Lee to "get good information before you attempt anything," Greene gave his consent to the operation.

Marion sent an officer under the protection of a flag on the pretense of returning some captured letters to Major Irvine and to discuss an exchange of prisoners. But the messenger's prime mission was to use his eyes while in the town and gather as much information about the strength of the garrison as possible. Although Campbell received the officer in a cordial manner, he did suggest that Captain Clarke, as a point of honor, should come into Georgetown and surrender himself as one who had broken his parole.[11]

Putting all intelligence together, it was estimated that the garrison at Georgetown numbered about two hundred men. Frequent patrols in the area added the information that most of the troops were quartered in barracks outside the redoubt. All outposts were on the land side, while the water approach was left unguarded.

Marion and Lee decided to split their force, with the legion infantry being transported downriver by boats, while the legion cavalry and mounted militia rode overland. At dawn on January 22 Captains Patrick Carnes and Michael Rudulph ordered the ninety men under their command into the boats that had been collected. They shoved off and, guided by several of Marion's men, began the ninety-mile trip down the river. The mounted troops waited for twenty-four hours after the departure of the boats before they moved out. Messages ordered Postell and other patrols to rendezvous at Kingstree—by forced marches if necessary.

Carnes and Rudulph, rowing and drifting, reached the mouth of the Peedee during the dark hours of January 23. They pulled ashore on a small island where they rested in concealment for the remainder of the day. That night they floated down to Georgetown, timing their departure to arrive outside the village between one and two o'clock in the morning. They arrived early, while the mounted troops, delayed by bad roads, did not come in until later than planned.

Carnes and Rudulph came ashore at Mitchell's Landing around midnight. Fearing delay would mean discovery, they began the attack before the designated time. They trotted across a rice-field dam to the outskirts of the town. Rudulph slipped quietly into town and posted his men between the barracks and the redoubt to shoot down the garrison as they ran for the protection of the fort.

Carnes sped silently through the streets to the quarters of Lieutenant Colonel Campbell. The commanding officer was fast asleep when the intruders crashed into his room and took him prisoner. He was given his parole. Lieutenant James Cryer led his militia to take the other prisoners. Major Crookshanks, the adjutant, and Major Irvine, said Peter Horry, were discovered asleep "at a tavern belonging to a genteel family, with whom they had spent the evening with great hilarity."

Lieutenant Cryer held little love for Major Irvine, who had once sentenced him to five hundred lashes for trying to smuggle his horse out of Georgetown. When Irvine, awakened by the sound of running feet, rushed onto the porch and fired his pistol at the shadows racing through the night, Cryer drove forward and sank his bayonet into Irvine's chest just as the major was raising his hands in surrender. Similar intentions were held for Major Crookshanks, but his doxy, the innkeeper's daughter, saved his life by throwing her arms around his neck, screaming "Save Major Crookshanks." Her frantic pleas saved the adjutant, who was granted a parole.

When Lee and Marion had taken their positions on the outside of town, they rushed in at the burst of firing. Everything now seemed quiet. The British soldiers, instead of panicking, had wisely barricaded themselves within their quarters. Those within the fort prepared to resist an assault.

The redoubt was too formidable to storm with infantry without artillery support. It was likewise evident that at daylight the Americans would be subjected to a murderous crossfire from the barracks and the fort. The order to withdraw was issued. On the surface, it appeared that the raid had gained little other than serving notice on the enemy that if his small posts were to be safe from attack their garrisons would have to be strengthened.

Lee and Marion fell back on Murray's Ferry. Neither was discouraged by the failure; in fact, they convinced themselves that they had achieved "a little success," especially since they had no artillery. They had worked well together, and Marion admitted to Greene that "Col. Lee's Interprising Genius promises much."

Privately, Lee took most of the credit. He was convinced that Georgetown could be taken and declared that if Greene would but send him reinforcements and a field piece, he would guarantee a victory. He felt that he could have handled the situation better; Rudulph's troops should not have been placed so as to intercept the men from the barracks but should have been ordered to take the fort with bayonets, maintaining the element of surprise. Perhaps it was because of Lee's boasting that Greene, in writing to Sumter and Colonel James Campbell, did not mention Marion's name but stated that the raid was staged "by Lt. Col. Lee and his Legion." [12]

They had no more than settled in camp when they received the electrifying news that Daniel Morgan had inflicted a crushing defeat on Banastre Tarleton at a place called the Cowpens in western South Carolina on January 17 and even now was retreating northward with his prisoners. "After this," Greene exulted, "nothing will appear difficult." Unaware that the attempt on Georgetown had been carried out, he suggested that if the news of Tarleton's defeat could be circulated in that garrison it could create some panic among the loyalists.

Although it was not realized at that time, Francis Marion had played an indirect role in the defeat of Tarleton. Balfour had detached so many men to protect the lines of communication in the low country that he could not send reinforcements to Ninety Six when requested. As a result, when Morgan took such a position as to threaten that post, Cornwallis had been forced to send Tarleton out to drive him off.

So exhilarated was Greene over the Cowpens victory that he considered cutting across the rear of Cornwallis's army and hitting Ninety Six with his entire army, including Marion's brigade. An express brought the news that even now Greene was hastening to Charlotte for a council of war with Generals Morgan, William Lee Davidson, and Andrew Pickens. Greene did not reveal his future strategy to Marion; he told Lee to sound out Marion on all points, but "Dont let no mortal have the least intimation of what I have in contemplation." Until future operations were fully developed, it was suggested that Lee and Marion utilize their talents in the impressment of all horses, either cavalry or draught, between the Peedee and Little Peedee rivers for the use of the Southern Army in its next big move. Greene wanted enemy magazines destroyed and suggested Lee and Marion attack Colonel Watson, for he was a "most inviting object." He did assure Marion that the question of rank and command would not come up.

In carrying out these orders, Marion ordered Captain John Postell and thirty men across the Santee to make a forced march to Santee Bridge, not only to take up horses and provisions of all kinds, but to burn all British supplies and provisions he came across. On his return he was to burn the stores and wagons at Monck's Corner. Marion, remembering Horry's troubles in the past, cautioned Postell, "Take care that your men do not get at liquor, or clog themselves with plunder so as to endanger their retreat." A similar order instructed Major James Postell and his thirty riders to sweep northward up the far side of the Santee to burn the enemy supplies stored at Colonel William Thomson's plantation on the Congaree. To both Postells he emphasized the necessity of speed and the importance of not encumbering themselves by taking prisoners.

Lee and Marion, awaiting the return of the Postells and encamped at Cordes Plantation, began to plan another joint venture, this time against Fort Watson whose, garrison was reported to consist of only forty-one men. They had framed only the preliminary stages of their scheme when they were forced to give it up. Greene had not taken the time to attend the planned conference at Charlotte. Intelligence reported that Cornwallis was now in pursuit of Morgan in an attempt to recover the prisoners taken at Cowpens and avenge the humiliation suffered by Tarleton. Placing the Army of the Peedee under the command of Brigadier Isaac Huger with orders to march for North Carolina, Greene, with only a sergeant's guard, rode across country to join Morgan's retreating forces. Orders came across the river for Lee to rejoin the army immediately.

Lee didn't want to leave, for he visualized a campaign, supported by reinforcements from Greene, that would allow him to carry through his own plans, plans that would allow him to gain that martial glory he so ardently sought. He noted that "the posture on the other side of Santee, and in the State of Georgia, held out to a proper attempt, was so pleasing, that I regret exceedingly my recall from that country." Nevertheless, on January 31, 1781 he saddled up and led his legion out of the camp at Cordes Plantation.[13]

Marion was once again on his own.

Chapter VIII

Lee was gone when the Postells returned. Their successful raids had been carried out with "great spirit and good conduct." Major Postell had found no stores at Thomson's Plantation; they had been carried off several days earlier. As he was returning, he received intelligence of a quantity of rum, salt, sugar, flour, pork, and British uniforms at Manigault's Ferry. All but four of the guard had gone chasing off after Captain Postell. The Major rode in, took the redoubt, destroyed the supplies, leveled the post, and rode off.

Captain Postell had destroyed the supplies at Watbo Bridge and had then surprised the depot at Keithfield Plantation near Monck's Corner. After a lively action he had burned or destroyed fourteen wagons loaded with clothing and twenty barrels of rum, killed two of the enemy while wounding two, and taken a captain, a subaltern, and twenty-four grenadiers prisoner. He did not lose a man; according to Postell, "Nothing indeed appeared difficult." [1]

Marion reorganized his brigade. Each militia regiment in the brigade raised a troop of light horse of forty-eight men who were to be armed with swords and pistols. They were to be uniformed in short blue homespun coats with different colored facings to indicate the regiments from which they had been drawn. Peter Horry was given command of the unit and was given a warrant to impress suitable horses on which to mount his men. To replace Horry, Captain John James was promoted to major.

Marion kept shifting his position, moving his camp each day. Inasmuch as he usually was on the march during the day, he usually appointed "officers of the night" rather than officers of the day. He was forced to take some precautions to protect his reputation. He discovered that plundering parties moving through the countryside gave out that they were members of his brigade. Denying this, he also issued a statement to the effect that he would publish the names of all such men, "after which it Will be lawfull for any man to put them to Death where ever they are without being able to be called to Account for it." [2]

Some of the plundering was the result of the activities of Captain William Clay Snipes. Snipes had been active and had behaved well while acting under the command of Peter Horry. Having suffered at the hands of the loyalists, he hated them with a passion. With the creation of the brigade when Marion had been named a brigadier general of militia there had been no command for Snipes. He had ridden off to Greene's camp to present his grievances to Governor Rutledge. The governor had listened, was courteous, and was impressed enough to write to Marion, "I have no Objections to giving him a Company . . . ," but he implied that those men who were enlisted by Snipes were to be brought in to serve under Marion, if Marion so directed.

Snipes, however, was so angry with Marion, whom he accused of being unfriendly to the cause, that he had no intention of serving under the brigadier and requested that he be allowed to serve under Colonel William Harden who was raising a regiment in the Beaufort area. Snipes had gone as far as Georgia to recruit, and General Huger, before he had marched the army northward to join Greene, had given him permission to serve under Harden. Snipes also claimed that he had Greene's permission to cross the Santee and operate independently. Perhaps Snipes felt that he could operate freely under Harden, best explained by Rutledge's later evaluation of the man as "a very worthy brave man, [but] keeps up no discipline or authority over them—he just lets 'em do as they please." Snipes, Marion felt, "Certain will do no other Service than plunder the Inhabitants, which will make more Enemys. . . ." He was equally certain that Snipes would cause more trouble in the future.[3]

But there was more favorable news to counter the bad. Since December 20, Captain John Postell had made himself a source of irritation to Colonel Campbell by collecting rice, cattle, Negroes, and horses along the lower Peedee and disrupting communications with Georgetown. To rid himself of this nuisance, Campbell detached Captain James De Peyster and twenty-nine grenadiers of the King's American Regiment. Their first act was one of retaliation. Captain John Postell, Sr., seventy years old, had been taken and paroled after the fall of Charleston. Near the middle of January, De Peyster and his men had stripped the Postell Plantation of everything that could be moved. In reporting this to Marion, Postell had lamented, "My honour is all that I have left. My family has been reduced to beg for their bread." He felt that his parole had been broken by the British. The elder Postell had been imprisoned, and Marion's letter to Saunders offered an exchange "on Account of his Age & hope Humanity will Induce you to treat him like a Gentleman."

Young Postell was to get his revenge. He had but fourteen men, but he had an advantage in that he knew the ground, and his anger at the treatment of his father added a bit of rashness to his planning which at other times may have been overruled by prudence. Early in the morning of February 21, 1781, Postell and his men had stolen forward around De Peyster's sentries and managed to occupy the detached kitchen without being observed. De Peyster was summoned to surrender. He refused. To demonstrate his determination, Postell burned the kitchen and then sent in a second summons to the effect that if De Peyster did not surrender immediately he would next burn the house. The British captain asked for five minutes. Postell's answer was to have his men bring straw forward and begin to heap it around the house. The British filed out and piled their arms. In taking in his prisoners, Postell made them travel on foot and deliberately made them walk through every creek and mudhole along the way.[4]

Then Marion received what for him was distressing news. From Guilford Court House in North Carolina, Greene had written on February 11 congratulating the Postells and advising "Great Activity is Necessary to keep the Spirits of the people from Sinking, as well as to Alarm the Enemy Respecting the safety of their posts." The general then went on to say that Thomas Sumter had been directed to call out the South Carolina militia and employ them in the destruction of British stores and "perplexing their affairs in South Carolina." Then he added the line that troubled Marion: "Please to Communicate & Concert with him your future operations." Matters were not helped when Governor Rutledge suggested that he do everything he could to further Sumter's ideas.

It wasn't that Marion held no respect for Sumter, but they were persons of clashing personalities. Sumter was a man of strong opinions and an inflexible mind. His aggressive, and often incautious, actions were not those in which Marion could feel comfortable.

Sumter attempted to rouse his emotions by reporting that

Negro patrols organized by the British to bring in deserters were now being forced to make frequent sallies against the countryside, which "alone is sufficient to rouse up and fix the resentment and detestation of every American who possesses common feelings."

Marion was not impressed. He sulked. Until he received further orders, and perhaps because of his pique at being forced to act under Sumter's direction, Marion dismissed the greater part of his brigade, telling Sumter that he could not march because the "enemy is too strong for me to move." Then, with those few who formed the core of his brigade, he moved over into the general vicinity of Snow Island to await further developments.

Sumter lost little time in beginning his operations. He needed supplies for his campaign. There was a British depot at Fort Granby on the Congaree that held enough stuff to supply his needs. On February 11 he marched his brigade toward the Congaree and laid siege to the post. Fearing Rawdon would send reinforcements, Sumter suggested that Marion maneuver in such a fashion as to distract the enemy.

Marion's compliance was immediate although not overly enthusiastic. His intelligence as to the strength of the enemy had convinced him that Sumter could not possibly overrun the British posts. But Sumter was the senior officer and Marion, albeit reluctantly, moved to execute his instructions. He moved over to Indian Town and issued a call for his militia. But they had just returned from a campaign, the weather was cold, and they clung to the warmth of their firesides.

Rawdon, in the meantime, had dispatched Lieutenant Colonel Welbore Doyle and the New York Volunteers to the relief of Fort Granby. Sumter called off his siege on February 21 and fell back down the Congaree. He next attempted to surprise Belleville, the British outpost at Thomson's Plantation. He blocked all approaches, seized the boats, and then boldly stormed the stockade. He was driven back by the fire of the defenders. Sumter then moved over to Manigault's Ferry, leaving behind a detachment to occupy the attention of the garrison at Belleville. This group, however, was routed by Major Alexander McIntosh driving down from Camden. Sumter swung over to the east bank of the Santee. There he made a rash attack against Fort Watson, but he suffered so many casualties that he drew off to Farr's Plantation, near his home on Great Savannah.

The Gamecock's tail feathers had been ruffled, but his ambition remained unchecked. He suggested to Marion that their two forces should either be joined or that they should move close enough to each other to cooperate more easily. In fact he went so far as to suggest that Marion should come in "with all possible speed" for a consultation. Marion took his time and more or less made it obvious that he wished little to do with any scheme that involved cooperation with Sumter.

On March 1 Sumter learned that Colonel Watson was gathering a force at Fort Watson to crush him. He moved quickly to get out of the way. Riding hard, he moved to the High Hills to move his infirm wife and young son to safety. With his wife strapped to a mattress across the back of a horse, he rode forty miles to Bradley's Plantation on Black River.

Another dispatch urged Marion to make a junction with him as quickly as possible. After waiting for Marion for two days, he moved northward on March 6. Between Scape Hoar Creek and Radcliffe's Bridge over Lynche's Creek, he suddenly came face to face with Major Thomas Fraser and his Loyal South Carolina Regiment. After a sharp fire fight, Sumter drew off and left the field to Fraser. Behind he left ten dead and around forty wounded sprawled on the ground.[5]

This scuffle reminded Rawdon, since apparently Sumter was on the run, that he should devote more attention to Marion. Balfour had also planned for some time to free the country between the Santee and the Peedee "of those parties of the enemy which of late have so much infested it, and restore to the lower district of the province that peace they have for some weeks been deprived of." In carrying out Balfour's desires, Rawdon designed a net to entrap Marion, whose force he had heard was no larger than three hundred mounted men. He planned a pincer movement, with Colonel Watson moving down the Santee and then driving in on Marion's front. Colonel Doyle was to move to the east and down the Santee and then cross Lynche's Creek to cut off Marion should he fall back before Watson. By March 5 Watson and his "Buffs" were encamped below Nelson's Ferry. But Rawdon weakened his basic plan when he received information that a large force was advancing against Ninety Six, and temporarily concentrated the majority of his force in the vicinity of Camden, on the alert to move quickly.[6]

Marion had finally stirred himself to start his men on their march to join Sumter. He had crossed Murray's Ferry when Captain Zachary Cantey dashed up with the information that he had discovered Watson's camp. Despite the odds against him in pitting militia against well-trained and disciplined troops, Marion felt that he had to take the chance. He led his men back to Wiboo Swamp about halfway between Murray's and Nelson's ferries. It was a good place for an ambush, a quarter mile causeway bordered by Wiboo Swamp.

Watson had become wise in the ways of the Swamp Fox. He recognized the causeway as a perfect spot for an ambush. Scouts verified his suspicions. On one end of the causeway sat Watson on his horse surveying the situation. On the other end Marion sat watching him.

The fight began when Watson ordered Colonel Henry Richbourg and his loyalist cavalry to rush out across the causeway. Peter Horry and his mounted troops were sent to meet them. Horry stammered badly when under pressure. He leaned forward and waved his sword. He had ridden some fifty yards before he found that he could not come out with the word "Charge!" Sputtering as he reined up, he turned and bawled, "Damn it, boys, you, you know what I mean, go on!" The two groups clashed, fought briefly in a rattle of sabers, and then fell back to their own lines. As Marion deployed the remainder of his troops across the road Horry was once again ordered to charge. Watson's musketry and fire from his two artillery pieces sent them reeling backward. Taking advantage of the situation, Watson ordered forward Major Samuel Harrison and his loyalist dragoons.

As they sped across the causeway, one man stood in their path. Gavin James of Horry's light horse regiment, a giant of a man both in size and courage, sat on his great gray horse. He fired his musket; a Tory horseman spun from his saddle. The enemy fired a volley; James was unhurt. A trooper darted forward, swinging his saber and was spitted on James's bayonet. The third who came charging up saw this same bayonet redden with his own blood. As he fell he grasped James's musket, and as the husky man retreated the last fifty yards to his own lines, he dragged the dying trooper behind him, still tightly clinging to the weapon.

As Harrison's horsemen made their way across the causeway, Marion sent out the remainder of his cavalry under the commands of Captains Conyers and McCauley. They sent the Tories scampering back to their own lines. In a personal duel on horseback, Conyers mortally wounded Major Harrison.

Watson now ordered his infantry forward. They trotted across the causeway, bayonets at the ready. Feeling that his men, few of whom had bayonets, could not stand up to regulars, Marion ordered a retreat. That night he pitched camp at Cantey's Plantation.[7]

The following morning a rider came in with a packet of letters from Snow Island. Included was a dispatch from Captain

John Saunders who had succeeded Campbell as commandant of Georgetown. Following Marion's instructions, Colonel Hugh Ervin had released four prisoners from the Bull Pen on Snow Island and sent them, escorted by Captain John Postell and Lieutenant William Futhey into Georgetown to be exchanged. Postell had requested the assignment, hoping it would allow him to secure the release of his father. At Georgetown, although Postell was under the protection of a flag, he was recognized as the one who had caused the damage at Keithfield and who had but recently taken Captain De Peyster; he was seized and held as one of those who had taken a parole after the fall of Charleston and had then broken his oath by taking up arms again. Futhey had turned and fled to bring the story back to Snow Island.

Marion was furious. On March 7 he indicated his feelings to Saunders in a letter that was punctuated with expressions of his wrath. Not only did he protest the seizure of Postell, but he was critical of the treatment of Captain Clarke who had been taken up and carried into Georgetown for not following the conditions of his parole. According to Marion's information, Clarke had been confined in a place where he was unable to stand upright or lie down full length, and he was not even being fed half rations. Marion declared that those officers and men who had fallen into his hands had been treated humanely, but now he planned to write Balfour to inform him that unless Postell was released immediately and those officers and men of his who had been taken by the enemy were given better treatment, he would retaliate with every means in his power.

He sent a strong letter to Balfour protesting not only the Postell affair but the hanging of three members of his brigade by Watson and Rawdon. He promised that three of the British prisoners held by him would suffer a like fate. He deliberately insulted Saunders by forwarding the letter to Balfour through Watson, and then he sent it under an armed escort.

Watson felt that he should answer the charges against him but sent no reply that day. Instead, the following morning he marched down the Santee road with Marion falling back before him yet harassing his column in every way possible. That night at Cantey's Plantation, Watson composed his answer. In the first place, he was annoyed that Marion had sent an armed escort with the flag of truce. He was also angry because on February 22 Sumter had shot down seven British soldiers who had hoisted the white flag. In reply to Marion's charge that Saunders had violated the "Laws of Nations," he challenged Marion to name an instance when the British had violated such international rules of warfare. The detention of Captain Postell, he declared, "with all its Consequences, is Justifiable."

Marion cut off the correspondence, yet an undercurrent of rage still seethed within him. His retaliation was swift. His orders were that nightly patrols were to shoot down British sentries and to ride down pickets, something not customarily considered in the eighteenth century when wars were supposedly fought by gentlemen.[8]

Watson again began his forward movement, with Harrison's loyalists up front and the regulars trailing along in the column behind them. Marion backed slowly down the road as the enemy advanced. The bridge at Mount Hope Swamp was destroyed, and the riflemen of Hugh Horry and William McCottry were stationed along the bank to prevent a crossing. At their first fire, Watson unlimbered his artillery and fired several rounds of grapeshot. Marion's men fell away as the regulars waded into the stream.

Marion rode on toward Murray's Ferry to lead Watson away from the Lower Bridge, just twelve miles away, and then turned toward Georgetown. Watson was apparently following, but suddenly swerved toward the lower bridges and Kingstree. Marion reasoned that if Watson's men made it across the Lower Bridge he could effectively stifle Whig resistance in the area around

Indian Town, where the spirit of rebellion flowed in a heavy tide.

Major James was ordered off with seventy men, thirty of whom were McCottry's riflemen. His mission was to deny Watson the stream crossing. James was aware of the necessity of rapid movement, for there was little doubt that Harrison's loyalist dragoons would be rushing across country to secure the bridge. James set off across fields, leaping fences, threading his way through wooded areas, and crossing the Black River below the bridge. He won the race.

Upon reaching the east bank of the stream, the major had the flooring of the bridge removed and then set fire to the stringers on the east end of the structure. McCottry's riflemen were posted beyond the marshy area on the east bank so as to give them a good field of fire across the remains of the bridge. Those men with muskets were placed out on the flanks, not only to provide support for the riflemen but to prevent the use of the ford below the bridge. By the time all of this had been done, Marion and the remainder of the brigade had reached the site. Sending Captain Thomas Potts and his Peedee company to support James, he stationed the rest of his men to the rear to act in reserve. They waited for the enemy to come up.

It was a good place to conduct a defensive action. The roadway on the west bank cut through a bluff, making it difficult for Watson's men to approach the bridge without crowding together. Across the river, forty or fifty yards away, the water melted into a marsh, slowing up those who might attempt to ford the stream and, in turn, making them easier targets for marksmen. It was behind this morass that McCottry and his men lay waiting.

John Watson was a gallant officer, but he was not about to allow his men to walk into such an obvious trap. He brought his artillery up to the bluff with orders to drive off the defenders with grapeshot. But the gunners were unable to depress the muzzles of the field pieces, and, as a result, their blasts whistled harmlessly through the trees on the far bank. They manhandled their guns to the edge of the bluff; a burst of rifle shots drove them back.

Watson next attempted to force his way across the stream by way of the ford below the bridge. A captain, waving his sword forward, stepped out smartly in front as the British column straggled toward the edge of the stream. McCottry caught him in his sights and squeezed off a shot. As the officer fell, four men rushed forward to drag him to safety. All four tumbled as rifle balls found their marks. Watson recalled his troops. That evening, after collecting his dead and wounded, he moved off a mile above the bridge to encamp on John Witherspoon's plantation. It was later said that he told Mrs. Witherspoon that "he never saw such shooting in his life." British losses, though heavy, were not determined at the time, for the bodies of their dead were sunk in the river.[9]

That night Marion camped on the high ground above the ford. He awakened his men before sunup. Back across the Black River went the men of Conyers and McCottry with orders to creep up on Watson's encampment and pick off the sentinels and pickets. Redheaded Sergeant McDonald climbed high in the branches of one of the huge oaks bordering the lane leading to the Witherspoon house. There, from his lofty perch, and at a distance estimated to have been three hundred yards, he put a rifle ball through the knee of Lieutenant George Torriano of the Sixty-Fourth Regiment.

Young Mary Witherspoon was the fiancée of Captain Daniel Conyers. Apparently this was well known to the British officers who, after Torriano had been dropped, began to make degrading remarks about Conyers and all rebels in general. Finally the young girl could stand no more of this insolence; she reached down, removed her shoe, flung it in the face of one tormentor, and pointing outside, shouted, "Coward! Go meet him!"

That afternoon Watson moved just about half a mile farther

upriver and selected a large open area with no trees nearby to harbor sharpshooters. Even then, the best of Marion's snipers lay far back and threw the British off balance by sending an occasional rifle ball skimming through them and "kept [Watson] in a bad humour . . . and his regulars in constant panic."

Watson's wounded were beginning to suffer from lack of medical attention. Because of Marion's earlier whimsy in sending a flag under an armed guard, the British colonel burlesqued that trick by sending over a letter by young John Witherspoon. He requested that Torriano and the wounded rank and file be allowed to pass unmolested to Charleston where they might receive proper care.

Although Marion was still unhappy about the Postell affair, he sent back an answer by the lad, explaining that the only reason he had resorted to an armed guard for his flag was the seizure of Postell. He assured Watson, "I wish to carry on this War as Usual with all Civilized Nations." If Watson would submit a list of the wounded men Marion would issue a safe-conduct pass for them and their escort, and "you may be Assured I will not Act in any other way, than what I find is done by the British troops."

Watson immediately returned a list that included three men and a Negro to care for Lieutenant Torriano, but only two men were named to look after the six wounded rank and file. He also seized the occasion to blast the behavior of some members of Marion's brigade, citing particularly the atrocities he claimed were committed by one who bore the name of Maynard, who, with several companions, had brutally flogged a number of Tories. He likewise charged that Captain Conyers had whipped two loyalists, Thomas Wise and John Stillwell, almost to death.

In his letter accompanying the pass, Marion neither affirmed nor denied the whipping charges, but he did berate Watson for the plundering and house-burning that had been carried on under the guise of military expediency.

Watson's answer made reference to Marion's previous statement that he wanted to fight the war according to the customs of civilized nations. He then defended his own actions with the assertion, "The burning of Houses & the property of the inhabitants who is our Enemy is thought right & is Customary in all Countries." [10]

The Postell incident still remained an open question. On March 12 Balfour had sent a letter to Marion in answer to the complaint of restraining the partisan officer after he had come in under the protection of a flag. He included a copy of the parole signed by Postell and added, "I therefore trust when you represent the case to your Congress, you Accompany it with so essential a Document as the enclosed."

Balfour had sent the letter to Saunders for transmittal to Marion. In the covering letter he had assured Saunders that his behavior in the matter had been "Perfectly right," and warned that in sending on his letter to Marion a noncommissioned officer serve as messenger rather than an officer, "for fear he detains the person sent on Account of Postell."

But Saunders, perhaps to demonstrate his contempt for Marion's threats, ordered Cornet Thomas Merritt to deliver the letter. He rode off alone under a white flag until he arrived at Britton's Ferry. There he asked the ferryman, Britton, to guide him to the Snow Island hideout. When the two men arrived at Dunham's Bluff, the officer in command invited Merritt into the redoubt. A messenger was sent to Colonel Hugh Ervin. After a short interval Colonel Ervin and an armed party came across the Peedee in canoes, seized Merritt, trussed him up, and carried him back to the hideout as a prisoner.

Balfour was outraged, accusing Marion of an "impaction of the laws of Nations and of War, as you complain in the case of Captain Postell; and such a one as if not immediately addressed, I shall be obliged to punish in the most exemplary manner by the severest retaliation." Marion never took time to reply to this protest. He now had a hostage, and it should be clear to the British that if they went so far as to hang Postell for breaking his parole, young Merritt would meet a similar fate.[11]

While this paper war had been going on, Watson had remained at Blakely's Plantation. His foraging parties brought in swine, cattle, and grain from the surrounding countryside. Marion knew his every move, for if one of his scouts did not report an incident to him, a civilian did. Every day Watson expected to hear that Colonel Doyle was bringing up reinforcements, but messengers could neither get into nor leave his camp through the cordon that the partisans had thrown up around the British position.

Watson, with every passing day more in danger of becoming completely isolated, came to the conclusion that he must retreat to Georgetown. To conceal his losses, he sank the bodies of those wounded who had recently died into the deep, green waters of an abandoned rock quarry. Those wounded still alive were loaded into wagons. He marched at a fast pace down the road to Georgetown.

Seven miles from Blakely's was Ox Swamp, where the road crossed the marshy ground on a causeway and bridges. When he arrived at the swamp, Watson discovered that the bridges had been destroyed and that trees had been felled across the road. If he tried to skirt the obstructions he could become caught in an awkward situation, should the enemy appear while he was trying to negotiate the soggy ground. If he turned back he would be forced to fight, for Marion's brigade was trailing along not too far behind. He gave orders and had his column execute a sharp right turn through the open piney woods and make for the Santee road, fifteen miles away.

Marion expected such a maneuver. He sent parties to conceal themselves in the pine thickets and swamps along the way. They constantly peppered the trotting column, so much so that Peter Horry was led to chuckle, "Never did I see a body of Infantry ply their legs so briskly!" Occasionally, when the harassment became too vigorous, Watson wheeled his field pieces into position and fired a round or two of grapeshot at the unseen enemy. It did little more than strip the trees. Sometimes he had his men face about in a battle line, deliver a volley, and then stage a charge into the thickets. There was no one on whom to use bayonets.

As the British column crawled slowly toward the Sampit River, just nine miles from Georgetown, Marion ordered Peter Horry to ride around the enemy and take possession of the bridge over that stream. After destroying the bridge, Horry posted Lieutenant John Scott and his riflemen fifty yards beyond the Sampit.

The British column did not slacken its pace as it neared the river but waded in and pushed its way to the far side. As they came out on shore, they began to form ranks. For some reason Scott did not give the order to fire. Horry cursed him roundly, although he later stated that the strongest words he used on Scott that day were "coward" and "Infamous poltroon."

Even as the first of Watson's men were forming, Marion came up on his rear with a drumming of hoofbeats and a rattle of musketry. As Watson attempted to rally his troops, his horse, struck by a musket ball, collapsed beneath him. The colonel leaped upon another. Turning his cannon about, he ordered his gunners to present Marion's horsemen with a load of grapeshot. As the iron balls tore through their ranks, the men of the brigade fell back out of range. Loading his wounded into two wagons, Watson crossed the river, leaving some twenty dead on the field.

Late that night the British colonel allowed his weary men to pitch camp at Trapier Plantation. He was disgusted at the unorthodox method of fighting by the "damned rebels" and complained they "would not sleep and fight like gentlemen, but, like savages, were eternally firing and whooping around him by night; and by day, waylaying and popping at him from behind every tree as he went by." [12]

Marion and his men spread their blankets beside the Sampit that night. Few had fallen asleep yet when the clatter of hoofbeats announced the arrival of a messenger from Kingstree. The news that he brought led Marion to realize that the British could also utilize the quick strikes characteristic of partisan warfare to their own advantage.

Lieutenant Colonel Welbore Doyle and the New York Volunteers, on orders from Lord Rawdon, were even now driving to the rear of Marion's brigade. Marion had not expected that the British would forsake their traditional manner of fighting in formal formations in open fields. Doyle had already crossed Lynche's Creek at Witherspoon's Ferry and was even now striking for Snow Island. Marion was at best twenty-four hours of hard riding away from his hideout, and, even then, he could not persuade his weary men to climb back into the saddle before daybreak.

Colonel Hugh Ervin, commanding at Snow Island, received intelligence of the approach of Doyle. He prepared to make a stand, although the majority of the men under him were either sick or wounded or had been stationed there to guard the prisoners in the Bull Pen. Those men who were fit for duty were posted along Clark's Creek. Extra guns, ammunition, and supplies were dumped into Lynche's Creek.

Doyle drove his men hard, realizing that if he used too much time, Marion would hear of the raid and come riding down upon him. Guided by local Tories, he reached Clark's Creek by the middle of the morning. He spread his men along the bank of the stream so that his line outflanked that of Ervin's little band and by enfilading fire managed to drive them from the boats. For a while it was a bloody little skirmish. Seven of Ervin's men had been killed by the time they were driven back from the creek. Doyle led his men across the stream to Snow Island.

Cornet Merritt, as an officer, had been kept prisoner in the Goddard house rather than in the Bull Pen with the ordinary soldiers. When the firing broke out, he convinced himself that it was Watson coming to rescue the prisoners after having crushed Marion. Colonel Ervin, however, soon came to the house, gave young Merritt sidearms, and informed him that he was now in charge of the twenty-five other prisoners and the fifteen wounded who were too ill to travel. With this last chore assigned, Ervin led his men away.

Doyle had not lost a man, but he knew full well that he could not tarry on the island. Burning or destroying everything that they could find, including Goddard's cabin, the loyalists hurried back across Clark's Creek. By that afternoon they had crossed Lynche's Creek and had gone into camp on the north side of Witherspoon's Ferry.[13]

Leaving the Sampit, Marion and his men rode hard. But his troops had grown tired of the days of fighting and travel. It was near time for the planting of crops. As they galloped through the Williamsburg District, men began to drop out and ride toward home. Marion did not try to stop them, for he was aware of their concerns. By the time he reached Indian Town there were only a few more than seventy men under his command.

As usual, the general sent patrols ranging over the countryside seeking information of enemy operations. One detachment, sent to scout the Camden area, discovered a boat laden with corn at the mouth of Kershaw's Creek. They attacked the guard, killing two of the enemy, wounding four, and capturing eight British soldiers and one loyalist.

Doyle's foragers were reported plundering the plantations south of Lynche's Creek. Hugh Horry and seventy men were dispatched to spoil their fun. Near McPherson's Plantation they ran into a party of thirty foragers who were under the protection of another group of about the same size. Horry charged them, killing two and taking prisoner thirteen British regulars, two Tories, and two Negroes without loss to himself. Captain McCottry and his riflemen trailed the survivors as far as Witherspoon's Ferry. As they came up to Lynche's Creek, they saw the enemy rear guard on the far bank attempting to scuttle the ferryboat. At the sight of McCottry's, men they took to their heels.

Doyle's camp was within range on the far side of the flooded stream. McCottry spaced his detachment along the shore, and they began to pick out targets on the opposite bank. A private and an officer of the New York Volunteers were shot down. Doyle hurriedly deployed his men along the bank and delivered a rolling volley at the unseen foe on the far side. It amounted to little more than an exercise in bluster. Because of the wide spread of McCottry's men, it was difficult to determine just how many were delivering the harassing fire. Doyle hurriedly struck camp and moved off toward the Peedee.

Back at Indian Town, Marion was surveying the events of the last seven months, seven months of hard riding, hard fighting, and hard living. He had driven the enemy from Williamsburg, but like the heads of a Hydra, they kept returning. Doyle's raid on Snow Island had deprived him of a base of operations and badly needed supplies and ammunition. The impossible had come about, as Major Ganey had recovered from the wound inflicted by Sergeant McDonald and was even now issuing another call for his Tories to seek retaliation upon the wiry little brigadier. All of Marion's efforts now seemed worthless; he fell into a deep grayness of the spirit.

The general's dejection was noted by the men still around him, and their talk around the campfires was cast in dismal tones. Peter Horry was disturbed by the increasing moodiness and felt he had to do something. He berated them, ashamed of their long faces, but his tongue-lashing only added to their sullenness.

He went to the general, but Marion had already noted the mood of the men and had come to the conclusion that it was time to stop "sighing and croaking."

Horry remembered the general's talk, and probably added some noble thoughts, later supplemented by the saccharinities of Parson Weems. Marion began in bitter tones:

Yesterday I commanded 200 men; men whom I gloried in, and who I fondly thought, would have followed me through my dangers for my country. And, now, when their country most needs their services, they are nearly all gone! And even those of you who remain, are, if report be true, quite out of heart; and talk, that you and your families must be ruined if you resist any longer! But, my friends, if we shall be ruined for bravely resisting our tyrants, what will be done to us if we tamely lie down and submit to them. . . . when those armies, viewing you with malignant eyes, shall constantly be insulting you as conquered rebels; and under pretence of discovering among you the seeds of another rebellion, shall be perpetually harassing and giving up to military execution the best and worthiest of your fellow citizens?

Then, waxing even more eloquent, he described in vivid terms the past mistreatment of the American colonies by Britain, the outrages committed by the king's troops and the Tories and ended with a ringing: "And God is my judge this day, that I would die a thousand deaths, most gladly would I die them all, rather than see my dear country in such a state of degradation and wretchedness."

The men, who had first stirred uneasily, now began to fall in with the spirit of his words and as the speech drew to a close, they began to cheer wildly and shout that they would fight beside him until death struck them down. Marion, knowing full well that he would have to act quickly to take advantage of this spontaneous outburst, cried out, "Well, now, Colonel Doyle, look sharp, for you shall presently feel the edge of our swords."

Orders were given to break camp and ride. To get at Doyle Marion had to cross Lynche's Creek, but the stream was at high flood, and Doyle had destroyed all of the boats. Marion rode through the swamps until he came to a narrow place and then saying little, rode his horse directly into the roiling waters. The horse began to thrash about but soon fell into a smooth swimming motion as he made for the opposite shore. The men plunged in after him; some almost didn't make it.

Peter Horry felt "never so near the other world in my life." The swift current caught up his horse and swept him downstream. As they were carried near a tree whose branches overhung the water, the profusion of vines that twined themselves over the limbs seemed to reach down and "like Absalom," tangled themselves about the colonel's head. His horse was carried from beneath him. Horry bawled like a lusty fellow without receiving an answer "which made me begin to think my chance was bad." His bellowings finally penetrated the darkness to draw the attention of a young man on a stout horse who rescued the sodden officer.

Every man made it safely across the creek, although in some instances blankets, clothing, saddles, and weapons had been lost. Some of the men were thrown up on high ground and were isolated by the floor waters until daylight when they were able to make their way to the far shore. Once they were on the other side, fires were lighted to dry out clothing and firearms.

Once dry, they again mounted, some riding bareback, and took the muddy road in quest of Doyle. They ran across an old man named Burch who told them that Doyle and his men had camped on his place the day before. That evening, he said, a messenger from Lord Rawdon, riding hard, had come into Doyle's bivouac. Burch did not know the contents of the message, but immediately upon reading it, Doyle had broken camp, ordered his heavy baggage burned, and had galloped off toward Camden, some sixty miles to the west.[14]

With Doyle riding hard for Camden, Watson was now almost isolated at Georgetown. He was a tempting target. Marion issued a call for his militia. It was time to take the field again.

Chapter IX

Thomas Sumter, in the meantime, had been having his troubles. After his retreat before Major Thomas Fraser, he had kept moving until he had reached the Waxhaws, where his wife could travel no farther. His troops were also unhappy with him. Not only did they charge him with leading them on fruitless missions, but some claimed that he had constantly deceived them as to the strength of the enemy. He found himself forced to make excuses to them, a particularly galling thing for one of Sumter's temperament and soaring ambition, for he felt it to be a shameful thing to do and believed the men should accept his decisions without explanation.

Despite his lack of recent success, Sumter still outranked Marion. And Governor Rutledge, just before he left Greene's camp to confer with the Continental Congress, had suggested that both Marion and Andrew Pickens cooperate with Sumter. The governor hoped Marion would "cultivate a Good Understanding with Genls. Sumpter & Pickens, and do every thing in your Power to forward the former's views. . . ."

With no real force of his own to command, Sumter began to eye Marion's brigade. He was unhappy that Marion had not joined him earlier and had assured him that his absence was indeed "mortifying," while to Greene he complained that he could get "no assistance from Genl. Marion" and implied that this was the reason for his recent lack of success. To Marion he made the charge that he allowed his troops to plunder at will and decried "the disorders [that] are prevalent in your Brigade."

Sumter planned to raise several regiments of light dragoons among the militia and rather grandly suggested that Marion form at least two such units from his brigade and that they be ready to cooperate the next time he decided to operate along the Santee. He likewise ordered Marion, of whose strength he knew nothing, to move to a position higher up in Black River, not only to prevent cattle from being driven into the enemy at Camden "but also to facilitate my plans & designs on the west side of the Wateree—the more speedy your movements are, the better they will answer."

Marion could be just as stubborn as Sumter. He resented the senior general's implications and arbitrary orders, especially since he had lately been more successful in the field. He refused to have anything to do with Sumter's plans for raising a state militia for ten months of the year and paying it off in goods, slaves, and other properties taken from the loyalists, a scheme that was to become known as "Sumter's Law." [1]

Marion's men had not answered his call as speedily as he had hoped; many lingered at home long enough to get their crops into the ground. Others were just weary of riding and fighting, while still others feared for the safety of their families. Colonel Watson was on the prowl again, this time with a force of about nine hundred men made up of regulars, Harrison's Provincials, and Ganey's loyalists.

By April 7 Watson was across the Black River at Britton's Ferry and had gone into camp on the widow Jenkins's plantation. They plundered the place of all provisions, even going so far as to kill seven of the widow's cattle and, after skinning them, leaving the carcasses on the ground for the buzzards because they were too thin to eat. Watson's progress would not have been so leisurely had he realized how desperately both Balfour and Rawdon were trying to get in touch with him.

On April 9 Watson bivouacked on Catfish Creek, not too far from Marion's position on Wahee Neck. As Watson moved into the area, the militia left their fields and came trooping into Marion's camp. Not only were they fearful of Watson's force, but Lord Rawdon had begun to allow the Tory militia to hold mock courts and try all those rebels who were not held as prisoners of war. Their judgments were harsh. The strength of the brigade had risen to five hundred men, but Marion dared not strike at Watson. Not only was he outnumbered nearly two to one, but his ammunition was running dangerously low, with an average of no more than two rounds per man. The best he could do was to lead them in a few hit-and-run raids to keep the enemy off balance.

Another of his dark moods began to cloud his mind. He entertained the idea of throwing over the business in the low country and taking to the hills from where, from time to time, he could sally down and harass the enemy until either the British had left the country or he was killed. Then there was the possibility of riding northward to offer his services to Greene and the Southern Army.

He told Peter Horry to call into council the field officers—Colonels Peter and Hugh Horry, John Ervin, James Postell, and Majors John James, John Baxter and Alexander Swinton. He discussed his plans for leaving the low country. He made no mention of Sumter's demands, nor did he suggest that they had been a factor in his decision. The officers assured the general that they would carry on in any manner he should direct, although several let it be known that they were not happy with his proposed plans.

A number of company grade officers, along with a number of the men, were troubled when the news filtered down through the camp. Among them was Captain Gavin Witherspoon, whose enthusiasm for combat tended to overwhelm his prudence. As Witherspoon walked back toward his campfire, Ensign Baker Johnson tore into camp on a heaving, lathered horse. Knowing that Johnson had been out on scout, Witherspoon stopped by to learn the latest intelligence.

But Johnson was a hungry man, and in no mood to talk until he had filled his belly. As he threw himself off his horse, his first words were, "for God's sake give him something to eat." All that Witherspoon had was a pot of cold rice, and as he sat this before the famished scout he asked the news.

Between mouthfuls Johnson sputtered forth, "Fine news. I saw a great number of Continental troops, horse and foot, crossing Drowning Creek."

"Come and tell the general!" cried the excited captain. Johnson, something of a free spirit, paused long enough in his wolfing down the rice to answer, "No, I'm starving from hunger and if the general wants the news he must come to me."

Witherspoon dashed off to get Marion. The general came to his scout. The news was good. Lee and his legion were returning to South Carolina. Even as ripples of excitement spread through the camp, the steady thump of a drum was heard in the distance. Shortly afterward Captains James Conyers and Edmund Irby rode in, leading a detachment of Lee's infantry accompanied by an additional company under Captain Conway Oldham. Lee's mounted men were coming on behind, for upon leaving Greene's army along with some infantry, they had marched toward Cross Creek as a means of confusing the enemy. After that Lee had some difficulty in locating Marion. A guide was dispatched to help Lee in as well as bring out the boats that Marion kept hidden along the Peedee to ferry the legion across the river.[2]

Conyers not only carried a letter from Greene, but he was able to fill in the operations of the Southern Army since it had left the state. After Cowpens the commanding general had placed the army under Isaac Huger and had ridden across country to direct Daniel Morgan's retreat. Cornwallis had fallen in behind in full pursuit, hoping to recover the prisoners taken at Cowpens. The two units of the American Army had come together at Guilford Court House in North Carolina and had then crossed over the Dan River into Virginia. Cornwallis had turned back at the Dan and had moved over to Hillsborough where he had raised the royal standard.

In Virginia, at Halifax Court House, Greene's army had recruited its strength. He had recrossed the Dan on February 23, and, after maneuvering and skirmishing with each other, the two armies had clashed at Guilford Court House on March 15, 1781. Greene had been forced to leave the field to the British, but he had inflicted such damage on the enemy that the *Annual Register* had commented on Lord Cornwallis's claim to victory with, "That victory . . . was productive of all the consequences of defeat."

Several days after the battle, Cornwallis had marched southeast to seek sanctuary at Wilmington at the mouth of the Cape Fear River, a town already in British hands. Greene had pursued as far as Ramsey's Mill on Deep River. There he had turned back into South Carolina, hoping to lure Cornwallis after him. At Ramsey's Mill he had sent Conyers and Irby on ahead with the legion infantry before the army broke camp.

Conyers handed Marion a dispatch from Greene, which briefly recounted the events of the campaign in North Carolina through the "battle of Guilford, which finally terminated in the retreat of the enemy, and his lordship was obliged to run hastily." Conyers had been sent ahead to see to the collection of supplies for the Southern Army; Marion immediately detached Major Swinton and sixty men to round up cattle and swine. When the army reached South Carolina, Greene hoped "you will be prepared to support its operations with a considerable force," and he wished the partisans to gather all available information as to the enemy's disposition of troops. The commanding general had also written Sumter to issue orders to Marion and Pickens "to collect all the Militia they can to cooperate with us." [3]

Although Lee believed the British were ignorant of his return, they not only knew of his arrival but had received intelligence that Greene's army had turned south. It had been this information that resulted in Doyle's hasty recall to Camden, for it was Rawdon's feeling that Camden was a likely objective for Greene's next push. This was also the reason that Ganey's Tories and Watson's command had been sent into the area—to break up large concentrations of militia who might join Greene. Now, with the approach of Lee, Watson had felt it best to pull back. For one thing, as soon as Ganey's loyalists heard rumors of Lee's return, they began to drift off in increasing numbers. Lest he get caught between Lee and Marion, Watson acted with dispatch. His heavy baggage was piled high and was soon blazing in a great bonfire. His two field pieces, taken from Fort Watson, were pushed into Catfish Creek, for they could slow his march. He marched briskly for Georgetown, taking a roundabout route to escape interception. [4]

Marion suspected that Watson would be recalled to Camden, but if he could keep him penned within Georgetown, he could weaken Rawdon's force should Greene move against him at Camden. He crossed the Peedee at Mars Bluff and rode through the spring rains. He made the mistake of riding through the Williamsburg District. The men, perhaps with the knowledge that Lee was returning, felt they were no longer needed so desperately and began to fall out of the column as they passed near their homes. By the time the brigade reached the bridge over Black River, Marion had only eighty rank and file under his command. Yet it was rumored that there would soon be action and many of those who had slipped away began to make their way back to camp as soon as they had checked on affairs at home.

Lee was back, having made a junction with Marion on April 14 after marching from Ramsey's Mill in eight days. His presence gave a lift to everyone's spirits. They were an odd pair, the Virginia aristocrat in his dapper uniform and the gaunt little South Carolina militia general in his charred leather hat. Yet Lee had the insight to recognize Marion's military abilities and quite willingly placed his legion under Marion's direction, something he was loath to do with others.

After an exchange of pleasantries and experiences, the two took up their planning where they had left off at Cordes Plantation when Lee had been recalled to the Southern Army. Marion wanted to make a push against Watson in Georgetown. Lee opposed this proposal on the grounds that it would put their force to far to the east when and if Greene launched his proposed attack on Rawdon at Camden. Also Greene had suggested that Fort Watson would be the most likely target. Marion, realizing the prudence of Lee's objections, joined in planning the attack on Fort Watson. There was a bonus if that post could be taken, for it would supply a quantity of badly needed ammunition.

They wasted little time in preparations and marched for Fort Watson early in the morning of April 15 and invested the post before noon. Major John Rudulph, with a detachment of dragoons, was sent off toward Georgetown to observe and report any movement by Major Watson. That evening the remainder of the legion and the brigade were camped in the skirts of the woods around the open field behind Scott's Lake. The siege of Fort Watson had begun.

Fort Watson was no easy project. Not only did the post sit high on the Indian mound above the level plain, but there were three rows of abatis, the tangled trees making an assault difficult for infantry and practically impossible for cavalry. Within Fort Watson's walls Lieutenant James McKay commanded a garrison of eighty regulars and forty loyalists. Colonel Watson had earlier taken away the two artillery pieces, and they now lay at the bottom of Catfish Creek. Even without artillery, however, Mckay felt in no great danger. He was well supplied with provisions and ammunition, his stockade was strong, and there were no trees near to shelter riflemen. After the customary summons to surrender and the customary rejection, both sides settled down to a sporadic exchange of small-arms fire.

The supply of drinking water came from Scott's Lake. Several of McCottry's riflemen and a few Continental sharpshooters were detached to check this. They stationed themselves out of musket range, between the stockade and the lake, and picked off anyone who was so bold as to venture out. But James McKay was a man of some enterprise; he immediately set his men to digging a well. On April 18 they struck water. It began to appear as though the defenders might be able to hold out indefinitely with this supply, or at least until reinforcements could be sent from Camden to lift the siege.

The absence of trees near the walls to furnish cover for riflemen posed a problem. And there were so few entrenching tools that to attempt to dig siege lines would be impracticable. To make matters worse, Marion's men had less than two rounds of ammunition remaining each. Lee rushed off a letter to Greene, asking for the loan of an artillery piece for several days and promising that it would be returned shortly, as the general was assured, "Five minutes will finish the business. . . ." Lee reverted to his old form and in recounting the progress of the siege did not mention Marion and listed mostly the accomplishments of "I." Then a greater and more dreaded danger than the enemy swept through the camp—smallpox! Few of the militia had been inoculated, although most of the Continentals had been forced to undergo the preventive process. Marion's men began to creep out of camp. So many slipped away that his orders for April 21 declared that anyone who left would be classed as a deserter and his name published as "an Enemy to the united States and Suffer as such."

Greene reacted quickly to Lee's request for an artillery piece, for he was convinced that "for want of Cannon I am not a little afraid they will fail of success. . . ." A six-pounder and gun crew under the command of Captain Ebenezer Finney was started on its march escorted by a detachment commanded by Major Pinkethan Eaton. But Captain Conyers, acting as their guide, lost his way. While Lee chafed because the gun had not arrived, Marion became discouraged with the siege of Fort Watson. His militia continued restive, grumbling and hinting they were going to seek the comforts of home. Two of their number had been killed and six lay wounded. And the defenders appeared just as strong as they had in the beginning.

Lieutenant Colonel Hezikiah Maham of the St. Stephen's Parish militia, who had served as a captain in one of the South Carolina rifle regiments and now commanded an independent state dragoon regiment, came forth with an idea that was brilliant in its simplicity. His rather simple suggestion was that a tower be built high enough to allow the riflemen to fire at targets within the walls of the fort. Dragoons were immediately sent off to collect all the axes in the vicinity.

Men were ordered into the woods to cut and trim trees, with the logs to be piled out of range of musketry from the fort. For five days, the logs were cut to size and notched on the ends. On the night of April 22 they were carried forward to within easy rifle range of the walls and the construction of a rectangular log crib was begun. When the tower reached a height higher than the walls of the fort, a floor was laid. In front of this platform a shield of thick timber was thrown up to protect the riflemen from small-arms fire.

Before dawn on April 23, a detail of McCottry's riflemen with their first fire drove the defenders to cover. As these riflemen provided a covering fire, one Robert Lee, a volunteer serving with the legion, and Ensign Baker Johnson, each leading a party of men, rushed forward and began to pull away a section of the abatis and then moved in to chop away at the logs forming the wall of the stockade. Behind them, at a safe distance, stood the legion infantry, bayonets fixed, ready to make the final charge. With his men unable to expose themselves enough to return the fire from the tower, Lieutenant McKay ran up the white flag of surrender.

Captain Patrick Carnes of the legion and Captain James Milton for Marion entered the fort to arrange the terms of capitulation. The terms were generous. As a sign of respect for gallant adversaries who had managed to hold out for eight days, the officers were given paroles, were allowed to retain their side-arms, to keep their personal baggage, and to remain in Charleston on parole until an exchange could be effected. The soldiers were to be paroled and marched to Charleston, with the forty loyalists given the same terms as the regulars. In all, six officers and 109 rank and file laid down their arms. The losses of Lee and Marion were two militia killed and three militia and three of the legion wounded.

Marion, as the senior officer, composed the official report to Greene. He praised Lee for "his advice and indefatigable diligence in every part of this tedious operation." Robert Lee, Ensign Johnson, and "Major Mayham" were cited for their roles, with the latter receiving full recognition for his part in the reduction of the fort. The following day his orders carried his personal gratitude to Lee's legion, Maham, Ensign Johnson, Mr. Lee, and Lieutenant McDonald, who had but recently been promoted to that rank from sergeant.

General Greene gave Marion his due when, in his general orders, he reported that Fort Watson had "surrendered to Marion." Although the reduction of the fort represented a breach in

British communications, Lord Rawdon dismissed it as the loss of "a small Post where Lieut. Col. Watson kept his Baggage at Wright's Bluff." After leveling the walls, Marion moved over toward the High Hills of the Santee and bivouacked at "Bloom Hill," the plantation of William Richardson, near enough to Greene should the general wish his aid against Camden.[5]

But during this period there had been a regular spate of irritations, not the least of which was the continued arrogance of Major William Clay Snipes. Although Marion had issued him a commission as major, Snipes still held little affection for the brigadier. When a call had gone out for men to aid in the reduction of Fort Watson, Snipes had attempted to throw obstacles in the way. When Colonel Abel Kolb was gathering his men to answer Marion's summons, Snipes had appeared in the community, spreading wild and scurrilous tales about Marion and ordering those men who had responded to join William Harden instead. Kolb protested, stating that he had just received Marion's orders prohibiting anyone from leaving the regiment without the brigadier's express consent. Snipes was as rude to Kolb as he had been to Marion, answering Kolb's protests with, "This will inform you that I have Instructions from General Sumpter, who Commands General Marion, to Raise men where I can; & as to Gen'l Marion's orders, in the Case it avails nothing." Snipes continued to insist that he had General Greene's approval for what he was doing, an impression that the commanding general had been quick to deny every time he heard the report.

On April 18 Kolb's dispatch to Marion enclosed a communication he had received from Snipes. He also sent in a few men, explaining that most of the militia in his district were attracted to the state troops by Sumter's promise of a bounty. He also reported that a Lieutenant Lyons had been calling out militia and then sending them on to Sumter and had impressed the plow horses of some who had announced their intentions of joining Marion. Lyons's attitude had been as insolent as that of Snipes. When Kolb questioned his authority for sending Kolb's men to another unit, Lyons had snapped, "he Damnd himself if he wou'd serve any officer but whom he pleased, that he disregarded any Orders that might be issued to the Contrary."

The reference to Sumter and his seniority did little to ease Marion's concern. He immediately dashed off a letter to Sumter, complaining bitterly of the attitudes of both Snipes and Lyons. Throughout his letter there were implications that neither Sumter nor his subordinates should interfere with the men of Marion's brigade, and he protested as illegal Sumter's plans for paying state troops with plunder taken from the loyalists. He suggested that he might even go so far as to carry his complaints to the governor.

Sumter did not reply until April 30, and in a rambling letter he emphatically denied that he had interfered with the militia on the east side of Santee and assured Marion that Snipes was acting on his own and not at Sumter's direction. He defended his method of paying off state troops and then, in asserting his seniority, he reminded Marion, "As to the powers by which I Act, they Ought not to be Called into question by any man untill Gentlemen whom it might Concern, had used proper means to Obtain information."

An angry Snipes replied to Marion's charges by claiming that his conceit had blinded him in "that the commission you have received is really puft you up so much that you have Intirely forgot the Cause." Within a month, leading a party of twenty men, Snipes was surprised by enemy troops out of Dorchester. Snipes and two of his men escaped; the rest were put to the sword.[6]

Added injury came from the reprimand of Brigadier General Moultrie, whom Marion had always considered a close friend. As a result of a communication from Balfour, who had charged

that Marion had treated loyalist prisoners of war badly, Moultrie
had apologized, stating that such behavior was "contrary to his
natural disposition; I know him to be Generous & humane."
This was a particularly bitter blow to Marion, who prided himself on his ability to control his men, and the fact that Moultrie
believed Balfour's charge without further investigation made the
reprimand seem just that much worse. Moultrie twisted the
blade with, "you will Give such Orders as will prevent private
animosities from taking Revenge at this time, by such Unwar-
rantable practices, as can only serve to disgrace the Generous and
the brave." [7]

Such blows to his pride caused Marion's sensitivity to surface
once again, and he fell into one of his blue moods. Henry Lee
seemed to be about the only person who appreciated Marion and
the measures he had taken to prevent the British from securing
the state after Greene had begun his retreat through North
Carolina. No other partisan leader had been able to gain such
success as he had. On April 20, Lee had written Greene saying,
"I wish you would write a long letter to General Marion. His
services demand great acknowledgements and I fear he thinks
himself neglected."

Marion had begun to feel that Greene did not properly appre-
ciate his efforts. And Greene did not. He still had little use for
detached militia operations, and partisan strokes were still, to
him, but "garnish of a table." In fact to Joseph Reed, president
of the Executive Council of Pennsylvania, he was to note that
although both Marion and Sumter were good and brave men and
deserved great credit for their exertions, "Their Endeavours
rather seem to keep the contest alive, than lay any Foundations
for the Recovery of these States." He felt that the only reason
the militia came into the field was for plunder, and his distrust
had been increased by Sumter, whom he had tried "to get . . . to
join us, but this I know he will avoid if he can with decency."

However, Greene reacted quickly to Lee's suggestion that

Marion's spirits needed bolstering. From his flow of words, Greene gave the impression that the partisan was one of the most important cogs in his military machine: "I am at a loss which to admire most, your courage & fortitude, or your address and management." He promised that from his letters, not only General Washington and the Continental Congress but the "World in general" would hear of Marion's great merit. "To fight the enemy with a prospect of victory is nothing," wrote Greene, "but to fight with intrepidity under the constant impression of a defeat, and inspire irregular troops to do it, is a talent peculiar to yourself." Two days later there was another letter, congratulating him on the success against Fort Watson, approving of the articles and capitulation, and saying, "[I] feel myself particularly indebted to you and all the officers and men under you, for their spirit, perseverance and good conduct upon this occasion."

These letters, coupled with the self-satisfaction brought on by the fall of Fort Watson, did much to lift Marion's spirits. He began to operate with much of his old abandon in his loose, yet cautious fashion. His camp at Bloom Hill was so located that he could either slide over to aid Greene before Camden or by a hard march go against Watson in Georgetown. Greene wanted him to prevent Watson from reinforcing Rawdon at Camden. All traffic on the river was under his control as was most travel along the Santee road. Colonel John Ervin and eighty mounted men were dispatched to the vicinity of Rafting Creek in the High Hills to awe the Tories and prevent them from sending provisions into Camden.[7]

And Greene had been having his own troubles. When he had arrived within a mile and a half of Camden, he had his army pitch camp in battle formation on Hobkirk's Hill and on the slope facing the town. Just before daylight on April 19, a supply of provisions had arrived and his men were sitting around eating newly issued rations when, near ten o'clock, there was a burst of musketry. Lord Rawdon, having intelligence that Lee, Marion, and Sumter were on the march to join Greene, and that Watson was blocked by the partisan position, had come to the conclusion that his only chance lay in surprise. Arming his cooks, drummers, and convalescents to support his regular garrison, he had sallied out and caught Greene unprepared for battle.

The Battle of Hobkirk's Hill had been fierce. In the beginning Greene's troops had recovered from their initial surprise and had pushed the British, but an order issued by Colonel John Gunby of the Maryland Continentals had been mistakenly executed and the entire line had collapsed. Rather than risk defeat, Greene had withdrawn his troops and reassembled them three miles from the site of the battle. He was not discouraged, although he had once again been forced to give up the field of battle to the enemy. To General von Steuben he explained that "this repulse, if repulse it may be called, will make no Alteration in our general plan of operation."

To Marion, Greene said: "By Mistake we Got a Slight Repulse, the Injury is not Great" and assured him that he was going to invest Camden again within the next few days. Among the ill effects of the battle were the rumors that Greene's army was "routed and totally dispersed." Marion and Lee were to spread the word that it was only gossip.

Greene was unhappy with Sumter's refusal to join him before Camden. The general had come to the conclusion that the Gamecock was in the field only to plunder and even went so far as to consider placing him under arrest. On the other hand, Sumter's justification to Greene was "How far the Militia Coud be Depended upon to act with the Regulars, I am also at a loss to Determine—But am Rather of oppinion they Woud not behave well as they have Never been accustomed to oppose the enemy openly." [9]

Because of his desperate need for men, Greene concluded that he must make greater use of the militia. He ordered Marion to move his men up to within seven miles of Camden. His respect for militia operations had been increased, not only by the fall of Fort Watson but by another success on April 18.

Colonel William Harden, acting on Marion's orders, went against Fort Balfour at Pocotaligo. It was an easy conquest. On April 14 he struck a Tory gathering at Four Holes, paroling the captain and twenty-four men that he captured. The following night he took a Captain Barton and six privates in the captain's home. Harden sent out a small group to lure the enemy out of Fort Balfour and was able to capture Colonels Fenwick and Letchmere at Vanherst. Surrounding the post, Harden sent in a flag to demand the surrender of the garrison. It was refused. A second summons stated that if Harden were obliged to storm the walls, he would give no quarter. The commandant, Colonel Fletcher Kellsal, asked for half an hour to consider; Harden gave him twenty minutes. Within the next two hours, eight officers and sixty infantry, along with a lieutenant and twenty-six dragoons with their horses marched out as prisoners of war and piled their arms. Fort Balfour was destroyed.[10]

Despite Nathanael Greene's abiding dislike for militia and their often haphazard operations, Francis Marion had gained military respectability.

Chapter X

It was spring at Bloom Hill and the mud and chill of the winter campaign had waned into an unpleasant memory. Marion rested his men until he received Greene's dispatch of April 28, 1781.

Greene, on the advice of Captain Conyers, had changed his mind about having Marion move up near Camden. Conyers, in fact, had done Marion a favor, for he persuaded Greene that Marion's contributions would be greater in individual action, away from the main army. Conyers realized the value of good leadership, for he had been detached to lead a group of militia but had asked to be recalled "for Volunteers are not to be made Soldiers of without Officers."

The commanding general had come to the conclusion that the enemy must not be allowed to consolidate their forces and "we must again resume the partizan war." He was convinced that if the various outposts protecting the supply lines to primary posts were closed, the enemy would be forced to pull their lines closer to Charleston. First, Greene suggested that Marion leave fifty men some fifteen or twenty miles below Camden to disrupt the delivery of supplies to that place. Then Marion and Lee were to concentrate on the reduction of the posts lying between Camden and the Congaree River: Fort Motte, Bellesville, and Fort Granby. Marion, if the conditions were right, could go against Georgetown. In addition to this, Greene implored Marion to collect dragoon horses for the use of the army.

Lee had even bigger ideas. He had rather grandly promised that he and his legion could perform great deeds if only they had more men and proposed that one hundred picked riflemen and fifty infantry be detached from the Southern Army. An irritated Greene dismissed the suggestion with "You write as if I had an Army of fifty thousand men. Surely you Cannot be unacquainted with our real situation." He ordered Lee to work closely with Marion for the time being, for if they separated each would be too greatly exposed.

Upon receipt of his orders, Marion broke camp and marched down to Salem to encamp near Lee. But Marion discovered that he had little time for planning an extensive campaign against the posts, for the Tories were out, perhaps because of the rumor that his brigade had been "routed and totally dispersed." [1]

Earlier, when Marion and Lee had left the area, Ganey's Tories had begun to assemble at Drowning Creek. Colonel Abel Kolb, fearful of the mischief they might cause if left alone to grow in strength, called out the militia companies of Captains James Gillespie and Josiah Cantey. Marching swiftly into the district, he surprised and routed them. As was customary in the vicious little civil war then raging in eastern South Carolina. the victors held few qualms about plundering the vanquished.

Just as soon as Kolb pulled back out of the community, the angry loyalists began to reassemble. When they became strong enough to make their presence felt, Kolb once again issued a call for his militia and started marching for the Little Peedee with the commands of Major Lemuel Benison and Captain Joseph Dabbs. At Hulin's Mill, John Deer and Osburn McLean, two of the better known of Ganey's confederates, were flushed in the woods. Springing up from their concealment, the two raced for Catfish Creek. Rifles cracked. Both fugitives fell; Deer was dead and McLean gravely wounded. Another of Ganey's men, Caleb Williams, was captured; his reputation was so flecked with blood that he was immediately and unceremoniously strung up to the nearest tree. Leaving these Tory casualties as examples to their comrades, Kolb turned back toward the Peedee.

Kolb was mistaken in his impression that the loyalists along Drowning Creek would be awed into complacency without an occupying force to insure their good behavior. The intense Tory outrage and desire for retaliation took form when Captain Joseph Jones put out a call for volunteers. On April 28 at least fifty loyalists had assembled at Maidendown Bay, and that afternoon they galloped off toward the Peedee. Late that night they silently surrounded Kolb's house. They called for Kolb to come out. Kolb refused, resolving to sell his life as dearly as possible. Two brothers by the name of Evans who were spending the night at the house grabbed muskets. The attackers drew back out of range when they felt the combined fire of the three defenders. Jones gathered his men for an assault upon the house.

Before exposing his men to the fire from the house, Jones called out that he would burn the defenders out if they did not give themselves up. In response to the weeping entreaties of the women in the house, Kolb shouted back that he would surrender. As he stepped across the threshold of the front door, accompanied by his wife and sisters, and with his sword held hilt forward in submission, he was immediately shot down by one Mike Goings. After the Evans brothers suffered a similar fate (Thomas was brought down while running for his life), the house and stables were plundered before they were put to the torch. Then, in the light cast by the leaping flames, the Tories rode happily off toward Catfish Creek.[2]

As soon as he heard of this action, Marion dispatched Colonel John Ervin's regiment to punish Jones and his men. He wished to alert the brigade, but there was no brigade to alert. His men were near enough to their homes to labor under an emotional conflict. Under local law, South Carolina militia could not be kept in the field longer than two months at a time and some had already served beyond that period. Others were just homesick. As his men wandered off, Marion discovered that he had no more than 150 men with him. Marion blamed Greene, for not giving him more to do and complained that his men had "Dropt away, waried with Duty & I believe Dispirited, in not seeing greater Support."

The flamboyant Lee, without consulting Marion, had informed Greene that the partisan chieftain could spare at least sixty dragoon horses and perhaps as many as 150, "if he will." Marion had done nothing about the general's previous request for mounts—for one thing, the horses in his brigade were usually the personal property of the men, while those taken in battle were considered legitimate prizes of war to be divided among the victors. Without the promise of some booty, the militia would have been reluctant to turn out on a volunteer basis—especially since so many of them had been plundered by the Tories, or seen their livestock confiscated by British foragers. When Greene increased his request from sixty to eighty dragoon horses, Marion became irritated, especially by the sentence, "If the object of the People is to Plunder altogether, Government can receive but little benefit from them." [3]

Greene had also learned that Cornwallis had marched out of Wilmington. His destination was unknown, but the general suspected he would be turning back into South Carolina, and Marion was requested to send scouting parties to watch the progress of the enemy general. If Cornwallis did turn south, it was Greene's opinion that Tarleton and his legion would ride on ahead, and this could mean that the Southern Army could be caught between Rawdon and Tarleton, or that Tarleton might race directly into Camden to strengthen that garrison. With these possibilities facing him, Greene wished Lee and his legion to rejoin him immediately. He sought a stronger defensive position by crossing the Wateree above Camden and moving to Twenty-Five Mile Creek. There he remained until he learned that Cornwallis had taken the road to Virginia.

Lieutenant Colonel Nisbet Balfour, as commandant of Charleston, was now the ranking British officer in South Carolina, although he kept in as close touch with Cornwallis as communications would allow. With Greene hovering in the vicinity, he feared for the safety of Camden. To strengthen Rawdon, changes were made in military dispositions. Major Archibald McArthur, captured at Cowpens but now exchanged, was assigned the task of collecting all the replacements then in Charleston. With three hundred infantry and eighty dragoons, McArthur moved up to Monck's Corner. Watson, who had remained at Georgetown to supply cover for Cornwallis should he return to the state, made a forced march across the Santee to make a junction with McArthur. Then, with McArthur's pickup force providing a screen, and with Harrison's Provincials furnishing the vanguard and scouting the flanks, Watson moved at what appeared to be a leisurely pace toward Camden, but he was determined to fight his way into the town if necessary. After crossing Lenud's Ferry, he suddenly slanted his march toward Monck's Corner. Then, feeling that he had sufficiently confused those watching his movements, he turned again and started for Nelson's Ferry.

From Major Rudulph, Marion learned of Watson's movements, but he could not make an attack without orders, and he was also waiting for Eaton and Finley to bring up the artillery. He did send Colonel Ervin to watch the enemy march. When Eaton came in on May 2 he brought orders for Marion and Lee to leave the Black River and cross the Santee to stop Watson. During the night Marion's men were ferried across Scott's Lake and by daylight he was astride the Santee road. He was too late, for Watson had already passed and was nearing Camden. Lee was equally "mortified," for both he and Marion had been confident of success. They moved on up the road to Fort Motte.[4]

Fort Motte was strategically located in the triangle where the Congaree and Wateree came together to form the Santee. It was the principal depot and strongpoint on the British line of communications between Charleston and the interior. Its garrison had been active in dispersing bands of Whigs who were so bold as to venture into the area. The post had originally been located at Colonel William Thomson's plantation, a mile away, but had been moved to take advantage of the better terrain at Mount Pleasant Plantation, owned by Mrs. Rebecca Brewton Motte. The large mansion house, located on Buckhead Hill, had been strongly fortified by a stockade, a ditch, and an abatis. Mrs. Motte, a widow, had been forced to take up residence in an old log cabin formerly occupied by the overseer. Her son-in-law, Major Thomas Pinckney, had been wounded at Camden and was now a prisoner of war of the British.

The garrison, numbering around 140, was made up mostly of British regulars and Hessians under the command of Lieutenant Donald McPherson. They had just been strengthened by a small detachment of McArthur's dragoons who had been escorting provisions from Charleston to Camden when Lee and Marion approached. Although only a lieutenant, McPherson had performed well in command and had been so diligent in controlling plundering parties that he had received a commendation from Balfour. But McPherson had no artillery and his prime hope was early relief from Camden.[5]

Lee and Marion came up on Fort Motte on May 6. That same day, while they were looking over the lay of the land, Marion received a letter from Greene. It carried a tone of reprimand, or even of censure, and if one read carefully between the lines, the commanding general was blaming the partisan for the way he handled his men. After stating that he well understood that the militia claimed all horses taken from the Tories, Greene condemned the practice as little more than plundering. It is to be suspected that this letter was the result of a letter to Greene from Sumter, who had stated, "Genl. Marion is also in the way of Getting good horses—but how far you may succeed in applying to him I know not."

Greene wasn't too happy with Marion; he had earlier told Lee that Marion's personality was not adequate to do the job at hand. Lee had replied that he was far better than Sumter. Yet the general had written Sumter that "It is a pity that good horses would be given into the hands of People who are engaged for no limited time."

Marion was already irritable, and this letter from the general did little to soothe his ruffled feelings. Not only was he unhappy that so many of his militia had left him, but he was annoyed that Greene had been so long in sending him orders that Watson had been allowed to slip into Camden.

His unhappiness overflowed in his answer to Greene. He stretched the truth a bit when he stated that the horses taken from the loyalists had "been kept for the service & never for private property." He suggested that the only way he could furnish dragoon horses was to dismount his militia now with him, which would not only limit his operations, but "we shall never git their service in future." Then he drove his arguments home with a threat of his own. As for dismounting the militia, he said, "This would not give me uneasiness, as I have some time determined to relinquish my command in the militia as soon as you arrived in it & I want to do it as soon as this post is either taken or abandoned." He solicited leave to go to Philadelphia. Then, with this off his chest, Francis Marion got on with the business of the siege of Fort Motte.

Perhaps Greene would never have made his suggestion had he better understood Marion's tactics, and he would have realized the importance of horses to the partisans had he been able to check with Rawdon. One of the reasons for Marion's success had been the swiftness of his mounts and Rawdon had admitted this was why "we have never been able to force them to a decisive action." [6]

Opposite Fort Motte was another hill, on which Rebecca Motte's cabin was located. Lee took post on this ridge, while Marion's brigade of only 150 men was moved across the valley to occupy the slope of the hill on which the fort stood. Finley's six-pounder was located behind the militia lines, resting on a small mound of earth thrown up by the brigade. Mrs. Motte almost daily entertained Lee and his officers as well as giving generously of her time to the sick and wounded.

Regular siege operations were initiated, with slaves from neighboring plantations employed in throwing up earthworks. On May 10 a formal demand of surrender was sent in to the enemy. McPherson, a brave man, hoped to hold out long enough for the arrival of reinforcements from Camden and refused to entertain any such proposal. With that, the six-pounder opened up a methodical fire.

Meanwhile, things were happening as a result of Marion's failure to prevent Watson from reaching Camden. The weary British column had trudged into Camden early in the morning of May 7. When he learned that Watson had made it safely into town, Greene had written Marion that same day, declaring it to be a most unfortunate circumstance, "as the enemy will begin to act impudent and to show themselves without their works, which they have never ventured upon since the morning of the 25th." Because of this increase in enemy strength, Greene moved five miles upriver to take a strong defensive position behind Sawney's Creek.

With his confidence strengthened by Watson's arrival and his ambition inflated by his victory at Hobkirk's Hill, Rawdon moved out of Camden on the night of May 7 and crossed the Wateree at the ferry in an effort to mount a drive on Greene's flank. But Greene had anticipated such a move and had fallen back four miles to Colonel's Creek, leaving his pickets, light troops, and mounted men to operate in the vacated area as a patrol in force.

Moving on to Sawney's, Rawdon fell under the impression that Greene's patrol was the main Southern Army and deployed his force in battle line. After surveying the ground he came to the conclusion that the position on the far side of the creek was too strong and, after a couple of hours, turned back to Camden, still under the delusion that he had made contact with Greene's full force. Because of the strong position, he felt he "could not hope to force it without suffering much Loss, as must have crippled my Force for any future Enterprize. . . ."

Greene still felt that Rawdon was too strong to meet in an open field, and feared that the British would next make a strong move against Lee and Marion. Rawdon, however, was not that confident of his own strength. He had never felt that Camden was so important a post that it should be held at all costs, or that its location was of great strategic importance, especially since Marion had demonstrated how easily its supply lines could be cut or disrupted. The garrison was even now suffering from an acute lack of salt. Cornwallis was of the same opinion, and was to express his view that "the weakness and treachery of our friends in South Carolina, and the impossibility of getting any assistance from them, makes possession of any part of the country of very little use, except in supplying provisions for Charlestown," and was convinced that "it is doubtful whether we can keep the posts in the back parts. . . ." If Rawdon ventured forth to take on Greene, Camden would be left so lightly defended that it could be easily overrun. Rawdon decided to abandon the post. Orders were also sent out to blow up the British post at Nelson's Ferry. After releasing all prisoners, he burned the jail, mills, some dwellings, and all of his surplus supplies. Thirty sick and wounded were left behind, as were thirty prisoners who were to be exchanged for them. Taking between four and five hundred Negroes and all the most "obnoxious" loyalists, he moved down the road toward Charleston on May 10, planning to relieve Fort Motte along the way.[7]

That evening, May 10, word was received at Fort Motte that Rawdon had evacuated Camden and was on the move, although Marion felt that the rumor was false and that someone was only reporting a foraging party. But soon beacon fires on the distant hills along the Santee conveyed the cheerful news to those inside the fort that help was on the way. They gave out a lusty cheer. Lee and Marion, knowing that there was no time for regular siege operations or for building a "Maham Tower," concluded that McPherson would have to be burned out. Lee, as the more persuasive and personable of the two, went to tell Mrs. Motte.

Their idea was to employ an Indian trick and shoot fire arrows onto the roof to set the mansion house in flames, an act that should not prove too difficult as the shingles were tinder dry from a long spell of hot weather. When an apologetic Lee broached the scheme to Mrs. Motte, she is said to have replied, "If it were a palace, it should go." Rebecca Motte took one look at the crude bow and arrows that had been prepared, went into her house, and presented Lee with a "bow and its apparatus imported from India." Doctor Mathew Irvine of the legion carried in another flag demanding that McPherson surrender. It was refused as curtly as had been the first.

Lee and Marion moved their troops into the lines in preparation for an all-out assault on the stockade. They waited until noon to allow the sun an opportunity to suck the shingles dry of the dew. Flaming arrows, tipped with resin and sulphur, arched through a brassy sky. Some say that the bow was pulled that day by Nathan Savage, a private in Marion's brigade whose home had been burned by Wemyss.

As the roof began to blaze in at least three places, McPherson ordered men up to rip off the burning shingles. A charge of grape from Finley's six-pounder sent them tumbling off. About one o'clock, his efforts to extinguish the flames frustrated, McPherson hung out the white flag. Marion accepted the surrender, although Henry Lee was to comment that proper "policy commanded death."

As soon as the fort surrendered, men were sent rushing in to put out the blazing roof. McPherson was granted honorable terms because of his gallant conduct. For some reason friction had sprung up between Marion's militia and Lee's legion, so much so that Lee received the formal surrender of the regulars while Marion accepted that of the loyalists.

It had been an action remarkably free of casualties. Only two men from the brigade had been killed: a Lieutenant Cruger and, unfortunately, the loyal Lieutenant McDonald. In the post were found a large supply of provisions that had been forwarded from Nelson's Ferry and were destined for the garrison at Camden. That night Mrs. Motte entertained the officers of both armies in a brush arbor thrown up before her cabin, with Peter Horry commenting, "It produced the happiest effect on us all." [8]

More casualties occurred during the next twelve hours than during the entire siege of Fort Motte. It had been rumored that the Whigs planned to seek retaliation upon Tories in British service. After the surrender the loyalist rank and file had been confined in a mill belonging to Colonel Thomson at the foot of the hill on which the fort had stood; some of the Tories claimed they had been stripped of their clothes by the Americans. According to one of those imprisoned, "Little Lee" (Robert Lee) had come to the prison and on Colonel Lee's orders had taken nineteen-year-old Lieutenant Fulker of the loyalist militia, who was told that he was to be hanged on Mrs. Motte's gate. When the young officer asked why, and pleaded that he at least be given a trial, he was told that he was charged with being the cause of the death of a Mrs. Tate on Poplar Creek who, although suffering with smallpox, was turned out of her home, and "she catched cold and died." Despite Fulker's denial, he was taken to the gate, stripped of his clothes, and hanged.

John Jackson, accused of killing one of Sumter's men, was next. He was likewise stripped of his clothes, hanged from the gate, and left there all night. The following morning, while Lee's and Marion's men were leveling the fortifications, the bodies of Fulker and Jackson were dragged by the halters still around their neck and buried in the moat. As soon as their bodies were cleared from the place, Hugh McKelly, accused of acting as a guide for Doyle, suffered the indignities of being stripped and hanged with only an old dirty hunting shirt wrapped around his private parts.

Levi Smith (termed by Peter Horry as "a most furious tory") had accepted a British commission as Justice of the Peace and had commanded the militia in Fort Motte. He was named as the next victim and claimed to have been shown a note by Lee ordering him hanged. McPherson and other British officers protested that his militia commission should be respected as valid. Smith was a neighbor of Mrs. Motte, and his wife and children came rushing over but were told not to come within a hundred yards of the spot of execution. As soon as McKelly was dead, Smith was stripped, and the old shirt taken from McKelly's body and given to Smith to cover his nakedness. He tried to compose himself for the end.

Lieutenant Cooper of Marion's brigade, whose brother, Sam, a prisoner of Lord Rawdon's, was supposed to be exchanged for Smith, feared the consequences and rushed off to find Marion. The noose was adjusted about Smith's neck when Marion rushed up, a naked sword in his hand, shouting, "In the name of God! What are you about, what are you about here?"

"We are hanging them people, sir," was the reply.

His voice rising even more, Marion asked them who ordered them to hang any person. The answer was "Colonel Lee."

"I will let you know, damn you," shouted a livid Marion, "that I command here, and not Colonel Lee. Do you know that if you hang this man, Lord Rawdon will hang a good man in his place; that he will hang Sam Cooper, who is to be exchanged for him." But despite such an assertion of his authority, Marion was unable to have the lynching party punished.[9]

Greene, accompanied by a small escort, rode into Fort Motte shortly after the surrender. He and Marion met for the first time. They were on better terms now. Greene needed Marion, and the little brigadier's threat to resign his militia commission had a sobering effect upon the general. On May 9 he had written from Colonel's Creek that he had no intention of taking horses from the militia if Marion was of an opinion that such action would hamper their effectiveness, and "render your situation less agreeable with them." He expressed his unhappiness that the militia had deserted Marion, but he pointed out that the partisan's task, by its very nature, was difficult.

Greene then went on to list his own privations and difficulties since the beginning of the war: "I have never had leave of absence an hour, nor paid the least attention to my own private affairs. . . . I left a family in distress and every thing dear and valuable, to come and afford you all the assistance in my power." He had attempted to touch Marion's conscience by declaring, "Your State is invaded, your all is at stake. What has been done will signify nothing unless we persevere to the end. . . . and if you leave us in the midst of our difficulties, while you have it so much in your power to promote the service it must throw a damp upon the spirits of the Army, to find that the first men in the States are retiring from the busy scene to indulge themselves in more agreeable amusements." But then he tempered his criticism with a bit of flattery: "You have rendered important service to the public with the Militia under your Command, and have done great honor to yourself; and I would not wish to render your Situation less agreeable with them. . . ."

In Marion's reply on May 11, he complained that he was tired of trying to do something with the peripatetic militia, and although he still hinted that he might relinquish his command and go to Philadelphia, he did send Greene a fine horse for his personal use and added, "as far as it is in my power to procure more I will send them." Now, with misunderstandings behind them and a victory to celebrate, threats of resignation seemed forgotten as they planned their next moves.[10]

Happy once again, Marion led his militia across the Santee, intending to move against Georgetown should an opportunity present itself. Lee was ordered to go against Fort Granby, thirty miles west of Fort Motte. Thomas Sumter, who liked so much to conduct a war of his own, had forced the surrender of the enemy garrison at Orangeburgh on May 14—the British complained that his men had shot down sixteen of the loyalists in cold blood after they had been taken prisoner. Brigadier General Andrew Pickens was carrying out raids in the vicinity of Augusta. Greene's overall strategy was to bring about the fall of the various posts as near the same time as possible, thereby preventing the enemy from sending any large reinforcement to any one of the besieged garrisons. Without these posts to protect their supply lines, the enemy would be forced to retire into Charleston.

Sumter had been irked when Lee and Marion had taken Fort Motte, for he had wanted to add the fall of that strongpoint to his laurels. His vexation ripened into anger when he heard that Lee had been sent against Granby, and he suggested to Greene that the legion be recalled since his own command would be able to reduce the post. Lee had marched May 13 and the next morning Finley's six-pounder was within six hundred yards of the fortified frame building. Fort Granby was heavily garrisoned by 348 men (sixty of whom were Hessian) under the command of a Maryland Tory, Major Andrew Maxwell of the Prince of Wales American Regiment. Outside the fort Lee found Colonel Thomas Taylor and a small force left by Sumter to "amuse" and harass the enemy. Henry Lee was well aware of Maxwell's reputation as a person who lacked courage and whose prime military talent was for plundering.

On the morning of May 15 Finley fired a round or two at the fort while the legion infantry moved forward to open fire on the pickets. Maxwell was summoned to surrender, with Lee giving the word that Motte had fallen and that the main southern Army was on its way to join the siege of Granby. Maxwell immediately agreed to surrender on condition that the garrison be allowed to keep their plunder and could remain in Charleston as prisoners of war until they were formally exchanged. Lee agreed, except he demanded that all horses be given up. Maxwell at first agreed and then reneged because of the angry protests of his mounted troops. Negotiations were suspended until a patrol came in with the word that Rawdon had crossed the Santee and was moving in the general direction of Fort Granby. Lee agreed to Maxwell's demands.

After the capitulation had been signed late in the morning of May 15, Maxwell moved out toward Charleston with his men and their plunder—the major's personal share was two wagon loads. A number of Taylor's men and some of the legion grumbled against such leniency for marauders and threatened to kill the prisoners. Others whispered that the only reason Lee had granted Maxwell such generous terms was to rob Sumter of the glory, or to prevent his command from getting booty. The noise died down when Greene sent word that the first person who violated the surrender terms would be executed.

On the surface it would appear that Lee had been outbargained by Maxwell, but it should be remembered that not a single man had been lost on either side and the material left behind by Maxwell included two artillery pieces, the weapons belonging to the garrison, ammunition, salt, and a quantity of liquor. The fall of Fort Granby increased the number of prisoners taken since Greene came to South Carolina to eight hundred rank and file and fifty officers. The victory also released Lee for another quick strike. The taking of Motte and Granby had deprived Rawdon of two primary magazines and thereby limited British maneuverings.

Greene, who had moved down to the general vicinity of Fort Granby, ordered Lee and Eaton to march the same afternoon of the surrender to assist Pickens in the taking of Augusta. Sumter rode in the following day, and, when he learned that Lee had allowed Maxwell to go off with his plunder, the Gamecock threw a tantrum. So far was he wrapped in his anger that he dashed off a letter of resignation and sent it, along with his commission, to Greene. Since the general now planned to utilize the partisans to a greater extent, Greene was once again forced to exercise his literary talents to calm ruffled feelings. He had no authority to accept the resignation of a militia general, and the next day he returned the commission with, "I cannot think of accepting it & beg you to continue your command." [11]

Marion, in the meantime, had trailed along behind Rawdon's column as the British "blowed up" the post at Nelson's Ferry. The enemy had seemed to wander almost aimlessly, and Marion reported to Greene that Rawdon seemed "in Great fright" before his lordship finally circled around and made for Monck's Corner by way of Eutaw Springs. When Rawdon split off his baggage and sent it by way of Wadboo, Marion followed in hopes of intercepting it. Greene had started the main army on its march to lay siege to Ninety Six and he instructed Sumter to recall Marion should it appear that Rawdon showed any inclination to come to the relief of that post.

With not enough men to raid the baggage train, Marion retired to his new hideout. Like Snow Island, Peyre's Plantation was also a high ridge surrounded by turgid streams and oozing marshes. Now that his primary function was cooperation with Greene's army, Marion enforced a greater appearance of order and discipline, although the brush arbors and lean-to's sheltering his men looked much like those in the old camp. He now depended upon a militia draft to fill out his brigade, with each district drafting a certain number of men for a specified length of time. Many of those so selected refused to come into camp, and Marion published their names as enemies of the state, "after which their persons & property will be taken & authority Given to the friends of America to apply them to their own use." He allowed a number of those with him to go home to attend to their personal affairs.

He was now angry and wished to vent his spleen on the enemy because of the treatment of some of his men. The guards who had been sent to escort the British officers paroled after the fall of Fort Motte to Georgetown had been ill treated. They had been stripped of their clothing, held in confinement a short while, and when released, were told that they would be cut to pieces if they were not out of sight in ten minutes. This, coupled with the Postell affair, was too much for Marion, and he threatened he would retaliate in every instance.

Patrols worked over the area, gathering intelligence and holding the loyalists in such terror that they did not become active. Lieutenant Colonel Maham was assigned the duty of observing and reporting the movements of Lord Rawdon. Among the intelligence reports received was one stating that the garrison of Georgetown now numbered only about eighty regulars and five Tory militiamen.

Georgetown held a strange fascination, almost an obsession, for Francis Marion. On May 19 his letter to Greene carried the request, "I beg leave to go & Reduce that place." Shortly afterward he was pleading, "I wish to hear from you as quick as possible that the Garrison at Georgetown may not slip through my Hands." Although he had allowed many of his militia to return to their homes, he was certain that when the word was out that he was moving against Georgetown, they would turn out in even greater numbers. As late as May 22 he was still insisting to both Greene and Sumter that he could take the port, and if his militia did not turn out as briskly as expected, he would take those available with him and hang close to the enemy in harassing actions. He assured Greene that if Georgetown fell the Tories along the Peedee and Waccamaw Rivers would remain quiet.

Neither Greene nor Sumter seemed to care too much about Georgetown, although Greene was to write Sumter on May 26 that he might allow Marion to go against the port if it were certain that Rawdon was making no preparations to go to the aid of Ninety Six and if such a move would not expose Sumter's flanks. But this letter had no immediate impact on Sumter. Greene also wrote Marion that he had no objection to his proposal, although in his opinion Georgetown was "but an Inferior object." But Marion, fearful that Sumter would veto the expedition, had moved several days before Greene wrote this dispatch.[12]

Marion could not abide the gnawing ambition within him, and he crossed the Santee and went into camp on Cantey's Plantation. A call went out to his militia. Their response was even better than he had anticipated, for the reduction of the posts had brightened their spirits and there was a smell of victory in the air. The numbers under his command swelled until he had the unusual satisfaction of commanding a brigade that was near full strength. On May 24 he led them off on a march toward the coast, leaving Hezikiah Maham to keep an eye on Lord Rawdon's movements.

The brigade arrived outside Georgetown on May 28. The men

were deployed and began to throw up entrenchments. The size of Marion's force was too great for the enemy garrison, and at nine o'clock that night they slipped out to their vessels—a galley, two gunboats, and an armed schooner anchored in Winyah Bay. Once aboard they fell down the bay toward the bar at the entrance of the harbor. Marion marched into the town. In the redoubt were found three nine-pounders and a carronade, all spiked and with their trunions beaten off. The men were put to work leveling the fortifications. A search was conducted for the cache of arms rumored to be hidden in the town, and all the liquors, clothes, and salt were ordered taken up as legitimate prizes of war. A large store of salt was found and taken away to be hidden in various magazines around the countryside. Just as soon as he finished, Marion planned to recross the Santee and edge closer to Monck's Corner to continue his observation of Rawdon and await the further orders of Greene.

The move was gratifying to Marion, but Sumter was outraged. He didn't like Marion, or any subordinate, going over his head to Greene, for he was still the ranking general of the South Carolina militia, and was insistent that all orders and dispatches should first be cleared through him. He had granted no permission to Marion to move against Georgetown, and, in an angry letter to Greene, he accused Marion of misconduct, stating, "I Requested that he would cover the Country, & prevent the Enemy from Ravaging it—he however proceeded against Georgetown."

Marion did not leave Georgetown so early as he might have wished, for the vessels carrying the refugees from the garrison lingered near the bar, suggesting that they were awaiting reinforcements to retake the town. Because of the delay, he now planned, after destroying the works, to leave a small guard to observe the actions of the enemy ships while he led the remainder of the brigade across the Santee to make a junction with Maham who was still hovering near Rawdon. To calm any aggravation Greene may have felt, Marion sent out parties to round up dragoon horses for the Southern Army.

The general also felt that it was time to improve his personal appearance in a fashion to befit his rank. From the plunder he not only fitted himself out with a new suit of regimentals, but also acquired two mules to transport his baggage. He replaced his old half-burned blanket but still clung to his charred leather helmet.[13]

It began to appear that the enemy might take the offensive again in South Carolina. Marion received intelligence that seventeen transports from Ireland had arrived in Charleston on June 2 with two thousand troops of the Third, Nineteenth, and Thirtieth Regiments on board. A rider on a swift horse relayed the news to Sumter with a request to forward the information to Greene. Sumter did not seem to be worried; when Marion sent in a more extensive report the following day, Sumter's laconic reply was, "I am sorry to hear of a reinforcement having arrived, I have hopes it may not be so considerable as is suggested."

To Greene, however, the arrival of fresh troops was a most important development. Henry Lee, after leaving Fort Granby, had taken Fort Galpin, and then he and Andrew Pickens had forced the capitulation of Augusta. Greene had been pushing the siege of Ninety Six, and now the news of the reinforcement meant that the garrison there could benefit from a relief force. Sumter had been unable to attract the militia into the field to the number that he had promised Greene. Since May 1 Greene had been attempting to persuade Marion to join Sumter, and now his orders were more positive. Marion was to call in Maham as planned and then "Act in Conjunction with Genl. Sumpter" in slowing the march of possible reinforcements for Ninety Six. Greene expected to finish off that post, and then turn and drive against the relief force, but "I wish them to be

Crippled as much as Possible before we have a general Action."
Greene held some doubts as to Marion's trustworthiness after
the latter had gone against Georgetown without waiting for
proper authorization. He told Sumter to "give positive Orders to
Genl. Marion's Force to join if the Enemy attempts to penetrate
the Country."

Sumter immediately ordered Marion to leave behind his
heavy baggage and join him on the march for Ninety Six. Lord
Rawdon, on June 7, left Monck's Corner and began a ponderous
march toward Orangeburgh. Sumter sent word for Marion to
take a position in the High Hills of the Santee from which Rawdon might be intercepted.

Marion left Georgetown on June 6, leaving Peter Horry in
command of the general area. A call went out to the brigade, but
his militia were their usual fickle selves; the word seems to have
gotten around that they might have to march as far west as
Ninety Six. Few responded to the summons. Sumter wanted
Marion to move no matter how strong or weak his force, but his
orders fluctuated between the insistent and the indecisive. On
June 13 he ordered Marion to move directly to Ninety Six, but
on the following day he assured him that the enemy were not
moving up and advised him to halt until British plans were more
obvious. On June 15 he had changed his mind, as the enemy
was pushing, and Greene wanted the militia to be employed in
"galling them as they advance." On June 16, Sumter reported to
Greene that Marion was moving up, "but at a great distance,"
and his "force but Inconsiderable." [14]

Marion felt it important that his past work not be undone
by an absence that allowed the Tories to gather strength, and
he had no time to devote himself to making sure they were subdued. Maham was sent out to keep the loyalists under control,
while those along Drowning Creek who had been acting up
were put down in a skirmish with Thomas Wade. To make sure
that matters would be quiet while he was gone, Peter Horry was

sent to negotiate a treaty with Major Micajah Ganey, who controlled the Tory militia between the Great Peedee and the North Carolina border. On June 17, 1781 Ganey and his officers agreed to lay down their arms and remain neutral for the next year. They agreed to deliver up those who refused to comply with the terms of the treaty as well as all deserters from the American Army who sought refuge in the area. And because there was no longer a British force at Camden to furnish protection, they agreed to give up all Negroes and property they had plundered from the Whigs, although Ganey later refused to give up property taken by the British and then placed in the hands of the loyalists. There was one interesting provision—that those accused of plundering should be tried by a five-man jury, made up of two Tories, two Whigs, and an officer from the side of the complainant, who were to determine the guilt and punishment of those convicted.[15]

Greene was not doing well at Ninety Six. Because of the obstinacy of John Harris Cruger and his Tories, the siege had dragged on well beyond the general's timetable. After he received the information that Rawdon had left Monck's Corner, and a messenger disguised as an ordinary countryman had managed to slip into the fort with the news, the tempo of operations was stepped up. The word that Rawdon was marching spread through the American camp. Apprehensions among the men were such that Greene's general orders on June 14 carried the assurance that the enemy reinforcements would be driven back into Charleston by the militia of Sumter and Marion.

Rawdon had swept wide on his march to avoid Sumter who, in turn, had disregarded Greene's orders to retard the enemy's march by hanging in front of their column. Although intelligence stated that Rawdon was marching for Ninety Six, because of his original direction Sumter had assumed that he was going to retake Fort Granby and moved over to protect that place. By June 19 the British relief column was near enough to Ninety Six for Greene to organize and execute a hasty assault. It was thrown back after a bloody fight. Then, because of what he termed the "Circumstances of War," Greene had cleared the area the following day. On June 21, Rawdon's column arrived, having marched two thousand troops two hundred miles through quivering heat. He pursued the American Army as far as Fish Dam Ford. After making arrangements for the evacuation of Ninety Six, Rawdon marched for the coast. Fifty men died from sunstroke on the return march toward Charleston.[16]

Greene was not pleased with the response he had received from the militia generals. To Lee he penned an angry complaint: "It is next to impossible to draw the militia of the Country from different parts of the State. Marion is below, Pickens I can get no account of, and Sumter wants to make a tour to Monck's Corner, and all I can say to either is insufficient to induce them to join us."

Marion did not escape the bitter criticism of the general. Greene told him that he had hoped that Rawdon would have been beaten off before he reached Ninety Six, and "could I have collected your force and that of Generals Sumpter and Pickens, I could have done it, and I am persuaded we should have defeated him, but being left alone, I was obliged to retire." Stating that Sumter was planning to operate in the low country, the general added a firm, "You will therefore call out all the Force you can, and Cooperate with him in any manner he may direct." [17]

The regular army had finally caught up with Francis Marion.

Chapter XI

One of the things that Nathanael Greene disliked about militia was their insistence in coming out on horseback, thereby creating a forage problem. He did like the mobility they added to his overall operations, but he had become unhappy with their unreliability, especially since they had proved so reluctant to come out of late. He had come to the conclusion that the Southern Army would be greatly strengthened if two temporary regiments of dragoons could be recruited who would act in the same capacity as regular troops. After a consultation with Marion, Peter Horry and Hezikiah Maham were selected to raise the units, with the regiments eventually to be placed on either the state or continental establishment.

Greene had been waiting for Governor Rutledge's official authorization, but he felt that he had to go ahead, for the enemy was raising too many mounted troops, and the need to counteract their maneuverings was immediate. Although originally there was the suggestion that the new units be taken into the

Continental establishment, the regiments were to be raised as State troops. Each regiment was to be composed of 160 rank and file, enlisted for not less than a year and organized into four troops. All horses thought fit for dragoon use could be impressed from loyalists, or even friends of the cause who were not in service. Both Maham's and Horry's commissions were dated June 22, 1781, with each officer designated a "Lieutenant Colonel Commandant of a Battalion of Light Dragoons for the State of South Carolina, to be employed in the Service of America." Maham was to recruit the area below the Santee while Horry was to seek his men along the Peedee.

Hezikiah Maham had long proposed that he be allowed to raise such an elite unit. His appetite for such a service had been whetted back on March 21, 1781, when Marion had appointed him "Major Commandant" of a light horse troop for the brigade, to be raised on the south side of the Santee. Since even earlier he had been pestering the commanding general to allow him to form a legion similar to that of Lee's.

Peter Horry's command was to be similar, although he was to have a company of riflemen attached to his regiment. Horry hesitated, fearing his acceptance of such a command would endanger his Continental commission. Greene assured him that such was not the case. Horry had wanted to enlist his men by using "Sumter's Law," giving a confiscated slave as a bonus to those who enlisted in his corps, but Marion would not hear of it. Horry continued in his present command, melding his recruits in with his old men until he had enough men to formally organize his mounted regiment. Major Lemuel Benison was his second in command.

From the beginning Maham was angry because he felt that he should have the only such regiment, and that Horry was not fit to command inasmuch as he had been "throne out as a supernumerary officer." When Greene stated his opinion that Horry's old commission of Lieutenant Colonel gave him the right to issue orders to Maham, the latter refused to accept the judgment. This innocent attempt to increase the mobility of the Southern Army contained the seeds of a festering feud that was to become a disrupting influence rather than a positive gain.[1]

Marion had enough on his mind without having to act as a mediator between two swelling egos. Despite the positive tone in Greene's letters, he was also finding it difficult to carry out the commanding general's orders. In the first place, he did not particularly care to work with Sumter; neither did his men. To some Sumter was too impetuous and reckless. Marion still held an active Continental commission as Lieutenant Colonel and he had no desire to accept directives from a militia brigadier general, especially one who had resigned his own Continental commission in 1778. When Marion's call went out, only a few men turned up at the rendezvous. Sumter guessed the truth and took umbrage at what he considered an insult. To Greene he complained, "You will find no assistance is to be expected from him, at least not soon."

Marion's men seemed to sense when he was to lead them personally, and they were reluctant to operate as a segment of a larger force under the direction of someone else. Perhaps Marion's own moods conveyed the message; he demonstrated little enthusiasm for acting under the direction of the Gamecock. When the men were slow in coming out, Marion suspected chicanery by the enemy. He felt that they had deliberately paroled men with instructions to begin a whispering campaign against the Fox. On June 28, he ordered all such individuals to repair to the nearest enemy post and remain there until exchanged.

He tried to lose himself lest he be forced to make the junction with Sumter. So completely had he disappeared, that on June 23 Greene was asking Sumter, "Where is General Marion?" [2]

An unexpected opportunity promised a way to avoid acting with Sumter. It began when Colonel William Washington's dragoons from Greene's army captured a rider carrying dispatches for Lord Rawdon while on patrol south of the Congaree. A hasty reading revealed that Lieutenant Colonel John Watson had relinquished his command and had sailed for England. His replacement was Lieutenant Colonel Alexander Stewart, who was already moving supplies to Rawdon's force who was now maneuvering in the area between the Edisto and Santee rivers. Washington, perhaps exceeding his authority, sent the intelligence on to Marion, suggesting that his brigade prevent the two enemy forces from making a junction.

The word got around, and Marion soon had some four hundred men coursing up the road from Nelson's Ferry. After receiving the news, Greene, on July 6, left his army and with a small escort rode hard to meet Marion at Ancrum's Plantation. To block Stewart he ordered the brigade down to Monck's Corner.

Riding in a great loop to avoid Rawdon's weary column, Marion drove toward his quarry. Scouts were sent out to hang off the enemy's flanks. Frequent dispatches to Greene reported, "They have no idea of any force being near them." Reporting that the enemy troops were so tired that their march had slowed to a crawl, he suggested that Rawdon's three regiments would mutiny and lay down their arms if they had to march another day. Despite Horry's hundred troopers following his march, picking up stragglers, Rawdon was too tired and too sick to know or care of the proximity of the enemy. But he was not Marion's concern; the immediate objective was Stewart.

It was one o'clock in the morning of July 8 when Marion mounted and rode down the Orangeburgh–Monck's Corner road in search of Stewart. Scouts ranged out far ahead to give adequate warning should they meet the enemy. Perhaps Stewart anticipated such a move, perhaps he had been warned, or it is even possible that he lost his way, but he selected a less frequently used road more or less paralleling the more popular thoroughfare. Sometime in the night the two groups passed each other. At dawn Marion realized that Stewart had managed to elude him, and Peter Horry was sent off in search of the enemy. Horry managed to cut three wagons loaded with rum and wine out of the British column but was too weak to inflict serious damage before Stewart made his junction with Rawdon at Orangeburgh. Marion placed himself on the Orangeburgh road, and, when two "intelligent" prisoners were taken and gave information as to Rawdon's strength, Marion sent the intelligence on to Greene.

This swelling of Rawdon's numbers forced Greene to strengthen his own command. Messengers were sent to Lee, Washington, Sumter, and Marion ordering them to bring in their troops to the main army. Greene then prepared to offer battle to the British. Marion, riding hard, had reached Colston's Plantation by July 10, worried because his men had only six rounds of ammunition each. Greene waited until Marion joined, and on July 11 his army lay in a strong position on the north slope of Turkey Hill, three miles above Orangeburgh. He waited, hoping that Rawdon would be tempted to sally out of the town. Rawdon, however, was equally well prepared, with his men stationed around and within the brick courthouse and jail in Orangeburgh. To the north of the town a narrow bridge across the Edisto not only furnished a route of withdrawal but could also present the risk of slaughter to any group trying to force its passage across the stream. Greene felt the enemy too strongly posted to make an all-out attack, and the terrain was unsuitable for an effective use of mounted troops. It was soon apparent that Rawdon had no intention of leaving a secure position and risking his army in an offensive action. Greene's army was weary from the siege of Ninety Six and the subsequent maneuvering. He marched them off toward the High Hills of the Santee.[3]

Francis, Lord Rawdon, had grown weary of the war in South Carolina, for his persistent illness had continued to sap the strength from his tall young body. At Orangeburgh, he turned over the command of the field forces to Lieutenant Colonel Alexander Stewart and made his way down to Charleston. He sailed for England on July 20, only to be captured by a French privateer and held a prisoner in Brest until he was exchanged the following year.

For some time Thomas Sumter had been anxious to attack the British outpost at Monck's Corner. The proposal made some sense to Greene, for there was the possibility that such action would draw the enemy toward the coast and prevent the reestablishment of their posts in the upper country. Greene gave Sumter permission to use both Marion and Lee in the venture, and soon all three mounted units were moving into the low country. Shortly after they left, Greene received word that John Harris Cruger and his loyalists from Ninety Six had joined Rawdon. Fearing an attack against his army, Greene urged Sumter to get on with the business at Monck's Corner as quickly as possible and rejoin the Southern Army.

Sumter's basic plan was not at all bad, but it was a bit too complicated for a combination of Continentals and militia. Marion was to seize all approaches and routes of retreat. Lee and his legion swept forward toward Charleston to take Dorchester and "thunder even at the gates of Charlestown." Colonel Henry Hampton was to take Four Holes Bridge while Peter Horry and Hezikiah Maham raced down the east side of the Cooper River to secure the fords and destroy the bridge over Wadboo Creek. The design was to block relief from Rawdon above or Balfour below.

Even with the prospect of action, the continuing feud between Horry and Maham surfaced. When Sumter ordered Horry forward and placed Maham under him for direction, Maham demanded to see Horry's commission. When he discovered that Horry's date of rank was the same as his, he refused to serve under him and finally insisted that the controversy be settled by drawing lots. Horry, as might be expected, disregarded the suggestion.

Lieutenant Colonel John Coates commanded the British garrison at Monck's Corner, made up of the unseasoned Nineteenth Regiment and some mounted loyalists of the South Carolina Rangers. The Nineteenth had only arrived in Charleston on June 1, and its rank and file were "all raw Irishmen." Realizing that Sumter was attempting to isolate him, Coates, feeling his position at Monck's Corner was weak, had withdrawn a mile and a half to Biggins Creek on July 14. He sought refuge in St. John's Church, the parish church of St. John's Berkeley, a sixty- by forty-foot, practically impregnable building whose brick walls were three feet thick. On an elevation controlling the approaches to the church he threw up defensive works, and an abatis surrounded the church. After receiving reports of Sumter's maneuverings, and under the impression that Greene's entire army was moving against him, he realized that his position could leave him exposed and cut off from all possible aid. He began preparations to abandon his position and retreat toward Charleston on the east side of the Cooper.

Meanwhile, Sumter's grand scheme was gradually falling apart. For one thing, Hezikiah Maham did not follow his orders to destroy Wadboo Bridge. He became too involved in burning the two schooners he found moored there. The bridge was only partially destroyed before he turned back to watch Coates. When Lee came up on Dorchester there was no sign of the enemy, but he was able to gather up three hundred horses and four wagons, one filled with ammunition, all of which he immediately sent off to Greene. Hampton surrounded Goose Creek Church, taking some of the congregation prisoners, giving paroles to others, and carrying off all of their horses. At the Quarter House, a detachment of Hampton's riders took nineteen prisoners of the Loyal South Carolina Dragoons, and although he had surrendered, they executed a Lieutenant Waugh because he had allegedly killed Captain John Wright in a skirmish at Wassamassaw. When Lee arrived outside Charleston, he found that the enemy had been warned of his arrival and were battened up tight within the walls. He rejoined Sumter on July 16, having been forced to return by the long way because of the enemy hold on Biggins Bridge.

The same afternoon that Lee returned, Peter Horry's command was involved in a skirmish. Major Thomas Fraser led his South Carolina dragoons out and caught Horry's detachment at rest, either cooking or eating their evening meal. Fraser charged in what Horry termed "a most confused cowardly attempt." As most of Horry's men fled, Colonel Edward Lacey's riflemen broke the enemy charge. Horry rallied his men, killing several of the enemy and taking ten prisoners without loss of his own. Fraser fled back to Biggin Church. As he neared camp, Coates sent out infantry to meet Horry's pursuing horsemen, who wheeled and returned to their camp to finish their supper.

Fraser's dragoons had been sent out as a cover for Coates's evacuation. It was effective, for Sumter pulled up, fearing a sally in force. Despite his "mortification," he did take the time to boast to Greene, "Noble militia! What think you now of their charging British Dragoons with Rifles & pursuing them to their lines?" [4]

About three o'clock on the morning of July 17, Coates burned his stores and the church and moved eighteen miles down the Cooper in the direction of Charleston. Maham had left enough of the bridge to allow him to get his men across. Once across, he completed the demolition in order to slow pursuit. By that afternoon he had reached Quinby Bridge and posted his men in strong positions behind the creek. The bridge flooring was loosened, but the planking had not yet been taken up, as the baggage and rear guard had not yet crossed the stream.

The glow of the burning church against the sky was seen in Sumter's camp. The troops were marched at double time to Monck's Corner to try to get to the bridge over the Cooper before the enemy, but there it was discovered that Coates had retreated along the east bank of the Cooper. They set out in pursuit, with Lee's cavalry out in front of the slower units. Lee and Hampton were delayed at Wadboo because of the destroyed bridge and lost time seeking out a ford farther upstream. On the far bank the road forked and it was discovered that the mounted troops had taken the road for Strawberry Ferry while the infantry had struck for Quinby Bridge. A detachment was sent after the dragoons but failed to come up with them before they crossed the ferry.

Unknown to Coates, Lee's legion and Hampton's militia had cut off and taken his rear guard, who had laid down their arms without firing a shot. Coates was still expecting them and was taken by surprise when Captain Armstrong, leading the first section of the legion cavalry, and Lieutenant Carrington, the second, charged across the bridge. The loose planking flew up from the stringers, but the first two sections managed to leap across the interval. However, in doing so, they created a greater gap, too wide for Captain O'Neale, leading the third section, to jump. Armstrong drove off the gunners from the howitzer that had been placed at the end of the bridge. Frightened by the sudden charge, most of Coates's green troops fled, leaving Coates and a few of his men standing with their backs to a wagon defending themselves with their swords as best they could. A number of those British who had fled now returned and stood firm. The howitzer was rolled back to protect the bridge, wounding several of Lee's men by its fire. O'Neale stood by helplessly. The creek banks were too marshy to allow good footing for his horses, and those men who had been sent into the stream to repair the bridge had found the bottom too deep in silt to gain a firm footing. Armstrong and Carrington were driven off and rode to find a ford to rejoin the legion. The action broke off.[5]

Coates fell back to Quinby, the plantation of Thomas Shubrick. He formed his men into a hollow square, their front supported by the howitzer. The flanks were afforded some protection by some of the plantation outbuildings and a rail fence behind which he posted men.

It was about three in the afternoon when Marion came up with his men and the legion infantry. They crossed a stream some distance above Quinby Bridge and marched for Shubrick's. He and Lee surveyed the position of the enemy and concluded that it was too strong to attack without artillery. Near five that afternoon Sumter came up with his militia. He had not brought along his field pieces because, he said, he did not wish to be held up by artillery when he pursued the retreating enemy. Disagreeing with the estimate of the situation by Marion and Lee, and over their protests, he declared he "would go into battle, whether or not, live or die." He wanted an immediate assault upon the enemy and refused to wait until his artillery piece could come up.

Sumter stationed his battle line in a great half-moon. Horry was posted on the far right, with Marion's brigade on the far left. Between these two points were the commands of Charles Middleton, Thomas Polk, Thomas Taylor and Edward Lacey. Since the ground was not conducive to cavalry operations, the mounted troops of Lee and Hampton were held in reserve. Sumter's own men sought the protection of slave quarters as the initial fire of the enemy drove them to seek cover.

A little after five, on Sumter's orders, Thomas Taylor led his forty-five men forward in a charge to gain the rail fence. A countercharge with bayonets sent them reeling back. Marion's infantry, over on the left, seeing Taylor's men falling back, obliqued over toward the fence and opened up a galling fire upon the enemy formation to cover Taylor's retreat. The brigade held firm in the face of the musketry and howitzer fire, although a number were struck down. A large number of the enemy fell back into the mansion house and began a steady fire from the doors and windows. When his ammunition ran low, Marion pulled his men back to a distance of three miles from the field.

His losses were two officers and six privates killed, with six officers and thirteen rank and file wounded.

Among those wounded was the gigantic Major John Baxter who had been serving under Horry's command. As he fell, he called out to Horry, "I am wounded, colonel."

"Think no more of it, Baxter," replied Horry, "but stand to your post."

"But I can't stand, Colonel—I am wounded a second time!"

"Then lie down, Baxter, but quit not your post."

"Colonel," cried the wounded man, "they have shot me again, and if I remain any longer here, I shall be shot to pieces."

"Be it so, Baxter, but stir not."

The major obeyed orders and was wounded a fourth time for his attention to duty. Happily he survived his wounds.

The fight has lasted no more than forty minutes. Sumter's brigade losses were twelve killed and twenty-three wounded. The British suffered an estimated seventy casualties. During the heat of the battle, twelve of Lee's cavalry and four mounted volunteers had circled around to the rear of the enemy and had taken over fifty prisoners.

Many of Sumter's men had been firing from the protection of the outbuildings, and many could not understand why he had not waited to bring up his artillery to give them an even chance. Many of Marion's brigade were livid with rage, for it was obvious even to men in the ranks that the affair had been badly mismanaged. Flushed with anger because Sumter had not furnished his men with artillery support, and feeling that he had been a "sacrifice," Thomas Taylor walked up to the Gamecock and flatly stated, "I will never more serve under you!" [6]

The disgust of both Lee and Marion was obvious. Neither informed Sumter when they drew off fifteen miles before pitching camp that sultry night. There they buried their dead in a common grave. The talk around the campfires that night was of the exposed position of Marion's men while Sumter's men had been allowed to seek the protection of the Shubrick slave quarters. Both Marion and Lee agreed that victory could have been achieved had the fight taken place in a more open field where mounted troops could operate properly.

Lee led his men off to join Greene in the High Hills, convinced that "General Sumpter is become almost universally odious as far as I can discern. I lament that a man of his turn was ever useful, or being once deservedly great, shall want the wisdom to continue so, and preserve his reputation."

But to give Sumter his due, he was by no means a complete failure. He had forced the British to give up the post at Biggin, a number of stores had been taken and destroyed, and 141 prisoners had been taken along with wagons and horses. Furthermore, Rawdon had been forced to abandon Orangeburgh to come to Coates's aid. Perhaps Sumter would have fared better had he and Marion gotten along better.

Marion rode off with his fewer than one hundred troops into camp at Peyre's Plantation to give both men and mounts a much-needed rest. Many mourned their dead, feeling they could never forgive Sumter. So disgusted were some that when Marion, acting on a suggestion by Greene, tried to persuade them to remain in the field longer than one month, they flatly refused to even consider the proposal. Marion allowed many of his men to travel to Greene's camp in the High Hills to receive one-half bushel of salt as pay, "after 26 long and tiresome sultry Days being spent in the utmost hunger and fatigue to man & Horse that ever poor wretches endured."

Sumter was forced to withdraw when word was received that seven hundred men were on their way to rescue Coates. The Gamecock had no intention of giving credit to Marion for the efforts of the brigade during the battle. In his original dispatch to Greene he failed to mention the brigade, and in his second he implied that they had been worth but little because of their small numbers. There was also the suggestion that Marion had attempted to persuade his men to walk off rather than have them serve under Sumter. In his fifth letter to the commanding general regarding the affair, he indicated that Marion had acted rashly in his advance against the enemy and had suffered, "by Supposing the enemy Coud not fire upon his Men, when moving up in a Certain direction—he soon found his Mistake." Sumter was forced to admit that Marion had brought his men off in good order, and personally "behaved well upon every occasion."

His slighting treatment of Marion was partially rectified by Lee's personal report to Greene who, in turn, complimented Marion with, "The Gallantry and good conduct of your men reflects the highest honour upon your Brigade," and "I only lament that men who spilt their Blood in such noble exertions to serve their Country could not have met with more deserved success."

By the first of August Marion, acting on Greene's orders, made a quick dash to Georgetown, arriving in the port before most of his troops. He could only watch as eleven British vessels swung into the harbor and began to take on provisions from the vicinity. The landing parties were commanded by Doyle, and Marion would have liked to go against him, but he was far too weak and could only remove stores from Doyle's reach. The British left the area on August 8.[7]

Sumter was soon to fall from grace. At Quinby Bridge he had confiscated a British paymaster's chest containing £800. He divided the money among his men as a bonus, with each receiving a gold piece. But still his men complained about their arrears in pay. He had recruited too many under "Sumter's Law." Back in April he had gone so far as to persuade a number of North Carolina Continentals, promising them slaves as bonuses. To pay off his unhappy soldiers, he turned to outright plundering, and on July 25, Captain William Ransome Davis was ordered to seize the slaves, horses, salt, indigo, and medical supplies in and around Georgetown. This was Marion's territory, and he was angry with the invasion upon his authority, but Marion replied that it "may Interfer with my Command but suppose I must Submit." When informed of this act, Greene noted, "General Sumpter's taking the goods at Georgetown was certainly wrong, but it is not too late to prevent it. . . . It is uncertain how far disappointed ambition may carry a man."

The British struck back. They had kept a galley near the bar at the mouth of the harbor to control the water traffic of the port. On August 2 Captain Manson maneuvered his ungainly vessel opposite Georgetown and began to lob shells over among the buildings. After the townspeople had been forced to seek shelter, he sent a landing party ashore. They burned stores and warehouses, along with forty-two private dwellings. After the buildings were blazing, Manson resumed his bombardment to prevent the natives from extinguishing the flames.

Marion rushed all the aid he could to the people of the town, but he could send only a token of what was actually needed. Many of his men had left his brigade after Quinby Bridge, and by late July they had just begun to trickle back into camp. Since the middle of May Greene had been urging Rutledge to reestablish his government as quickly as possible, "as it is of importance to have the minds of the people formed to the habits of civil rather than military authority." On August 1 Governor Rutledge had returned to Greene's camp from Philadelphia. He agreed with Greene in decrying the "horrid practice of plundering." Feeling that much of the ill feeling and atrocities of both Whigs and Tories had been brought about by plundering, the governor issued a proclamation outlawing the practice. To Marion he said that everyone taken up for plundering should be regarded and treated as a felon.

Sumter took the proclamation as a personal rebuke, especially since he had utilized the practice as a means of enlisting and paying off his ten-months' soldiers. Perhaps he had become aware that his own popularity was fading, and he retired into North Carolina where he endeavored to gather recruits, supplies, weapons and provisions to forward to Greene's army. Before he left he furloughed a large segment of his brigade. He gave his command temporarily to Lieutenant Colonel William Henderson, former commandant of the Sixth South Carolina Continentals. Henderson reported, "On my arrival to take command of them I found them the most discontented set of men I ever saw, both men and officers," and he went on to complain that "The thirst after plunder that seems to prevail among the soldiery makes the command almost intolerable." [8]

Francis Marion now became the senior active militia brigadier general in South Carolina. Both his duties and responsibilities were greatly increased, with many of his new duties involving civil authority as well as military. Although Greene still called on him to perform such duties as driving cattle in to the Southern Army, he also added to the brigade strength by detaching an experienced artillery officer, Ensign McQuire of the Virginia Continentals, to Marion's brigade. The brigade was enlarged to include the militia from Britton's Neck to Charleston, but the governor requested that he keep those officers commissioned by Sumter "while they behave properly."

From his temporary capital in Camden, Governor Rutledge had Marion name the justices of the peace in the Georgetown, Cheraw, and Charleston districts, and he was also asked to recommend persons for other positions in the interim state government. Nearly everything needed by the governor in reestablishing his authority he asked Marion to secure for him, including a printing press, paper, and ink. In short, Brigadier General Francis Marion became something of an executive assistant without portfolio.

To remedy the fluid condition of his manpower, the governor attempted to provide Marion with a stable force, decreeing that he divide his brigade into two divisions with each alternately remaining in the field for a month at a time. Just as positive were his orders that the general curb the plundering of his men—henceforth all loyalist property was to be kept for the use of the state.

Insofar as the Tories were concerned, Rutledge harbored a

vindictive turn of mind. His idea of orderly government was one in which the loyalists were either swept away or awed into submission. Marion was ordered to initiate a campaign of harassment against all those who were beyond the protection of the British. Wives and children of the loyalists in Marion's districts were to be hustled off to the British lines around Charleston. Rutledge was so intent on clearing the state of undesirables that he requested an alphabetical list of all known loyalists. From this time on Marion was to receive periodic orders to take up some specifically named Tory, confiscate his property, and send him under guard to the governor.[9]

Among other things, Marion was ordered to look into the facts behind the execution of Colonel Isaac Hayne. Hayne had been an active revolutionary who had been paroled to his plantation after the fall of Charleston. After being ordered to join the British army he considered his parole to have been violated by the enemy and felt that he was no longer obligated to abide by its restrictions. In April he had received commissions for his subordinate officers from Marion and had recruited a regiment. On June 5 he had been so bold as to lead a small troop of horsemen almost to the skirts of Charleston to capture the turncoat Brigadier General Andrew Williamson, the "Arnold of Carolina."

Nisbet Balfour had been furious, especially after it was reported that Williamson "was to have been hanged in the camp of General Greene." Major Thomas Fraser was sent out with ninety dragoons, and at Colleton's Plantation they captured Hayne while he was bearing arms. Williamson was freed. Hayne had been brought before and questioned by a court of enquiry on charges of inciting an "insurrection," espionage, and treason. On August 4, 1781 he had been hanged without further trial. The *Royal Gazette* gave the event a short paragraph, stating little more than that he had been "executed as a Traitor."

Some said it was British retaliation for the execution of Major

John André, who had been hanged as a spy for his role in the treason of Benedict Arnold. In fact Balfour had earlier suggested to Clinton that rebel officers who, as prisoners of war, had kept up a spirit of revolt, be made "most striking Examples of such as having taken Protection, make every Occasion to rise in arms against us."

The entire American Army, both Continentals and militia, had been greatly disturbed, and there was much talk of a mass hanging of Tories, something that Greene did not wish lest it ignite an all-out civil war in the state. There was some fear that Marion, who had issued Hayne his commission, would turn his men loose on the loyalists, and it was rumored that he had vowed retaliation. Greene was quick to warn the brigadier not to seek retaliation upon the Tories, "for I don't Intend to Retaliate upon the Tory officers, but the British." He explained that retaliation upon the loyalists would be playing into British hands, for increasing the hostility between the two factions would cause the Tories to fight with greater vigor. He not only sought an explanation from Balfour but published a proclamation promising retaliation upon regular British officers rather than "those deluded inhabitants who have joined their Army." He notified Balfour of his intentions. The clamor began to subside.[10]

The execution of Hayne, however, did have a sobering effect and led to the reluctance of some militia to respond to calls. The Tories grew bolder. Some rode in large groups, as great as four or five hundred, rampaging through the countryside below Charleston. To furnish protection, Balfour sent Major Thomas Fraser and two hundred dragoons into the area. A plea for help from Colonel William Harden, commanding militia south of the Edisto River, came into the hideout on Peyre's Plantation. He could no longer cope with the situation. Marion forwarded the request to Greene.

Since most of the men of Sumter's brigade had been furloughed, Greene's solution was to dispatch Marion to the aid of Harden, "if practical." Major George Cooper, with a party of mounted militia, was sent into the neighborhood of Monck's Corner and Dorchester to create a diversion and occupy the attention of the enemy. Cooper performed his task well. Riding swiftly, he had routed a band of Tories and had driven off the cattle in the neighborhood of Dorchester. Within twelve miles of Charleston he had driven out another loyalist group who had been well posted behind a brick church. Then, swinging down into the Goose Creek area, he had circled around the British post to Monck's Corner to rejoin Marion at Peyre's. He brought in a number of prisoners and had not lost a man.

While the enemy's attention was still centered on the site of Cooper's raid, Marion stole south with two hundred picked men, marching at night over seldom-used roads and paths. So quietly did he slip out of Peyre's that the British received no intelligence of his departure or march. After a circuitous march of near a hundred miles, he came up with Harden on August 22 at the village of Round O but discovered that the colonel was still recovering from an illness and had not yet called out his men.

During the evening of August 26 he arrived at Horse Shoe and was joined by 230 men, which brought his total command to something over four hundred. Marching across the great swamp at the head of Ashepoo, he camped at Middleton's Plantation within five miles of Fraser's command. Hugh Horry and his men were detached to ride across country to Cheraw to take three schooners reported taking on rice for the Charleston garrison, but they learned of his approach and dropped down the river.

Marion's scouting parties reported that the enemy force consisted of 180 Hessians, 150 British regulars, and 130 Tories supported by eighty dragoons of the Queen's Rangers and that they were too strong to be attacked. He placed a guard on the causeway at Godfrey Savannah, but they fled when a detachment of the enemy approached the far side. Marion trailed along behind Fraser when he marched to Hyrne's Plantation on August 28. He drew up his men in battle formation, but the British were too strongly posted to attack, and after an exchange of scattering fire between the forward units and the enemy pickets during the next two hours, Marion's men filed off.

The following day Fraser crossed the river and camped on Isaac Hayne's plantation. Marion lay within three miles of them. He learned that there were about a hundred Tories under Colonel William Cunningham waiting to join the enemy at Parker's Ferry. To frustrate this junction, he laid an ambush.

The causeway leading to the ferry seemed a likely spot for a surprise attack. The greater part of his men were concealed in the heavily wooded swamp on either side of the road. He sent a division of eighty men under Harden over about a hundred yards to the right; they were to come in on the flank when the firing began. Major Cooper was to circle around to the rear with orders to charge once the action became general. As decoys he sent forward a small detachment mounted on swift horses.

The trap was almost given away by the penchant of one of his men for self-decoration. The white feather he always wore in his hat was spotted by some passing Tories from Cunningham's group at the ferry. They first challenged and then fired into the woods. There was a burst of musketry before a few horsemen charged from the woods and drove the loyalists back to the ferry.

Meanwhile Major Fraser had been marching into the ambush. When he heard the burst of firing and sighted the decoy squad, he shouted an order to his dragoon. Marion's detachment turned in seeming flight. As the pursuers neared the ambush, they were wedged inward by the width of the causeway into a compact mass. As they galloped past Marion signaled his men. Muskets loaded with ball and buckshot blazed forth. Horses reared as their riders plunged to the ground. The dragoons turned. Fraser rallied them. Wheeling again, he led them on a charge toward the swamp. Another volley met them, once again the air was filled with the screams of men and their mounts. Fraser's charge carried him past the ambush. Now, as he turned back toward his main force, he once again had to expose his riders to the ambush as they raced back across the causeway. The survivors galloped wildly from the scene.

Marion had no opportunity to pursue as a column of infantry, supported by a field piece, advanced. Marion's men stood fast and exchanged fire with the enemy until, said Marion, "some villains cryed out, they were flanking us on the right," which threw them into some confusion. Marion, after about three hours, and now low on ammunition, faded back through the marshy ground two miles to allow his men to eat. That night he camped at Jenkins's Ferry.

Marion claimed that the enemy had lost at least eighteen dead and an estimated eighty wounded. There were no bodies on the causeway the following day when Captain Melton led a detachment back to survey the site, but the carcasses of twenty-seven horses lay bloating in the hot August sun.

Marion had nothing but praise for Colonels Stafford, Ervin, and Horry, who had behaved like "Sons of Liberty," but he was out of patience with Harden, who had not carried out his orders, "by which means I lost above one-third of my force." Actually by "force" he meant manpower in the field, as he reported casualties of one private killed and three wounded.

Marion remained in the area until August 31 to render aid to Colonel Harden, and on September 1 left Round O and rode thirty-two miles that night. The following day he arrived in St. Stephen's and heard that the enemy under Colonel Alexander Stewart was camped at Eutaw Springs. He reported to Greene that as soon as his horses were rested, "I shall endeavour to annoy them." [11]

That annoyance was to come soon.

Chapter XII

Greene had already received some intelligence of Stewart's movements and was working his way toward him, but as yet was not aware that the British had moved to Eutaw Springs. He did take time out to write Marion, congratulating the brigade on their success at Parker's Ferry and assuring him that the exploit would be called to the attention of the Continental Congress.

On August 22 Greene had called in all the different forces under his command except those of Francis Marion and William Harden who, at the time, were busy with Fraser. He had his army on the march, with Lee's legion scouting the countryside before them. Lee had been out since early August and on the thirteenth he sent back information that the heat and humidity apparently had sapped the will to fight from the enemy and that many of the British soldiers would desert if given an opportunity. He urged the general to make an early attack upon Lieutenant Colonel Alexander Stewart, Lord Rawdon's successor in the field when the latter had fallen ill and had taken passage for England. Stewart, ran Lee's report, had run across a Negro who had agreed to lead the British army against Greene by way of a secret trail through the swamps. There were also recurring rumors that Lord Cornwallis was returning to South Carolina from Virginia.[1]

Stewart had nearly two thousand men under his command, the greater part of whom were British regulars. Three artillery pieces were parked in his camp. He had gone into bivouac on the west side of the Congaree near Center Swamp, not too far from the now-deserted Fort Motte. The two rivers that lay between the two armies were swollen into near lakes by the recent heavy rains. The river, Stewart felt, would serve as a protection against surprise, and he had sent out few scouting parties. Despite Lee's vigilance, Greene had not yet received the word from Marion that Stewart had moved down to Eutaw Springs, a position better calculated to protect the supply trains from Charleston.[2]

Because of the flooded canebrakes on either side of the river, Greene was forced to take a circuitous route to make contact with Stewart, marching only during the cooler hours of the early morning or late afternoon. On August 30, after a march of ninety miles, they reached Howell's Ferry on the Congaree, where all invalids and convalescents were left to guard the heavy baggage and tents. The army, well rested, were confident, with many agreeing with Colonel Otho Williams's observation: "If Colonel Stewart . . . thinks proper to risk an action, he will be beaten." It was at Howell's Ferry that Greene had learned that Stewart had moved to Eutaw. Several days were spent at Fort Motte while waiting for Marion to come up; the men spent their hours resting, repairing weapons, washing clothing, and being drilled in the patterns of basic warfare.

On September 5 Marion received orders to join the Southern Army. The South Carolina brigade marched swiftly up the Santee, swinging wide to bypass Stewart. The following day he rested, waiting for Greene at the plantation of Henry Laurens, seventeen miles above Eutaw Springs. When Greene came in the following day, the addition of Marion's brigade raised the total strength of the army to 2,300 effectives. On the night of September 7, after a twenty-mile march, the army encamped at Burdwell's Plantation, only seven miles above Eutaw. That night Greene's general orders ran: "This Army will March at 4 oClock tomorrow Morning by the right to attack the Enemy." [3]

Stewart had grown too comfortable and had allowed his intelligence to lag. He had no idea that Greene was on the move and was enjoying his bivouac. Eutaw Springs was a delightful spot, not too far from Nelson's Ferry and just off the road leading to Monck's Corner. Its name came from the two springs that boiled upward from an underground stream to form Eutaw Creek. The creek wandered along between steep banks bristling with heavy thickets of blackjack oak until it flowed into the Santee near the ferry. Near the head of the creek stood Patrick Roche's fine brick mansion house of two stories and an attic, looking out over a cleared area of some eight acres. The clearing before the house was bisected by the east-west river road, one branch of which, just beyond the house, split off toward Charleston, sixty miles away. A palisaded garden lay between the mansion and the creek. Little underbrush grew beneath the great oaks and cypresses in the woods surrounding the open area. In the field there was a mound, the result of a battle between the Indians and whites a hundred years earlier, and "said to have been erected over the bodies of the brave Indians who fell in defense of their country."

At four in the morning of September 8, Nathanael Greene set his army in motion toward Eutaw Springs. The army marched in four columns, designed to allow them to swing quickly into battle formation with the least possible confusion. Out in front rode Lee's legion, followed by the South Carolina state troops (Sumter's former command) led by Lieutenant Colonel William Henderson. The second column was made up of the North

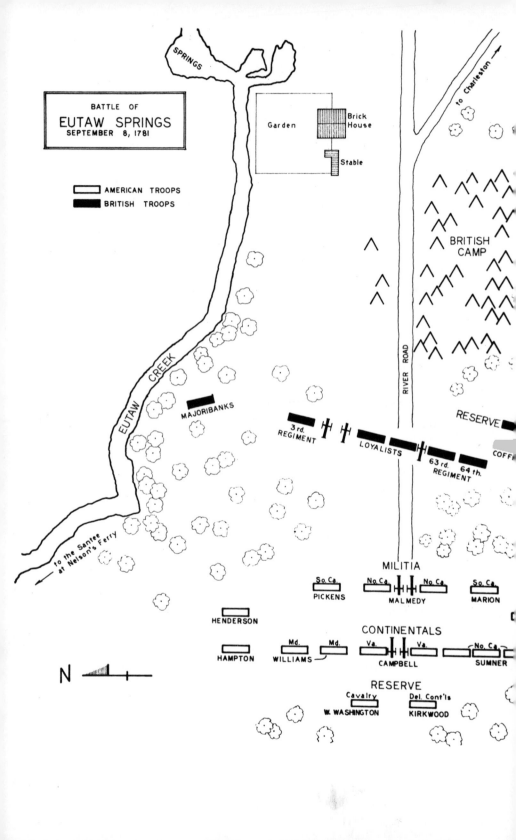

BATTLE OF
EUTAW SPRINGS
SEPTEMBER 8, 1781

SPRINGS

Garden   Brick House

Stable

to Charleston

☐ AMERICAN TROOPS
■ BRITISH TROOPS

BRITISH CAMP

EUTAW CREEK

RIVER ROAD

MAJORIBANKS

RESERVE

3rd. REGIMENT

LOYALISTS

63rd. REGIMENT

64th.

COFF

to the Santee at Nelson's Ferry

MILITIA

So.Ca. PICKENS

No.Ca. MALMEDY   No.Ca.

So.Ca. MARION

HENDERSON

CONTINENTALS

HAMPTON   WILLIAMS   Md.   Md.   Va.   Va.   CAMPBELL   No.Ca. SUMNER

RESERVE

Cavalry W. WASHINGTON   Del. Cont'ls KIRKWOOD

N

and South Carolina militia under the Marquis Francis de Malmedy, Andrew Pickens, and Francis Marion. The third consisted of three Continental brigades, the Marylanders under Colonel Otho Williams, the Virginians under Lieutenant Colonel Richard Campbell, and the North Carolinians under Brigadier General Jethro Sumner. The fourth group held William Washington's dragoons and Robert Kirkwood's little band of Delaware Continentals, who were to act as the reserve. After three miles the columns were halted, and Greene emptied his rum casks and allowed his men to partake of "a little of that liquid refreshment which is not unnecessary to exhilarate the animal spirits upon such occasions." The men were briefly drilled in forming their battle lines to teach the "raw troops to form with coolness and recollection."

For his strategy Greene adapted the basic battle formation as used by Daniel Morgan at the Cowpens and which the general had modified and thrown against Cornwallis at Guilford Court House. The militia were placed in the front line to absorb the initial shock of contact with the enemy, with the better trained and better disciplined Continental troops making up the second line. When formed, the first line consisted of Marion's brigade on the right, Malmedy's two battalions of North Carolina militia in the center, and the South Carolina militia commanded by Pickens on the left. Captain-Lieutenant William Gaines, who had just ridden in with dispatches the night before, was placed in charge of the two three-pounders in the middle of the first line.

Sumner's brigade of 350 North Carolina Continentals was on the right of the second line. Campbell's Virginia brigade of 250 men under Williams was posted on the left. Captain William Brown of Maryland was given command of the two six-pounders centered in this line.

Lee's legion protected the right flank, while over on the left were the South Carolina mounted troops led by Lieutenant

Colonels Wade Hampton, William Polk and Charles Middleton, the whole under Henderson's directions. Washington's cavalry and Kirkwood's Delawares were in reserve. Once formed, the columns moved slowly through the trees for fear of losing contact with one another.

Despite all this activity so near his camp, Stewart was still unaware of the approach of the American Army. Because of the shortage of bread, the British commander had been sending out foraging parties each morning to dig sweet potatoes. Nearly one hundred men had been sent out at five o'clock on the morning of September 8. Two hours after their departure, two deserters from Greene's army came in with the report that the American Army was marching to the attack. Although Stewart thought them spies and ordered them confined, he sent out Major John Coffin with 140 loyalist infantry and fifty cavalry to reconnoiter and recall the "rooting party."

Around eight o'clock, and within four miles of the British camp, Coffin's party was spotted by the North Carolina mounted militia who were scouting out ahead of Greene's main body of troops. Coffin, sensing an easy conquest, surged forward. John Armstrong, leading the Americans, sent word to Lee and began to fall back, leading the Tories on toward the main force. Lee threw together an ambush, with the legion infantry stretched across the road and the mounted men concealed in the trees on either side. Coffin came up and immediately charged. He was met by a shower of lead. Major Joseph Eggleston, leading the legion's mounted troops, swung around to the rear of Coffin. In the short skirmish that followed, Coffin managed to escape, but no less than forty of his men had been killed or taken prisoner. The rooting party came out of the woods as the skirmish began and suffered an estimated sixty casualties. The survivors made it back to camp at Eutaw after the ensuing battle.[4]

When Coffin reported a large body of mounted troops with the enemy, Stewart had no alternative but to stand and fight, for if he attempted a withdrawal there was a possibility his marching columns would be cut up by the horsemen. His strength was almost equal to that of Greene, and in general his men were battle tested. He formed his troops with the right flank resting on the creek, the left "in the air" but supported by Coffin's infantry and cavalry. Major John Majoribanks, with the guards and grenadiers, was stationed at a distance from the right flank in a blackjack thicket near the creek, the tangle of underbrush a good insurance against harassment by mounted troops. His artillery, two six-pounders and a four-pounder, were posted in the road, flanked on either side by Cruger's veteran loyalists from Ninety Six.

To gain time Stewart sent out skirmishers to slow the American advance. They were not too effective, and when they made their presence known, Greene sent up similar detachments to aid Lee, who was working out in front of the army. A small guard accompanied Gaines when he was ordered to roll his little three-pounders forward to aid Lee. Even as the artillery came up with Lee, the vanguard of the enemy came in sight. Gaines unlimbered his grasshoppers and loaded them with canister shot. He held his fire until the enemy were between fifty and twenty-five yards away and then staggered them with a blast. By the time the British elements had reformed, Greene arrived with the first line. The little field pieces continued to bark until they became disabled when the iron straps holding the trunions broke under the strain.

Never in the South had the militia performed so well as they did on that sultry September day. Marion felt that the greatest weakness was in the center of the front line where Malmedy's North Carolina militia were posted. He was to later declare that they began to drift toward the rear after firing only three rounds. On the other hand, his own men fought like veterans, perhaps steadied by the number of British deserters fighting in the brigade. They advanced about half a mile, firing slowly and with a great deal of accuracy. In general, British volleys flew high. When the enemy charged, the militia fell back, few having weapons with which to parry British bayonet thrusts. When they did break, they reformed quickly and drove forward again. Although he had issued orders that his men stand fast until they had fired at least twelve rounds, Marion estimated that they fired an average of seventeen rounds a man that day. As enemy fire was adjusted and brought lower, gaps began to widen in the line, and his men began to stray toward the rear. Greene brought up the North Carolina Continentals to steady the line. Stewart brought up his infantry reserves to counter this shift in strength.

The situation on the left was critical. The flank of Pickens's South Carolina militia, under the protection of Henderson's state troops, fell short of the British right flank, thereby exposing them to an enfilade fire, especially from Majoribanks's men in the blackjack along the creek. Henderson requested permission to change his position, but Greene held him back to protect the flank and the two remaining artillery pieces. Shortly afterward a musket ball broke Henderson's leg and he was no longer able to sit on his horse. The line sagged a bit, but Wade Hampton, who had succeeded Henderson, steadied them, and they "resumed their station in perfect tranquility."

Sumner's North Carolinians were subjected to a galling fire and began to waver and fall back. The British, sensing victory, sprang forward and in so doing, broke their formation. Greene sent word to Otho Williams to bring his Marylanders forward and "sweep the field with his bayonets." The Marylanders, along with the Virginians, who had not yet been actively engaged, moved up under a shower of grapeshot and musket balls. They trotted into position, their arms at the trail. The roll of the drums and the shouts of the advancing men added a new element to the din, and for a brief moment the battle seemed to hang in suspension.

In the face of this additional opposition, the British line began a slow withdrawal. Lee's infantry was thrown in to bolster the North Carolina Continentals, and that segment of the line rallied, poured in a volley, and fell in with the general charge. Stewart's left wing was thrown into disorder, and his men began to slough off.

The British center held firm until they too were thrown into confusion by the fugitives from the left flank. They began to yield. With a shout, the Americans renewed their forward advance; Lieutenant Colonel Campbell fell mortally wounded at the head of his Virginia Continentals.

It appeared that this was the proper moment to hit the disordered left flank of the enemy with a cavalry charge to turn the withdrawal into a rout. But Lee was with his infantry and his mounted troops remained where they had been posted, awaiting directions. With Majoribanks holding firm in the thicket and the left flank giving way, the British line had executed something of a quarter wheel, and both armies were now in the open ground before the mansion.

Greene had become convinced that the key to victory lay in the dislodgement of Majoribanks. William Washington was ordered to charge the enemy's right flank with Hampton to act in cooperation. Before Hampton came up to the line of departure, Washington led his men forward in a headlong charge; it was impossible to penetrate the snarled underbrush. Washington then discovered what he thought to be an opening between the right flank and Eutaw Creek. If gained, this position would allow hits on both Majoribanks's flank and rear. As his troops executed the order to wheel to the left, they fell under the concentrated fire of the enemy. Horses stumbled as their riders were swept from the saddles; all officers except two were either killed or wounded. Washington was taken prisoner when his horse was killed and pinned the colonel to the ground beneath its body.

The overall scene was one of classic warfare: horses rearing, plunging to the ground, or coursing wildly through the field; the ground was littered with human wreckage sprawled in the dust. Majoribanks's men, bayonets at the ready, sallied briefly from the thicket to kill or take prisoner the unhorsed riders. Hampton gathered up the survivors of Washington's troop and charged. Kirkwood's little band of Delawares drove into the blackjacks with their bayonets. Majoribanks, still holding to the protection afforded by the thicket, moved into a new position with one of his flanks resting on the palisaded gardens.

As the British army now appeared to be in full retreat, those in their camp became frightened lest they be overrun. Commissaries destroyed provisions and supplies, while a number of loyalists and deserters leaped aboard draught horses and clattered off down the road toward Charleston. Some of those on the field of battle threw themselves into the palisaded garden, while others sought the protection offered by a ravine or "hollow way" where they were able to reform. Major Sheridan, of Cruger's New York Volunteers, ordered his men into the brick mansion. Lee's infantry were so close on their heels that Sheridan was forced to slam the door against several of his own officers and men. Those unfortunate fellows were taken prisoner, and the men of the legion used them as protective shields when they pulled back from the house.

The remaining British troops retreated directly through their camp. Their tents contained much in the way of booty "to tempt a thirsty, naked and fatigued soldiery to acts of insubordination." The tents offered some concealment from the fire from the mansion house. A number of American officers had rushed through the camp in pursuit of the enemy, only to look back and discover their men looting the tents. The officers, in plain view of the house, became prime targets for Sheridan's sharpshooters. By then, the soldiers had "fastened upon the

liquors and refreshments they afforded, and became utterly unmanageable."

Majoribanks and Coffin, taking advantage of the general confusion, emerged from the thicket on the right and the woods on
the left. Greene, unaware of the collapse of discipline among
his soldiers, sent orders for Lee to charge Majoribanks now that
he was out in the open. Lee could not be found, and the order
was passed on to Major Joseph Eggleston. As Eggleston led the
legion in a charge against Majoribanks, Coffin dashed out and
drove him back.

Coffin then wheeled to charge those Americans scattered
among the tents in the British camp. Wade Hampton met him
and, after a sharp encounter, drove back the Tories. In pursuing
Coffin, Hampton led his men across in front of Majoribanks's
position. They were subjected to such a heavy fire in which William Polk thought "every man killed but himself."

Stewart personally rallied those of his men who had been retreating, shouting that if they would but follow him, he would
guarantee victory. He drove forward simultaneously with
Majoribanks.

In the excitement of the moment, the field pieces of Captain
Brown were run too far forward, although they were of such light
metal that they could do no damage to the brick house. But they
were also within musket range of the defenders. Nearly all of
the gunners manning Greene's two guns were either killed or
wounded. Noting this Majoribanks came onto the field and
dragged off the artillery under the covering fire of Sheridan's
men. Gathering those men who had taken refuge in the garden,
Majoribanks charged the Americans in the British camp and
drove them before him.

Greene collected his men within the protection of the trees.
Stewart's soldiers were too exhausted to follow their push
through the camp. After four hours of bitter fighting American

ammunition had run low, and the enemy still controlled the water supply. Greene also felt that it would be to his advantage if he could hit Stewart on the march rather than make another attempt to drive him from the field. Collecting all of his wounded except those who lay within musket range of the house, he moved out. A picket was left in the neighborhood to keep an eye on the movements of the enemy.

It had been a bloody affair. Greene's final casualty report totalled 574, of whom 119 had been killed, 383 wounded, and seventy-eight missing. Stewart's losses were uncertain, but, according to his official returns, the British suffered eighty-five men killed, 351 wounded, and 257 missing. On the other hand, Greene claimed that he had captured 500 prisoners, seventy of whom were wounded, contradicting British figures. Whatever his losses, Alexander Stewart was in no condition to fight another action in the near future. Marion had lost a number of his brigade, but not so many as at Quinby Bridge. Lieutenants John Simons and Holmes had been killed, and Colonel Hugh Horry had been wounded in the fleshy part of his leg. Three privates had also been killed. Four other officers and twenty privates had been wounded.

Marion's militia had fought well, and in official dispatches Greene praised them, stating that they had "fought with a degree of Spirit and firmness that reflects the highest honour upon this class of Soldiers." To Steuben he commented that "such conduct would have graced the soldiers of the great King of Prussia."

Charleston's *Royal Gazette,* on the other hand, had a little fun at the brigade's expense, with "By some mistake, Marion's corps, for this once, got themselves into danger, and it is said lost near one hundred killed and wounded." [5]

The day after the battle Lee and Marion were sent out to either intercept reinforcements or possibly slow Stewart should the British march for Charleston. On this same day, working in a steady downpour, Stewart's men smashed a thousand stand of arms, throwing many into the springs. Thirty casks of rum were poured into Eutaw Creek. Leaving seventy of his wounded on the field under the protection of a flag, Stewart marched for Charleston along the Nelson Ferry road, felling trees behind him to discourage pursuit. Greene followed slowly behind until he learned that Stewart had received four hundred fresh troops under McArthur from Monck's Corner to cover his withdrawal. Six men from the legion and Maham's regiment riding together on patrol managed to capture twenty-four British soldiers and four Tories as they straggled along behind the main column. But by this time Marion was reporting to Greene: "My horses are so tired they cannot Scarcely move."

As his men and their mounts rested, he reflected and grew proud of the way his men had stood up against the enemy. "My Brigade behaved well," he boasted to Peter Horry. And Governor Rutledge, perhaps thinking of Sumter, proudly observed, "That distrust of their own immediate commanders which militia are too apt to be affected with, never produced an emotion where Marion and Pickens commanded."

For the time being, Greene allowed Marion to act on his own. As soon as his men and mounts had rested, he rode down across Biggin Swamp to Laurens's Plantation at Mepkin. When he heard that the British were sending down their wounded and baggage by six schooners, he took a position on a high bluff above the Cooper River. The only vessel that he was able to take was a small open boat containing four white men and four Negroes. He destroyed the boat and released the blacks, who immediately reported his whereabouts to the enemy. Stewart held back his schooners. Marion rode on down through St. Stephen's to keep an eye on the enemy at Fair Lawn where Stewart had received reinforcements and was collecting Negroes to entrench and fortify the plantation house. His patrols did report that a British detachment had returned to Eutaw Springs on September 16, but he was convinced that this was little more than a "bravado," especially since he was in a position to intercept their supplies. He was right.

The Postell affair still rankled. Marion seemed to feel that Greene was deliberately avoiding arranging an exchange for the captive. He seemed obsessed with the idea of capturing enough British officers, refusing to parole them, and sending them on to Greene with an expression of his desire that there would be no further formal exchanges until Postell was returned. He had exceeded his authority by going so far as to attempt a private negotiation with Balfour, who refused to consider an exchange for Postell on the grounds "that he has been detained for being in Arms whereupon Parole Contrary to the Laws of all Nations." [6]

Marion had hoped to make a sweep over the Santee, but he had allowed a large number of his men to return to their homes because he had no ammunition, and Greene had been unable to furnish him with a supply since Eutaw Springs. Yet he was still a busy man. Both Greene and Rutledge kept him employed in a number of tasks, with the governor almost making a nuisance of himself, usually writing as many as one, and often three, letters a day from this time on.

Inasmuch as the British had pulled most of their forces into a small area around Charleston, Rutledge was attempting to stamp out the civil war that had raged so long and to restore domestic tranquility to his state. Marion was responsible for carrying the governor's decrees into effect. On September 3 he ordered Marion to send the wives and children of all known Tories into British lines, and on September 27 the governor had followed this with a proclamation promising clemency to certain classes of Tories as well as the right to reoccupy their property if they appeared before a brigadier general of militia within the next thirty days and, after taking an oath of allegiance, agreed to serve six months in the South Carolina militia. Exempted were those who had joined the enemy or held British military commissions, those who had signed congratulatory messages to Clinton or Cornwallis, and "all those whose conduct has been so infamous that they can not consistent with policy and justice partake of the rights of citizens."

In addition, there were the routine military obligations. As early as September 17 there had been reports that Lord Cornwallis was being invested by the French fleet and a Franco-American force under Washington at Yorktown in Virginia. Greene, who seemed always to anticipate the worst, feared that the British general might attempt to break out and fight his way back to South Carolina. This was coupled with persistent rumors that the British garrison were planning to drive out of Charleston to cross the Santee on a plundering expedition. And there were some indications of substance to the stories, for they were building boats at Fludd's Plantation. Some parties had advanced as far out as Murray's Ferry, rounding up Negro slaves. And the Tory leaders David Fanning and Hector McNeil were beginning to act up on Deep River. But Greene had not lost his confidence, and "If they will give us a few days to breathe, refresh and take care of our wounded, I shall have no objections to another touch."

Marion was ordered to call out the brigade. He tried, but a tenacious fever hampered his efforts. And the men appeared reluctant to leave their homes; some were harvesting their crops; others were just tired of war. Some with more money or influence than others were hiring substitutes to come out in their place when drafted for Continental or State troop duty, and considered themselves exempt from militia calls. The brigade had already been reduced, for Marion, on orders from the governor, had been forced to detach men to patrol around Greene's army to prevent the soldiers from strolling out to plunder the inhabitants of the neighborhood. And even if the men did turn out, there was no ammunition to issue them. Other parties were sent out to roam the roads leading into Charleston to prevent provisions from going into the city as well as to keep the British from venturing out to slaughter and salt down cattle for future use.

Greene had also dispatched Henry Lee to Virginia to confer with General Washington relative to sending reinforcements to the Southern Army. In his absence the discipline of the legion deteriorated. Major Joseph Eggleston, commanding the unit in Lee's absence, received a reprimand from Greene for the manner in which his men were treating the inhabitants. Greene feared the rise of a critical situation, for "It was this very Conduct which has made the british so odious."

Friends as well as enemies gave trouble. American privateers sailed up the rivers and plundered Whig plantations, using as their excuse the claim that the owners were Tories. Still more men had to be thrown out to patrol the river banks to scare off these predators.[7]

Francis Marion saw his brigade melt away, as detachment after detachment was sent off on the special missions. The victory at Eutaw Springs and the news of the investment of Cornwallis led many to feel that there was no longer a need for their services in the field. And to complicate matters even further, there was the continuing and raging dispute between Peter Horry and Hezikiah Maham that threatened the collapse of the brigade.

Chapter XIII

Greene's apprehension that Cornwallis might break out of the cordon at Yorktown and drive south led to a freshening of the Horry-Maham dispute. Greene had wanted to get on with the business of completing both their regiments so as to have a large body of cavalry to "frustrate [Cornwallis's] designs."

Maham had gotten the jump on Horry both in recruiting and the gathering of horses to mount them. By late September he had only fifty-seven men under his command, but this was greater than Horry's group. Most of his recruits had enlisted for only six months; many were former Tories taking advantage of Rutledge's proclamation. A number of their mounts had been seized from the farms of loyalists serving with the enemy; those unfit for dragoon service were traded away for those that were. When this method proved unsatisfactory, Greene proposed that planters of the community contribute at least one horse for a year or until the end of the war.

Horry had not done so well, although by September 20, 1781 he had enlisted five noncommissioned officers and eighty privates. For one thing, he did not maintain proper discipline over his officers, who were already beginning to act as though they were in the Continental establishment, although there was no real assurance that they ever would be. People were complaining of their rather arrogant behavior, especially with regard to taking up horses. Marion felt compelled to send a letter of reprimand to Horry. Although he had given Horry wide latitude in the impressment of horses to mount his men, Governor Rutledge, after reports that Horry's men were taking up "Plow Horses, breeding Mares, two year olds & yearlings" to trade for mounts fit for his use, sent an angry letter to Horry: such animals were to be immediately restored to their owners. Not only did he threaten to revoke Horry's press warrants, authorizing him to confiscate the animals, but he demanded that the officers stop their practices "to abuse, insult and exasperate the militia." "I think Col. Horry's conduct most extraordinary," the governor wrote Marion, "He is not yet a Continental officer and his Regiment is not yet on the Continental Establishment."

Although Horry's behavior presented difficulties, Marion found Hezikiah Maham almost unmanageable. Although his command, like Horry's, was neither on the state nor Continental establishment, he considered his rank to be Continental, and as Marion was only a militia brigadier (although he still retained his commission as Continental Lieutenant Colonel), Maham declared he would take orders only from Greene. His orders constantly referred to his command as "Legion Cavalry." A crisis arose when Maham impressed the horse of one John Oliver, and he refused to return the animal when commanded to do so by Marion. But he had discounted the temper of the little brigadier, and Marion straightway ordered Maham to return the horse or face a general court martial. "I think it is high time," he said, "that you and I should know whether I have the power of Commanding you or not. . . ."

The situation grew so tense and so volatile that Greene felt it necessary to intervene, especially after Maham began to confiscate the horses of the militia, and seize the saddles and equipment of Marion's light horse. It was "like robbing Peter to pay Paul," said Greene, and he ordered that militia horses be left alone unless they belonged to those who refused to take the field. At the suggestion of Rutledge, the general wrote to both Horry and Maham that "You will please put yourself and your Corps under the Command of General Marion and follow his Orders." And to Marion Greene suggested that he and his old friend sit down together and try to talk out the situation.

Horry, in camp at Indian Town, unfortunately had no sooner received Marion's invitation than he received three letters from Governor Rutledge. In these the governor repeated Marion's complaints about both Maham and Horry, since both were acting as if theirs were independent commands. Horry was so incensed that he refused to ride to Marion's camp at Cantey's Plantation. In a long reply, he denied each of Marion's allegations against him and declared that everyone who carried a tale to Marion was believed. He demanded either a court martial or court of enquiry and an opportunity of "Vindicating myself & Silence Genl. Marion's Complaints."

That same day Horry wrote Greene, stating that he and his officers were put upon by Marion and demanding to know whether he was on the state or Continental establishment—if Continental, he would take orders only from Greene. "I used to submit to Genl. Marion's Orders with pleasure," he said, "but at present I Assure you it is disagreeable to me & all my officers that have Experienced his late Usage."

Both Greene and Rutledge decided that something had to be done before the militia situation in the low country disintegrated into a shambles. Rutledge employed soft words in trying to smooth Horry's ruffled pride, but Greene adopted a sterner attitude toward the petulant colonel. He decried squabbling among officers of high rank. After assuring Horry that Marion would never intentionally have done anything to hurt a soldier who had done so much for the cause, Greene went on to say: "The General is a good Man, few of us are without faults. Let his Virtues vail his, if he has any."

It may well have been these letters that prompted Horry to go to Marion's camp. They talked. Although Horry still resented being "Censured, Severely reprimanded, & Condemned," after the meeting he reported to Greene that "we are both Satisfied." [1]

A possibility of renewed activity promised relief from accusations and rebuttals. Greene had ordered Marion to take a position to the left of the enemy, and he selected a spot near Huger's Bridge in St. Thomas Parish. Sumter had also taken the field again and had taken post at Orangeburgh. He and Marion were to prevent supplies from going into Charleston. Yet the commanding general's orders had been flexible: "You are at liberty to act as you think advisable. I have no particular instructions to give you, and only wish you to avoid surprise."

Marion had called out the brigade but had remained at Cantey's Plantation. He spent some of his time in taking up Tories who were not under arms to be held as prisoners and offered in exchange for those citizens held by the British. Both Greene and Rutledge ordered them released on the grounds that this was not proper warfare. [2]

When the overmountain men of John Sevier and Isaac Shelby had joined Greene's army, they had constituted an additional drain on provisions. They had been sent over to Marion, who was better able to feed them. When they arrived at Cantey's Plantation Marion, in turn, attached them to Hezikiah Maham, who was being sent on a "tour" down to Cainhoy to draw out the enemy cavalry supposedly stationed there and to disrupt traffic going in to Charleston. At Cainhoy there were only about a dozen enemy horsemen, and they would venture out only a short distance beyond their abatis, hastily retiring when they saw the size of the force against them. Maham captured one prisoner and burned a sloop and a schooner that had come up the Cooper to secure provisions.

Maham moved on over to Fair Lawn, the former home of Sir John Colleton, which had been converted into a hospital for the British wounded at Eutaw Springs. On November 2, 1781 he captured a subaltern, three doctors, and eighty-two privates. It was not much of a conquest, but he did manage to burn and destroy a number of guns, supplies, and stores because he had no way of bringing them off. Greene, upon receiving the report, praised Maham's success as "highly honourable to himself & Corps, & I hope will be followed by future Strokes of Good fortune."

With the British it was a different story. Colonel Doyle, on the instructions of Stewart, protested an attack "upon a parcel of sick, helpless soldiers in a hospital at Colleton house," who had not even a guard, and the burning of the building before "Dragging away a number of dying People to expire in Swamps, a Species of Barbarity hitherto Unknown in Civilized Nations. . . ." In his defense Maham declared that the place had been fortified and that soldiers had been stationed at that post in the past. Only twelve of the soldiers had been really sick, the remainder, he claimed, "was fit for duty," but he had carried away the sick on horseback rather than make them walk because the officer in charge had refused to take a receipt for them as prisoners of war. Although Greene felt the charges of inhumanity were groundless, and that burning the hospital had been the only means to destroy British military supplies stored there, the accusations were serious enough and appeared to hold enough truth to lead Greene to hold a court of enquiry. No final determination of the matter was ever reached, but William Moultrie later stated that Maham was "constrained to burn the house, because his men were making too free with the liquors." [3]

The bitterness of the bickering was somewhat dissipated in the joy generated by Henry Lee when he returned to Greene's camp from Virginia. In his saddlebags were official dispatches from Washington carrying news of the surrender of Cornwallis at Yorktown on October 19, 1781. Marion received the news on November 9; that same day he heard that General Alexander Leslie had landed in Charleston to assume command of British operations in South Carolina.

Equally pleasing to Marion was an extract from the minutes of the Continental Congress containing a resolution of praise by that body "for his Wise, Gallant, and Decided conduct in defending the Liberties of his Country and particularly for his prudent and intrepid attack on a Body of British troops on the thirtieth day of August last and for the distinguished part he took on the battle of the Eighth of September." To express his appreciation to the officers who had helped win this accolade, he gave a ball at the home of Major John Cantey on the evening of November 10.

Shelby, Sevier, and their men, after only three weeks with the Southern Army, left on November 25 since they, as did all militiamen, counted their time in the field from the time they had left their homes. Maham was sent down to attack the redoubt at Wappetaw Meeting House near Huger's Bridge in St. Thomas Parish, but found it empty, as its garrison had fled to the safety of Charleston. Marion followed him down with his brigade and lingered near Huger's Bridge, driving off the cattle and taking up supplies felt to be useful to the enemy.

To many it was obvious that the war was drawing to a close. The British no longer controlled any part of South Carolina other than the immediate area around Charleston, and General Leslie was forced to admit "We are entirely on the defensive," and he became even more convinced of that opinion when Greene took a "flying party" down to Dorchester where the enemy "took fright" and fled through the night to Charleston after burning their stores and fortifications.

But there were still enough enemy detachments outside

Charleston, such as at Haddrell's Point, that vigilance could not be relaxed. British galleys frequently sent out to collect fresh provisions had to be harassed. When Marion had the ammunition, he drove them off. His scouting parties worked almost to the very gates of Charleston. At one time the enemy sallied forth with five hundred men in an attempt to surprise him, but he moved quickly out of their way when he received intelligence of enemy moves from Greene.[4]

After the publication of Lord Cornwallis's surrender, the Tories appeared to have fallen into submission, and the people in general appeared anxious to resume the routine of peace. To counter discouragement on the part of the loyalists, Leslie, on December 15, 1781, promised in a proclamation that they could rely on speedy and effectual support being given them by the forces under his command.

Despite Greene's noting, "The British Army are very respectful," he was falling into a fit of despair because of the lack of support furnished him. Suspecting that the militia might be experiencing the same blue moods, he reassured Marion, "be not discouraged, I look forward to better days." He also knew well that Marion had been unhappy since the middle of November when Greene had written Sumter stating that Marion could "second him in an attack," and Sumter had suggested that the two "confer" at the first opportunity. Marion had not followed up the suggestion, and Greene had resolved the situation by having Marion hover off the left to protect that flank of the Southern Army.

There was also something of minor conflict between military interests. Rutledge feared that a number of the Tory "scoundrels" would not surrender in hopes of receiving a pardon and suggested that the most obnoxious of those who turned themselves in should be sent into Charleston to become a burden to their masters. Greene's greatest concern with the loyalists was to prevent them from supplying the Charleston garrison. To prevent a sudden sally, Peter Horry was sent down to the Goose Creek neighborhood to gain intelligence of enemy movements. But military operations were constantly hampered by the large number of Tory women and children who filtered into his camp to seek protection and who had to be fed until some decision was made as to their future.[5]

The Governor was convinced that now was the proper time to reestablish civil government. He issued writs of elections, which were sent to militia commanders who were instructed to set up and supervise elections. In his district Marion selected three men from each precinct as election supervisors. There was no trouble, although there were some murmurings when Rutledge excluded from the voting all those who had not borne arms in the American cause prior to September 27, 1781. Francis Marion was chosen by the people of St. John's Parish, Berkeley, as their representative to the state senate.

After first selecting Camden, Governor Rutledge chose Jacksonborough, a village on the Edisto, thirty-two miles from Charleston, as the site for the meeting of the Assembly. Greene felt the place to be too near the enemy and moved his army down to Round O to place himself between the legislators and the enemy. Marion was ordered to take a position in the neighborhood of Dorchester but at any rumor of enemy activity was to move over to Greene to insure that the Americans "might not be beat in detachment." When the governor planned to ride down to the bivouac the first of January, he gave Marion two weeks' notice that he wished the escort of an officer and twenty-five men, "well mounted as I shall travel Pretty expeditiously."

Greene had refused to allow the legislature to meet until he was certain that the enemy had not received a reinforcement in Charleston. In the meantime, Marion also was attempting to make sure that the Assembly could sit without disturbance, especially from stray bands of Tories. During the week before Christmas he rode down to Monck's Corner and across to Dorchester; there was no activity other than the fun of chasing several groups of loyalists back into Charleston. But when the Virginia Continentals left for home when their time of enlistment expired, Greene placed a greater part of the responsibility for the immediate protection of the Assembly upon the brigade, for the general could not weaken the Southern Army for fear the enemy might make a sally out from the city.[6]

But before the legislature met, there was a commotion down near Monck's Corner. Colonel Richard Richardson commanded an outpost at Cainhoy, keeping an eye on the British galley that lay in the Wando, as well as patrolling the roads down as far as Daniel's Island each day. From intelligence reports Leslie was led to conclude that a successful strike could be made against Marion. He detached sixty cavalry, and about three hundred infantry made up of the flank corps, which was supplemented by the Volunteers of Ireland under the command of Major William Brereton of the Sixty-Fourth Regiment. On Daniel's Island they were joined by a small detachment from Haddrell's Point under Captain John Roberts of the Sixty-Third. They had no sooner crossed over to the north bank of the Wando than they learned that the Americans were aware of their presence. Brereton sent the cavalry dashing on ahead of the main body.

When Richardson had learned of the expedition against him, he detached scouts to report on their movements and sent out a call for help. Marion, who had been summoned to Greene's camp, mounted and rode hard for the Wando. The following morning, January 3, 1782, Maham's horse under Captain John Caraway Smith arrived. Marion had sent them forward with orders to join Richardson who, in turn, had been ordered to make a junction with Colonel Benjamin Screven, with both to "scrimmage with them at every advantageous ground until I came up with them." Brereton, taking an unexpected route, managed to swing around Richardson and stop at Parson Garden's place to allow his men to cook their noonday meal. When Richardson discovered he had been bypassed, he turned and rode quickly to get around the enemy before they finished their meal.

Two miles from Garden's, at the St. Thomas Muster House, Richardson drew up his men. The British vanguard of twelve mounted men under Captain Archibald Campbell came in view. Captain John Caraway Smith, leading some of Maham's horse, raced forward. The British turned to flee, the Americans hard on their heels. Captain Campbell and three of his dragoons were killed in the running fight.

Maham's men, inadequately trained and poorly disciplined, galloped wildly along in pursuit with no semblance of order. They rode swiftly across a narrow swamp and bridge. At the far end of the bridge stood the British infantry. A volley sent Smith's men recoiling into a staggering mass of men and horses. Major Coffin followed this burst of fire with a charge of the fifty horsemen under his command.

The Americans fell back in terror and fright. Captain Smith with four officers, four dragoons and two mounted militia suddenly halted in their flight when they found themselves confronted by a steep embankment and with twenty-five of the enemy bearing down upon them. There seemed to be no alternative to surrender, but Smith suddenly shouted an order to charge. The enemy, taken aback by the maneuver, fell away before the mad men rushing upon them. Several lost their lives to swinging sabers as Smith and his men rode through them.

As they rushed back to their own lines, the British called off the pursuit when they received information that Marion was too strongly posted to attack. There was also the information that Greene had detached a sizable unit to attack Major James Craig on Johns Island. They fell back to Quinby Bridge and by daybreak had reached Cainhoy. In addition to the loss of Captain Archibald Campbell, Captain Alexander Campbell and two dragoons had been wounded, although Marion claimed that twelve of the enemy horsemen had suffered wounds. Brereton left one of his and two of Marion's wounded on the field and sent a letter to Marion requesting that his dead be buried by the Americans.

Too weak to press an attack, Marion fell back to Wambaw to collect his scattered men. It was impossible to determine his own losses. Officially he listed thirteen killed, six wounded and twenty-one missing. This may well have been wishful thinking, for Leslie claimed that Brereton took nearly a hundred prisoners, while another account stated that at least twenty-five of Marion's men were buried on the causeway where they fell.[7]

When the call went out for the Assembly to meet on January 8, Marion and the other brigadiers were delegated the responsibility of distributing the notices. Greene assigned to Marion's brigade the primary task of protecting the legislature, for fear the enemy would drive against him should he weaken his own force.

The command of the brigade was turned over to Peter Horry. At the time they were in camp at Strawberry Ferry on the Cooper River, but Horry was told that once the supplies in the neighborhood were exhausted, he should move around but always keep the brigade between Charleston and Jacksonborough. With these preparations the general rode off to take his seat in the Senate.

There were many familiar faces among the military men elected to office. In the Senate there were Thomas Sumter, Hugh Horry, Thomas Taylor, and William Thomson. Among those who had been elected to seats in the House were Andrew Pickens, William Henderson, Thomas Brandon, Wade Hampton, Richard Hampton, William Hill, Edward Lacey, James Lyles, John Thomas, and Richard Winn, all of whom had gained a degree of fame during the fighting.

Actually Greene had urged that they offer themselves as candidates, for it was his feeling that they could be of great service to the army, for there was "Nothing like the time present when gratitude is warm and danger not past, to get business of the sort approved." Others felt that the military was too strongly represented, and, although he wished that more business men had been among those elected, Governor Rutledge said of the military, "There is a great deal of Honesty among them." [8]

No sooner had Marion departed than Maham and Horry resumed their brawling. Although he had no claim to seniority, Maham flatly refused to obey orders issued by Horry and began to fire off letters to Greene demanding that his rank be elevated. Not even Greene's statement that "Rank is not what constitutes a good officer, but good conduct," made any difference. Marion begged Greene to step in, but the best the general would do was to note that he could not "imagine upon what principles Lt. Col. Mayam presumes to dispute rank with Lt. Col. Horry." Maham demanded that he be given an independent command; Marion said that if he was, he would want him attached to the main army.

To maintain some semblance of order in the brigade, Marion detached Maham, to be recalled by Horry if the enemy came out, but "wish he may not be called on for no other purpose." Perhaps it was to test his authority, but Horry almost immediately demanded that Maham submit a return of the strength of his command. On the other hand, it appears to be a sensible request in that Horry would need to know Maham's strength should he need his services. In an insulting reply, after pointing out Horry's inactivity as a Continental officer, Maham left little doubt as to his own position: "I had my Regt. three months in the field on duty before you had yours, as I cannot think of being Commanded by an officer of the same Rank—I think it proper not to make you a Return of my Regt. nor obey any order that you may be pleased to send."

A second letter on the same day declared that Horry had ventured far beyond his authority and ended with a threatening postscript: "You mention in yours that you would not wish to take any Advantage of me—I wou'd not advise you to Attempt any such thing, for fear you may fail in the Attempt." Even Marion felt that Maham had gone too far, but he was too busy in the Assembly to do much except write letters.

Both men were weary, as was most of the remainder of the army. Morale, even among the Continentals, was fading, and numbers shrank as many seized the first opportunity to walk off. Henry Lee, disappointed at not having received promotion, fearful that he had lost his future while serving away from Washington's army, and sulking because he had not received mention in Greene's dispatches of Eutaw Springs, applied for an indefinite leave on January 26. It was granted.

The same attitude prevailed among the South Carolina militia. Horry fell ill and was unable to maintain proper discipline. The militia, who could see little reason for sitting around camp, began to slip off. Horry began to feel sorry for himself, felt inadequate for the command, and suspected that the men were unhappy with him and uneasy when Marion wasn't around. He begged the Brigadier to return, writing, "Your brigade lessens daily." [9]

It was impossible for Marion to leave the Assembly. There were only thirteen senators present at Jacksonborough and that number was required to make a quorum. There were important questions before them: the raising of Continental troops, the organization of the militia, the treatment of loyalists, and the confiscation of their property. If Marion left the business of the Senate would grind to a halt, and it was still necessary that the members of the legislature elect a governor as successor to John Rutledge.

Peter Horry was too ill and too angry to consider political colorings. His troubles with Maham led him to once again request to be relieved. Marion showed Peter's letter to Hugh Horry, who agreed, "It seems to be wrote in too much haste." Marion promised to try to straighten out the mess. But he still could not leave. John Rutledge was no longer eligible for the governorship. It was expected that there would be a contest between the candidate from the low country, Ralph Izard, and Thomas Sumter, favorite of the upcountry legislators. Christopher Gadsden was elected, but he declined the honor, pleading the infirmities of age. The office was finally settled on John Mathews. Marion and Sumter were delegated the honor of waiting on the new chief executive to inform him of his election.

Disputes in the Assembly were almost as heated as those between Horry and Maham. When John Rutledge had delivered the opening address before the body, he had thrown the question of the loyalists into their laps with, "It is with you to determine whether the forfeiture and appropriation of their property should now take place." Marion grew unhappy with the bitter denunciations that surrounded the word "Tory" every time it was used. He didn't like the bill proposed by the colonels of Sumter's brigade, or the subsequent act, to confiscate four hundred loyalist slaves and other property to pay off Sumter's troops. He fought the bill at every turn. When Governor Mathews gave a dinner party and Marion was called upon for a toast, he rather facetiously raised his glass and proposed, "Well, gentlemen, here's damnation to the confiscation act."

So heated were the debates that Sumter considered the arguments a censure of his proceedings; he was likewise unhappy over the reorganization of the militia that required his brigade to serve on foot. On February 18, 1782 he resigned his commission as brigadier general of the South Carolina militia.

The new militia law placed every militiaman charged with disobedience or desertion in the Continental Line. Two Continental regiments were to be raised, with every recruit given one Negro slave, taken from loyalist estates, for each year of service. Marion seems to have accepted the law but must have felt a bit chagrined when he and Charles Cotesworth Pinckney were named as commanders of the regiments once they were raised.

Other business included such matters as voting ten thousand guineas to General Greene, to be spent either on land or slaves as he chose. A proposal to raise a battalion of Negro slaves was voted down.[10]

Marion had wearied of the flow of verbiage in the Senate and wished to hurry back to camp to try to straighten out the messy business of the continuing quarrel between Horry and Maham. Despite the general's orders that Maham cooperate with Horry, the latter was soon complaining, "Col. Maham interferes with my command so much I can scarcely act," and he renewed his plea to Marion that he return and take over. So intense had grown the feud that Horry suggested that he would resign if not supported, although he would not give up his Continental commission as lieutenant colonel. From the evidence it would appear Maham was at fault in the controversy, although Horry's quick temper must be admitted as a contributing factor.

Maham almost completely ignored Marion, directing most of his complaints to Greene. The commanding general attempted to act as a mediator; in fact it appeared that he was a little too soft in his dealings with the fiery leader of dragoons. When the colonel objected to the use of his dragoons by Marion, Greene's answer, as it had been with Horry, was couched in patient language, calculated not to offend. After explaining that the brigadier had to use troops to cover an extensive area, he said, "The Genl. is a good Man, and when you consider his difficulties and make just allowances, perhaps you will sense little to complain of but the sore necessity of service. . . . General Marion has been very useful and very necessary."

But no amount of patient explanation would placate Maham, and Greene finally had to interject his authority, stating that, as Horry had never relinquished his original Continental commission, he clearly outranked Maham, and issuing positive orders placing Maham under Horry's command. On the other hand, he was careful to warn Horry not to abuse his "triumph," for "Blinded by matters of interest and love of rank, he will yield to conviction unwillingly, and finding himself in this situation will feel with double force every unnecessary exercise of authority."

Marion even went so far as to petition the Assembly for leave to return to his command, but they refused to consider the request until those bills pending had been acted upon. He assured Horry that he was tired of legislating and "wish myself with you." And as Horry's complaints about his health grew more frequent, Marion played his trump card: "If your health is such as to Require your Absence from Camp, you will leave the Command of the Brigade to Colo. Mayam." With this he knew that only death could remove Horry from camp so long as Maham remained active in the field.

Maham, on the other hand, had settled the question by his own actions. Inasmuch as he also had been elected a member of the Assembly, he came into Jacksonborough and claimed his seat. His dragoons were placed under the direction of Captain John Caraway Smith. Horry relinquished his command just as quickly. With no sign of enemy activity and feeling secure, Horry, contrary to Marion's directions, gave in to his illness. The brigade, then camped on Wambaw Creek, was turned over to Colonel Adam McDonald. Then, on February 24, Horry rode off to his plantation on the Santee to nurse his ills and his bruised ego.

The effects of the long dispute between Horry and Maham were to be felt on the field of battle, for both had spent so much time in their quarrels that they had neglected to train their men properly.[11]

Chapter XIV

While Francis Marion stirred restlessly in his seat in the Senate, the enemy had taken the field. Perhaps because of intelligence reports of the confusion in Marion's brigade, they chose this time to sally forth in strength. Colonel Benjamin Thompson, whose detachment formerly had been used primarily in rounding up cattle, crossed the Cooper River on February 23, 1782, leading two hundred horsemen, five hundred infantry, and two field pieces. His preparations had been conducted with such secrecy that they had gone unnoticed by American informers, although as early as February 20, Horry had reported to Greene that there was movement by the enemy. The word went out that something was in the air. Greene hinted that an expedition might be sent out to hit Marion's brigade.

As he rode in search of the brigade on February 24, Thompson had come across the tracks of many horses in the road. Leaving his infantry, he trotted on ahead, following the hoofprints. Thompson lost the element of surprise when the scouting party of Captain Thomas Bennett spotted the fast-traveling column as it passed through St. Thomas Parish. Bennett threw the spurs to his horse and sped off to warn McDonald.

Major Lemuel Benison, commanding Horry's dragoons, was eating breakfast at Mepkin Plantation, about a mile in front of the brigade when Bennett galloped in. Benison felt that Bennett was overly excited and calmly continued eating. Bennett, with no effort to hide his disgust, raced away to the plantation of Elias Horry, where he found Colonel McDonald also eating a meal. The colonel refused to accept the rider's news, for he said he had ridden through Christ Church Parish just the day before, and there had been no sign of the enemy. Nevertheless, to be on the safe side, he did send out Major John James, who had arrived just the day before with troops from the Williamsburg District. He told James to assume temporary command of the regiment while he finished his meal.

James had served long enough under Marion to realize that he must prepare for any eventuality. He moved the brigade over to the right of the camp and formed the men in the skirt of the woods behind the causeway leading to Wambaw Bridge. As he was galloping across the field to the left to consult Colonel Benjamin Screven, the ranking officer on the field, James was startled by the distant thunder of heavy firing from the direction of Mepkin's.

Thompson had come up on Benison's corps a half hour before sunset. The vedettes had been killed in a brief action. A party of horse was crossing the causeway leading to the bridge. A charge scattered them, but Benison's horsemen stopped on a rise about a hundred yards from the end of the causeway and formed in good order. Thompson's loyalist militia drove to within thirty yards opposite them and invited them, by shouts and gestures, to come mix it with them. Thompson expected Benison to charge. After they had stared at each other for a few seconds, Major John Doyle blew his whistle to signal a charge and led his men forward, sabers swinging. Several of Benison's men managed a quick pistol shot before turning to flee. Among those cut out of their saddles was Major Benison.

Screven's command was composed mostly of reformed Tories who had taken advantage of Rutledge's proclamation and claimed clemency in return for serving six months in the militia. They heard the firing. They listened. They fled. Across Wambaw Bridge they scampered, throwing off the planks as they ran. The survivors of Benison's dragoons tore through the camp. James noted that the courage of his men was beginning to falter, and he gave orders to retreat to the bridge. Two British dragoons attempted to cut him down with their swords. Holding them off with his pistol, James suddenly wheeled and forced his horse to leap the gap in the bridge flooring, some say a distance as great as twenty feet. On the far side he managed to rally the men, who gave some check to the enemy.

In the middle of the American camp, just as the sun was setting, Thompson sounded the retreat and fell back to join his infantry at Drake's Plantation. He estimated that he had killed at least thirty of the rebels, several of whom he judged "by their dress to be officers of distinction."

Back at Jacksonborough, Marion received the intelligence that Thompson had crossed the Cooper. The Assembly was more than willing to grant him leave. On February 24 he had set out, accompanied by Maham, trotting across country to Mepkin Plantation. There they learned that the enemy dragoons, after making a feint toward that camp, had withdrawn. Feeling that there was no immediate danger, Marion stopped to refresh himself. Maham rode over to his own plantation to attend to personal business and recover from a light indisposition.

Marion had little time to rest; a messenger rode in with an account of the flight of the brigade. Calling out Maham's dragoons, he led them at a fast clip toward the Wambaw. After thirty miles of hard riding, on February 25, they halted to collect provisions at the widow Tydiman's Plantation between Echaw and Wambaw.

They were near enough to the reported position of the enemy to expect a possible attack. Marion gave orders to post the men in a posture of defense. The approach to the house was by a lane with high fences on either side. Before the house and beyond the land lay a sizable field flanked by a large pond on the right. Captain John Caraway Smith stationed his dragoons as pickets in the lane. All seemed secure.

At three o'clock that morning Thompson, leaving his infantry to follow, led his cavalry forward to survey the scene of his victory the afternoon before. He received information that Horry was ill at a house about nine miles away and that Maham's horsemen were encamped not too far away.

A little over a half hour after Marion's arrival at Tydiman's, the enemy suddenly appeared in the field, maneuvering into battle formation. They waited. Thompson, noticing the river to the rear of Marion's position cutting off a retreat, decided to attack. Marion stationed a company of dismounted men behind the rail fence to provide covering fire for Maham's dragoons once they had formed. Captain Smith led his men to the left to avoid the pond and reach the enemy. The lack of drill and proper discipline became evident as the riders fell into disorder at the unaccustomed maneuver. Thompson thought they were attempting to make their escape through the swamp and ordered a countercharge.

As they spurted forward, Smith's horsemen reined up their mounts, turned, and fled. Some attempted to escape by swimming the Santee. Lieutenant Smizer drowned; others disappeared beneath the water as British sharpshooters picked them off. Captain Smith was able to lead a number of his command to Wambaw Bridge and there steady them. Marion, with difficulty, rallied a number of others in the woods about half a mile from the field. He sent them back to cover the retreat of the foot soldiers. The enemy made no attempt to pursue but fell back to Wappetaw Creek.

Thompson felt that he had already inflicted considerable damage upon Marion, although he was not sure of the partisan losses. He was happy about the forty horses he had captured. Much officers' baggage had been taken, including "General Marion's Tent and his Canteens full of Liquor, which afforded a timely supply for the Troops."

It was some time before all the fugitives of the brigade were rounded up; some came forward with reluctance, others never did appear. Although the Charleston *Royal Gazette* said that Marion had lost about a hundred men and that he himself had been drowned, he reported casualties of eight killed, seven wounded, and thirteen missing, "but the disgrace was great." A number of men had lost both their mounts and their weapons.

It wasn't much of a brigade now under Marion. Maham's regiment numbered less than sixty, while Horry's was even less. With such a bedraggled force, Marion adopted the only course open to him and fell back to the old retreat at Cantey's Plantation. Although not completely at fault, Captain Smith resigned his commission the day after the skirmish.

Both Horry and Maham tried to place the blame for the defeat upon Marion. Horry declared that had Marion been with the brigade rather than in the legislature, the British stroke would have been unsuccessful. Maham was to blame him for Smith's misadventure, stating that as an "infantry officer," his orders were too vague and led the officers to believe that they were to retreat and not fight. Yet much of the blame should be laid to the fact that so many of Maham's "new-made Whigs" did not possess the proper enthusiasm for fighting against their former allies. There was always the lingering fear in the backs of their minds that if captured by the British they might well be hanged for desertion or even treason. Greene, however, dismissed the setback with "There is no guarding against so superior a force" and offered Marion a part of Sumter's brigade to swell his strength.[1]

Governor Mathews attempted to strengthen Marion's shadow brigade by utilizing the new militia law and calling out three classes of men, each to serve one month in rotation. The theory was better than the practice, for few men answered the summons. Still there was work to be done. There were provisions still going into Charleston and this flow had to be disrupted.

Now that Georgetown was an open port again, trading vessels were dropping anchor in Winyah Bay. Mathews ordered the harbor fortified and that Marion station a party there "under an Active & Vigilant Officer." This officer was to be granted near dictatorial powers in the regulation of prices of necessities sold in the town; those items considered to be luxuries were to be priced at whatever the customers would be willing to pay. The prices of such articles as salt, coffee, tea, and medicines were to be established by the officer in command, with Mathews specifying that salt should not be sold for more than four dollars a bushel. All public stores were to be removed to Black Mingo under guard. The governor directed that these operations be carried out under Marion's overall supervision.

Peter Horry was Marion's choice as commandant of Georgetown. Horry's regiment had ridden often and hard of late and were due for a rest, and the selection was a way of rewarding a good friend and an excellent soldier.

With his brigade reduced and the regiments of Horry and Maham little more than skeleton units (mainly due to a late rash of desertions), the general felt it best to combine the two corps. He proposed to Mathews that they be combined in a legion similar to Lee's. After discussing the matter with Greene, the governor gave his approval on March 12.

The idea was sound, although Marion should have realized that it contained the seeds of an internal explosion. The problem arose out of the selection of a commanding officer for the new legion. On the surface it would appear that Peter Horry would be the logical choice, on the basis of his long seniority and for the long and valuable service he had rendered to the cause. But the colonel had been ill, and, according to one contemporary, he "failed in one most essential requisite in the command of cavalry, and that was horsemanship." Horry loved the dash and the excitement that came with commanding mounted troops. Despite the grief he had caused Marion in the past, the general came to the conclusion that Hezikiah Maham would be the more effective officer to lead the new legion, a decision concurred in by Greene.

Horry was already irritable. Georgetown was being harassed by privateers operating out of North Carolina who practically blockaded the town, plundering those vessels seeking entry to the port. He was having his troubles with the merchants of Georgetown who had begun to "murmur" when the colonel had placed rather heavy restrictions upon their operations. When he learned that Maham had been given command of the new legion, his temper bristled. Although Horry had agreed to the consolidation of the regiments, he never dreamed that Maham would be selected over him; in fact it is to be suspected that Horry would have raised few objections had any other officer been selected for the post. He was also incensed because he was expecting to be made a brigadier general, and although Marion had attempted to secure the promotion for his friend, it had gone to William Henderson.

Marion was distressed with the colonel's reactions and suggested that he reserve judgment until they could discuss the matter personally. He quite frankly stated his opinion that Horry was the better leader of infantry while Maham was better suited for mounted troops, and that was why Horry had been appointed commandant of Georgetown, as it had been determined to hold that post at all costs. The horses, saddles, and cavalry weapons of his former command had been turned over to Maham, with the dismounted men sent into Georgetown, although Marion had given Maham's recruiting officers permission to try to persuade them to switch to the mounted corps.

When Greene confirmed Marion's selection, Horry's already worn conceit was not strong enough to absorb the blow. He gave notice that he no longer considered Marion as a friend, with "I am sensible to whom I am indebted for being turned out of Service and Mayham Continued." In a more dignified tone he assured Greene that he would accept the decision for "you say Genl. Marion, thinks it is for the good of the Service." He demanded an investigation. But the more he brooded, the more he convinced himself that he had been humiliated more than he could bear. He complained to Greene of the injustice put upon him by his country and, "Therefore I have not great ambition to persevere in her ill-treatment. Although she is welcome to what is past." Greene had already wearied of the dispute with "I have said all upon it I can say." Turning over the command of the Georgetown garrison to Captain William Allston, Horry mounted and rode home, out of the war he had fought for seven long years and away from the friend at whose side he had ridden.[2]

Hezikiah Maham served but a short while in his new command. Falling ill, he returned to his home in St. Stephen's Parish, escorted by a small band of militia to protect him from stray loyalists. The news that he was confined to his bed spread. Lieutenant Joseph Robbins of Cunningham's Tories was one of those who heard the rumor. Stealing a page from Marion's book, he led a party some sixty miles on a swift dash across country and on May 16 surprised the militia stationed around Maham's poorly guarded home. Bursting into the house, they found Maham, a Lieutenant Smith, and a doctor eating dinner. Robbins wanted to take Maham with him as a captive, but since his prisoner was too ill to travel comfortably, he allowed him to sign a parole. However, the Tory leader was so anxious to get on his way that he forgot and left the signed parole lying on the table. Maham felt that since Robbins was not a recognized commanding officer, and since the enemy no longer actually held the parole, he was no longer bound by its restrictions. When he recovered from his illness, he wished to resume the command of the legion. Marion, perhaps remembering Isaac Hayne, refused, reasoning that since the colonel admittedly signed the document, he was honor bound to abide by its terms.[3]

Although his brigade seemed to be slowly disintegrating, there was still much for Marion to do. Greene sent him first one place and then another and felt that he should range widely to protect the slaves, for the commanding general was convinced of the "enemy's intentions to steal all . . . they can, and carry them off." There were alarming reports that the British were going to make a sally in force out of Charleston and that seven hundred Negroes had been armed to take the field.

Marion had wearied of shifting around because of so much unconfirmed information, and felt that Greene's fears were groundless. He also felt that he was being put upon to serve the whims of an over-cautious general. When he was shifted to Bacon's Bridge between Greene and the enemy, he complained, "This place is a starving hole, where nothing can be had and nothing can be expected but hard knocks."

When there was a report that the enemy had sailed for Georgetown, Marion was ordered to march his brigade to that place. After a forced march of four days they reached White's Bridge where it was learned that this, too, was a false alarm. They had marched 160 miles with no provisions other than a ration of rice and the scrawny cattle they had been able to round up in the woods along the way.

When the Pennsylvania Continental Line, because of the lack of pay, provisions, and rum, grew restless, Greene put down a possible mutiny by the execution of the ringleader, Sergeant Charles Gosnall. Marion was rushed back to take a position between the Southern Army and the enemy for fear the enemy might take advantage of the confusion.[4]

Marion, along with almost everyone else, had grown tired of the never-ceasing civil war that had raged so long in South Carolina. So were many of the loyalists, but those who had been most active feared that they could expect no mercy from the Whigs once the British Army evacuated Charleston. Greene expressed his wish to avoid an "unnecessary effusion of blood."

The backlash of one event in North Carolina was to be felt in South Carolina. The notorious Tory partisan, David Fanning, along with Colonel Hector McNeil, had slipped into the town of Hillsborough during the early morning hours of September 12, 1781 and had captured Governor Thomas Burke. After a battle with the local militia under General John Butler, in which Fanning had been sorely wounded, the Tories had marched for the coast.

Later, not too long after his recovery, Fanning drifted south with McNeil and began to raise some of those loyalists who had formerly served with Micajah Ganey and who, disregarding the treaty made with Horry on June 17, 1781, began to work their way down the Waccamaw River, doing a great deal of michief. Large numbers of Tories from North Carolina, particularly from Bladen County, came into the "neutral ground" established by the treaty, paying no attention to the protests of the former loyalists who wished to live in peace. Ganey wished to drive them out but discovered that he was not strong enough; in fact some of the more unhappy in his own district forced Ganey to lead them into the field again. Ganey was not too reluctant to take the field as his people had been frequently subjected to the plunderings of the men led by Lieutenant Colonel Maurice Murphy. Whigs on both sides of the boundary were distressed by these raiders as they swung back and forth across the line, and according to Marion, did "Mischief, such as Robbing & Stealing & has Shot at some men & abused some with their Swords."

The small force under Colonel Baxter stationed in the area to keep the Tories under control was too weak to block the movements of a stronger foe. Mathews suggested that Marion send someone into the area to determine if "this fellow will bring us and himself too into trouble very soon."

The situation had grown so turbulent that Judge Aedanus Burke noted that "The very females talk as familiarly of Sheding blood & destroying the Tories as the men do," and declared that one member of the Assembly had twenty-five notches filed into the barrel of his pistol as a tally of the Tories whom he had personally killed. "Out-lyers" crawled out of the swamps to seek revenge before the British left. There was one pitched battle fought at night at Seven Creeks in North Carolina. Parties slipping swiftly through the woods constantly disrupted the Cheraw militia, and when Colonel Thomas Wade had come out, they had whipped him in a short fire fight. This activity on the fringes of major operations had to be subdued so that the regular forces could get on with driving the British from the state.

Greene had ordered Marion to come into camp to bolster his own strength, but the brigade had no sooner begun the march for the Ashley River than local conditions intervened. Governor Mathews and Governor Alexander Martin of North Carolina had agreed on a joint expedition into Tory country to put down the uprising. Marion was given the command. His force was to be supplemented by the North Carolina legionary corps of Major Joel Lewis, who was to rendezvous with him at Ami's Mill on Drowning Creek. Greene ordered him to attempt to renegotiate the truce, and even General Leslie sent a letter advising the Tories of the present "critical situation." Marion led Maham's dragoons into the Williamsburg District and up the Peedee. He moved with such dispatch that his presence was not suspected until he was well into the area.

The loyalists showed no real inclination to fight. Ganey sent in a flag asking for a brief armistice while disagreements could be worked out; he was unwilling to renew the agreement he had made with Horry. Commissioners from both sides attempted to work out details, but their first meeting was so rife with arguments, charges, and countercharges that it almost resulted in blows.

The breakup of the conference was followed by a brief but fierce skirmish, and it appeared that there would be no treaty in the near future. Marion's brigade was needed for operations along the Santee and the Cooper to prevent enemy foraging parties from coming out of Charleston. An invitation was sent across the Peedee for Ganey to come in for a conference at Burch's Mill. Several of the brigade officers protested that a personal confrontation with a man of Ganey's character was beneath the dignity of Marion; he quieted them with the statement that he "aimed at no higher dignity than serving his Country."

On June 8, 1782 Marion and Ganey met at Burch's Mill. The treaty they agreed to contained essentially the same terms that Ganey had submitted to the year before: all loyalists would restore plundered property when possible, declare themselves to be peaceful citizens, take up all deserters from the American Army and deliver them to the proper authorities and, after signing oaths of allegiance to both South Carolina and the United States, would agree to the laws of each. Some "atrocious offenders" were excepted from the benefits of the agreement. Those who preferred to remain with the British were to be permitted safe conduct, along with their families, into British lines. Joseph Jones, who had killed Colonel Kolb, along with David Fanning and his followers, were among those excepted, but they managed to escape capture.[5]

Micajah Ganey, despite his wrong-mindedness in political affiliations, was a man of principle. After requesting and receiving permission from Marion, he journeyed into Charleston and formally resigned his royal militia commission to General Leslie. Then he returned to Marion's headquarters where he and a number of his followers enlisted for the six months required by law to secure a full pardon. They were to distinguish themselves in future activities.

Greene was pleased with the result of the negotiations, telling Marion, "To save the effusion of human blood must be the wish of every human and generous bosom." The British, on the other hand, put out the word that only a handful of the Tories had agreed to the settlement.

And not all Tories were readily accepted back into the good graces of their former enemies. Old wounds were slow in healing. At Burch's Mill a Tory by the name of Jeff Butler had come in seeking amnesty. The camp began to murmur, as he was recognized as one at whose hands a number of good Whigs along the Peedee had suffered. Feelings were so strong that some of the members of the brigade stated quite frankly that no matter what concessions or amnesty were granted the man, they would see to it that he was killed. After giving Butler the sanctuary of his own tent, Marion issued a warning to his brigade, "The man you would destroy has submitted. Both law and honour sanction my resolution. I will take him to my tent, and at the hazard of my life, protect him."

Marion gave no reply when his men countered, "Butler shall be dragged to death from your tent. To defend such a wretch is an insult to humanity." The general quietly told his officers to send him those of their men in whom they placed the greatest trust. He told these men that although he personally held Butler in the highest contempt, he still had to defend him or perish in the attempt. The night they silently spirited Butler out of the camp to safety.

David Fanning also appeared in the neighborhood with a party of thirty men, hoping to recruit support and swearing he would get Marion "dead or alive." Marion spread his men out in a net of small groups to stamp out any brush fires of revolt that might spring up. Fanning went on into Charleston and sent out a flag asking that his wife be permitted to join him. Ganey supported the request of his former comrade in arms. Marion, over the protests of his officers, granted the request, explaining that if he refused, "we fix a serpent in our bosom." Although Marion gave Mrs. Fanning a safe conduct, the Tory leader complained, "He would not let her have any of our property, not even a negro to wait on her." His anger festered and from this time on he almost daily solicited General Leslie for a command, and allowed he would "for a handsome reward," bring the heads of both Marion and Greene into Charleston.[6]

By this time Peter Horry had become restless and had begun to long for the field again. He wrote Greene to give him another command, but the general, in a curt reply, suggested that the growing possibility of "an evacuation of Charles Town will I hope render your further favours unnecessary."

Greene, however, needed all the help he could get. Marion left the Peedee around the middle of July, leaving 150 men with Colonel Baxter "to over Awe those who have submitted & subdue the few which have secreted themselves." Greene, who had moved down the west bank of the Edisto and had taken post just sixteen miles from Charleston, requested him to station himself at Wadboo. Because of the supply situation, Marion kept on the move, shifting from one camp to another on the east side of the Cooper River, his primary mission to cut enemy supply lines and prevent a surprise of the Southern Army. One patrol of twelve men, led by Captain G. S. Capers, encountered a party of twenty-six Negro cavalrymen—one of the "dragoon" units formed by the enemy to round up deserters. They were escorting three men in irons whom Capers recognized as friends. He charged. The blacks were cut down.

Marion, despite the makeshift makeup of his command, was desperately attempting to whip his men into some semblance of a military unit. Almost daily there were orders urging the officers to check the excesses of their men in everything from the unnecessary firing of arms to plundering. Courts martial were frequent, including those of some officers who were brought up for disobedience of orders. His militia were grumbling about the nonpayment of wages and the lack of clothing and provisions. Many were going home.

At Lenud's Ferry in early August, because of his shrinking strength, Marion consolidated the remains of Maham's regiment into the cavalry commanded by James Conyers. Normally Maham would have assumed the command, but he was still on parole, and Major Conyers took over the direction of the troop.[7]

Marion made one quick dash to Georgetown when Greene received word that a water-borne force had been sent against that place. The enemy were recalled when a messenger carrying Greene's orders to Marion to station himself in a strong posture at that place was captured. As it turned out, the objective of the enemy was merely to collect rice for the Charleston garrison, and they had no designs on Georgetown.

In late August Marion moved to his favorite bivouac, Fair Lawn. The spacious house, with the slave quarters stretching out on either side, was ideal; the mansion house was utilized as headquarters, while the men were sheltered in the sturdy slave cabins. An open field, stretching nearly a mile to the rear, guarded against any sudden attack from that direction. Not only was the house of such strong construction as to withstand musket fire, but the cedars bordering each side of the lane leading to the house let down their intertwined branches to almost touch the ground. This offered excellent cover should an enemy attack the camp. The cavalry that still remained under his command were posted some six miles away because of a forage problem.

On August 29 Marion received word that an attack was to be made against him. Intelligence reported that Major Thomas Fraser, leading a hundred dragoons supported by a number of the black dragoons, had crossed the Cooper with an intention of surprising the guards at Biggin's Bridge. Fraser had come out on the twenty-first. At Biggin's Church he had captured several prisoners who told him that Marion was encamped on Wadboo

Creek at Fair Lawn. Fearing that Marion would attack him when he realized that he was in the area, Fraser moved toward the enemy in a probing action to determine his strength. Not daring to attack the partisans from the front, he swung around some four miles to come in on the rear of Fair Lawn. He ran into a picket, killed several men, and took two prisoners, while the others ran away to give the alarm.

As his cavalry were some six miles away, and the only mounted men with him were the officers, Marion formed them into a patrol and sent them out to scout under Gavin Witherspoon. Part of his men he stationed in the cedars along the lane. Others were posted in three small outbuildings on the left.

Emerging from the field at the back of the house, Fraser spotted Witherspoon's reconnaissance squad near a picket. He charged. Witherspoon wheeled his men and dashed back toward Fair Lawn. Witherspoon suddenly pulled up to the left as if to cover the flight of his men. A British trooper shot forward, and as he raised himself in the stirrups to deliver a fatal blow, Captain Witherspoon calmly raised his carbine and shot him out of the saddle. A Captain Dawkins was wounded.

Marion had spotted the enemy when the major began the chase. He called in his pickets. When Witherspoon shot down the enemy trooper, the men in the cedars loosed a mighty shout. Fraser threw his entire force in a charge. When they heard the shouts from the cedars, with an answering cry they veered left and charged toward the trees. They were met with a shattering volley from muskets loaded with buckshot fired a distance of only thirty yards. Twenty enemy dragoons dropped from their saddles, four of them dead. Ten horses were killed. One officer, Captain Robert Gillies, was among the dead. With the blast of the volley, the horses hitched to the American ammunition wagon bolted. Five of Marion's men leaped aboard horses taken from the enemy and actually regained possession of the wagon but were obliged to leave it when charged by a larger body.

Fraser rallied his men; they milled around in the field out of range and for the next hour and a half made no move to renew the battle. Several of Marion's men crept along the fence to get near enough to singe the British flank. Several times they formed and charged but always pulled up short before they were within musket range. They had been hurt badly. In addition to those killed, there were three officers and eight men wounded. Among those who had fought with Marion that day were Micajah Ganey and his ex-Tories, and the little general was pleased with the way they had stood fast and fought their ex-allies. Some of the former loyalists, however, had not been so steadfast but had wavered and then fled when the fighting grew warm. Marion would have liked to take on Fraser's dragoons on even terms, but his mounted troops had not yet come up and, since the loss of his wagon, he was low on ammunition. As usual, the claims of the enemy were inconsistent with Marion's own reports of his casualties. To Greene he wrote that the enemy had lost six men killed and fourteen wounded. His own loss, or so he said, was one member of the brigade wounded and three captured. He had also lost a pack mule laden with his tent and personal baggage. He gave the order to retreat over the Santee. It was the last order he was ever to issue on a field of battle.

Fraser moved off toward Huger's Bridge, taking five prisoners along and leaving five other badly wounded captives behind. As he traveled he collected about a hundred head of cattle and about fifty sheep for the Charleston garrison. Marion sent Major Conyers to trail and harass the enemy column.

Although he could not claim victory, Greene was pleased with the behavior of Marion's men and lent his praise: "I wish the militia in every part of the State was equally deserving the same applause." And Edward Rutledge, John's brother and a member of the Jacksonborough Assembly, was led to chuckle, "old Marion has foiled the Enemy of late in a very handsome Manner."

Conyers tracked the enemy as far as Huger's Bridge. It was his opinion that the enemy had suffered heavily because of the blood on the road. When he heard that Fraser had been reinforced he came back into the brigade.[8]

In early September there were recurring reports that the British were planning an expedition against Georgetown, because Fraser "was not satisfied with his last affair and determined to try another attempt." Marion did move down to the Georgetown area to keep an eye on it. Nothing happened.

In Charleston General Leslie, according to intelligence, was preparing to evacuate the city. The artillery had been removed from the fortifications. When the troops began embarking aboard transports, details came ashore at Lampriere's Point to fill the water casks before putting out to sea. There has been a story through the years that when Greene suggested that Marion ambush these parties, Marion replied that "not another drop [of blood] shall, with my consent, be lost. . . . I would rather send a party to protect them." Actually, he seems not to have held such noble sentiments. He explained to Greene that he was unable to attack the party in that the watering point was surrounded by a heavy abatis, it lay within range of the galleys and armed vessels lying offshore, and the working party was no farther than two hundred yards from their boats to which they could retreat. He dismissed the suggestion with "The Situation is too Advantageous to them, to Attack with any probability of Success. . . ."[9]

On December 14, 1782 the last British soldier left Charleston. Greene had agreed that there would be a peaceful changeover. Major General Anthony Wayne, with the report of the British morning gun, moved toward the British works, leading four companies of light infantry, a detachment of Lee's legion, and two artillery pieces. By three that afternoon Greene, accompanied by Governor Mathews, his Council, and other prominent citizens rode in triumphant procession into Charleston. The streets were crowded, as were the balconies, doors, and windows, with many shouting, "God bless you, Gentlemen! You are welcome home, gentlemen!"

The militia, however, were neither permitted to participate in nor witness the spectacle. There were some who suspected that there might be friction between the militia and Greene's army, although they gave no reason for their fears. Greene, on November 22, had taken particular pains to explain that he had been no party to an order excluding the militia, and he did say that Marion and three or four close friends could go in with the party that took possession of the town. Marion replied that the militia had no real desire to go into Charleston, but would much rather be allowed to go home. If put in the form of an order he would come, but he would rather not and gave as his reason that he had heard there was smallpox in Charleston and as he had never had it, he would prefer to remain outside.[10]

The militia were disbanded and told to go home. At Fair Lawn, beside the cedars, Brigadier General Francis Marion mustered his men. He spoke to them:

The General returns his warmest thanks to the officers and men who with unwaived patience & Fortitude have under gone the greatest fatigue & Hardships & with a Spirit & Bravery which must ever reflect the highest honour on them—no Citysins in the World Have ever done more [than] they have. He begs leave to give his Particular thanks to all the Officers & Men of the Country Militia for that Partiality to his Person, & ready Obedience to all Orders for two years And a half, which will be Remember'd with Gratitude to the end of his Life. He will always consider them with the Affection of a Brother & will be happy to Render them every Service in his power—he cannot doubt in the least of their Readiness to turn out Should this Country be ever again so unhappy as to be invaded by her cruel & Barbarous Enemys. He wishes them a long Continuance of happiness & the Blessings of Peace— [11]

With that he climbed aboard Ball and rode home from the wars.

Chapter XV

Francis Marion didn't have much to come home to. Pond Bluff was in ruins. Unfortunately, his farm was but a mile off the highway over which the British had marched many times; both friend and foe had pillaged and despoiled his belongings; his personal possessions were missing, his furniture was destroyed and his house burned. His cattle had been driven off, his horses stolen, and at least half of his slaves either taken up by the enemy or run away. Ten of his blacks were still living on the place.

As did many of his friends and neighbors as well as a number of his former enemies, Marion had to begin again almost from scratch. He did have his land and the remaining slaves with which to work it. He had been without pay for almost three years but hoped to be pensioned on half-pay. He was not. Somehow he managed to acquire seed, feed, and tools as well as food and clothing for his Negroes. Still, the memory of his accomplishments was green in the minds of the people of South Carolina. On February 26, 1783, before the formal peace treaty had been signed, his colleagues in the South Carolina Senate passed the resolution: "That the thanks of this House be given to Brigadier General Marion, in his place as a member of this House, for his eminent and conspicuous service to his country." They followed this by voting him a gold medal "as a mark of public approbation for his great, glorious and meritorious conduct." When it was moved that Thomas Sumter be accorded the same honor, the mention of his name occasioned such an acrimonious debate that the question was carried over until the following day. By that time tempers had softened enough so that gold medals were voted Isaac Huger, Andrew Pickens, and Sumter.

The following day the president of the senate made the formal presentation, extolling Marion in fulsome words of praise and ending, "Whilst the virtue of gratitude shall form a part of our national character, your important services to this country can never be forgotten." Marion, in his own way, expressed his appreciation for the honors conferred upon him and his officers and added: "I shall always be ready to exert my abilities for the good of the state and the liberties of her inhabitants."

As a Senator he remained obstinately faithful to his ideals. This became evident when a bill was introduced into the legislature to protect from litigation those officers who had confiscated the possessions of the inhabitants pay or reward their troops. Adhering to his continuing abhorrence of "Sumter's Law," he rose to his feet when the clerk called his name in roll call. He demanded that his name be withdrawn from the list of those officers who were to be exempt from prosecution. He explained in what for him were elegant terms, "If I have given any occasion for complaint, I am ready to answer in property and person. If I have wronged any man I am willing to make him restitution. If, in a single instance, in the course of my command, I have done that which I cannot fully justify, Justice requires that I should suffer."

Despite Marion's protests the bill passed, exempting Sumter

and his officers from litigation by those whom he had plundered, with the Assembly considering Sumter "as having acted with Honorable and upright Views, and highly Meriting the approbation of his Country. . . ." All those persons who put forth claims of mistreatment were directed to apply to the legislature for redress. Pickens was also granted this protection; Marion was not. Yet the controversy continued until finally, in 1788, the North Carolina Legislature passed an act protecting from suits those of the state's citizens who had joined Sumter and had been given confiscated Negroes.

Despite the former activity of the loyalists, Marion, along with Christopher Gadsden and Aedanus Burke, was ready to accept them back into the life of the community. They sponsored bills in the Assembly favorable to the futures of Tories and requesting the legislators not to sully their minds with thoughts of retaliation. Soon after the end of the war, an elderly loyalist petitioned the Assembly for a pardon. To the surprise of many and the distress of others, the general spoke in favor of the prayer for forgiveness. "God has given us victory," he declared, "Let us show our gratitude to Heaven, which we shall not do by cruelty to man." [1]

In peace Francis Marion received more recognition than he had in war, perhaps because men now had an opportunity to measure his operations in proper perspective rather than attempt to evaluate the effectiveness of a single, slashing raid. The Continental Congress, on September 30, 1783 promoted him to full colonel in the Continental Line, which wasn't so great as it might seem when it is realized that on this same date that body also appointed twenty-six brevet brigadier generals.

There was one possibility that he might be called into the field again when the Privy Council alerted his brigade for action during the Tory-Whigs riots in Charleston in July 1784.

A year later the South Carolina General Assembly voted to repair Fort Johnson and station a garrison therein. There is some reason to suspect that this post was created especially for

Marion, for his financial distresses were no secret, and an outright offer of money would have insulted the sensitive little brigadier. Governor Benjamin Guerrard went through the formalities of appointing Marion as commandant. The salary was generous, £500 a year, but within a short time the legislature, with some of the members urging economic reform, reduced the pay to $500. Marion grew unhappy that the existence of Fort Johnson had become a political football, "but his debts made it prudent to submit." The legislature often neglected appropriating operational funds and money for the garrison's salaries. Marion sent letters into town rather than go in person and risk exposure to the smallpox then reported in Charleston.[2]

His duties at the fort were not so strenuous that he neglected his family. His life as a bachelor was a lonely existence, and much of his free time was spent with relatives along the Santee whose children he had come to regard almost as his own. His nephew Theodore, son of Job, was the cause of romance entering his life. Theodore began to pay court to Charlotte, the daughter of the widow Ashby, whose husband, Anthony, had been a captain in the old Second Regiment.

Theodore became aware of the not-so-secret whispers being bandied about with regard to his uncle. It was said that Mary Esther Videau, Marion's first cousin and the daughter of Anne Cordes and Henry Videau, a personable spinster of St. John's Parish, had long been an admirer of the Fox and had been seen to blush when the general's name was mentioned in her presence. Theodore suggested to his uncle that Mary Esther was interested.

And so it was that Francis Marion went a-courting. Mary Videau was a large woman of forty-nine years and the general had known her since they were both children. Her disposition was similar to that of her fiancé, and some went so far as to note that she even looked like the general, which may explain why she had never married in an age when brides were at a premium. But she did have money, although there is no indication that her fortune was more attractive to the general than her personal qualities. His attentions were well received. He proposed. She accepted. On Thursday, April 20, 1786, at the age of fifty-four years, Francis Marion became a married man. Theodore married Charlotte that same day.

Francis and Mary Marion lived a life of contentment if not one of complete happiness. William Dobein James explained their frustration: "In short, nothing could have made this matrimonial connexion more happy, but its being more fruitful. They never had an heir." Marion did later adopt a grand-nephew, Francis Marion Dwight, in the hope of perpetuating his name. Dwight was required to change his surname to Marion, but two wives bore him only girls.[3]

The wealth of Mary Videau aided in the recovery of her husband's fortunes. Their worth was swelled some by a bit of nepotism practiced by Marion at Fort Johnson. Thirty-six Negro slaves, with Job Marion as overseer, had been hired from their owners to work in repairing the walls. Of the total number, four had been hired from "Mary E. Videau," while another ten had been employed from the estate of Gabriel Marion. But shortly afterward, feeling himself to be "an Old Alminack out of date with the Public," he resigned his post as commandant of Fort Johnson and returned to Pond Bluff. To replace the plantation home that had been destroyed during the war a simple unpainted one story frame building was constructed of cypress. The bounty of the land was good, and the Marions prospered.

Francis Marion could never erase the excitement of the war years from his mind, even after his health began to fail. When his memories became too overpowering, he would pack his camp equipage on his two old sumpter mules, and, with Mary and the faithful Oscar in attendance, he would wander over the High Hills of the Santee, visiting old haunts and reliving the past with those he had led along the road to adventure.[4]

Many of those who had followed him in the field still looked to their old general for advice and guidance. One was the hot-headed Hezikiah Maham. Maham had fallen into debt and had been declared the loser in a subsequent law suit. When served with an execution warrant he grabbed his sword and forced the deputy sheriff to literally eat the document. When Sheriff Daniel Stevens came to arrest Maham, he fled to the swamps. Afraid to come out of hiding, he requested Marion to come to see him. He detailed his misadventures, admitting that he was at fault. He asked Marion's advice as to whether he should seek safety in flight. Marion replied, "Go, submit yourself to the laws of your country, and I then will be your friend to the best of my ability. Resist—refuse—and we are separated forever." Maham gave himself up to the authorities. He was to die in 1789.[5]

Francis Marion grew old gracefully, something of a folk hero in his own time. He was a good citizen, performing those tasks in the community for which he felt he was qualified. Time after time the voters of St. John's Parish returned him to the senate of the South Carolina Assembly. He was a hardworking though not particularly skillful politician, nor did he exhibit political ambitions. Most of his interests were concentrated on local problems or were related to the militia.

He did, however, demonstrate more than a passing interest in public education, perhaps because of his own rather vague and inadequate preparation. It was his belief that free schools were the only means of reaching the poorest and greatest segment of the population and that the responsibility of establishing such schools belonged to the state legislature. It was his feeling that an educated citizenry was South Carolina's best defense against ambitious political demagogues. To his grandnephew and name-sake, he urged that every opportunity for learning be pursued, as "You are advancing in Years fast & Your time of Education is short."

In 1790 he spent twenty-five days as a member of the convention that drew up a new South Carolina constitution. After its completion, and acceptance, he withdrew from active political life. In his personal politics he remained a Federalist, although not a dogmatic one.

Most of his time during his later years was devoted to the improvement of the militia. He commanded a brigade and spent more time in training than did the average militia officer of his day. He retained this command until 1794, when the state militia underwent a reorganization and his health began to fail. Interestingly enough, under the reorganization, Peter Horry commanded the sixth brigade, composed of the militia in the vicinity of Georgetown. John Postell and John Baxter were colonels of the same brigade.

Upon Marion's retirement from public life, the people of Georgetown appointed a committee to draw up a resolution expressing their gratitude for his past services. William James, who had been little more than a lad when he served in Marion's brigade, but was now a successful lawyer, drew up the document. After a high-sounding recital of the general's military accomplishments, he concluded with: "Continue Citizen General in peace to Till those Acres which you once wrested from the hands of An Enemy. Continue to Enjoy Dignity, accompanied with Ease, & quiet & to lengthen out your days, blessed with the Consciousness of a conduct Unaccused of Rapine or Oppression, & of Actions ever directed by the Purest patriotism." The first name signed to this testimonial was that of Peter Horry.[6]

But now the years and the lasting effects of the hardships of partisan warfare began to take their toll. In November 1794 he was beginning to complain of a "Constant pain in my head for some time, by Great cold but No fevor." Peter Horry, who as long ago as August, 1783, had recovered from his pique, often came to visit and reminisce of those days they had spent in the saddle, riding side by side. On what was to be his last visit, the two had talked until ten o'clock in the evening. When Horry suggested that it was time for the sick man to go to bed, Marion replied, "Oh, no, we must not talk of bed yet. It is but seldom, you know, that we meet, and as this may be our last, let us take all we can of it in chat. What do you think of the times?"

He was a good prophet. Not long after Horry's visit, Francis Marion took to his bed with his last illness. As he began to grow weaker, he noticed Mary sitting beside his bed, trying to choke back her tears. With great calm he said, "My dear, do not weep for me. I am not afraid to die, for thank God, I can lay my hand upon my heart and say since I came to man's estate, I have never intentionally done wrong to any man." Death came for him at Pond Bluff on February 27, 1795.

He left his estate to Mary, but when she died, or remarried, it was to go to his adopted son, provided he never used his former name of Dwight again. His wife lived to the age of seventy-seven, dying July 26, 1815, at Pineville, St. Stephen's Parish. Her body was placed beside that of her husband. She had grown heavy over the years; when she died she weighed 230 pounds.[7]

Marion was buried in the family graveyard on Gabriel's Plantation at Belle Isle. The marble slab above his grave read:

Sacred to the Memory
of
BRIG. GEN. FRANCIS MARION
Who departed this life, on the 27th of February, 1795
In the Sixty-Third Year of His Age
Deeply regretted by all his fellow citizens
HISTORY
will record his worth, and rising generations embalm
his memory, as one of the most distinguished
Patriots and Heroes of the American Revolution:
which elevated his native Country
TO HONOUR AND INDEPENDENCE
and
secured to her the blessings of
LIBERTY AND PEACE
This tribute of veneration and gratitude is erected
in commemoration of

FRANCIS MARION:

the noble and disinterested virtues of the
CITIZEN:
and the gallant exploits of the
SOLDIER;
Who lived without fear, and died without reproach.

Although his career as an officer in the Continental Army had
been relatively drab, aside from the sieges of Charleston and
Savannah, Francis Marion always cherished his commission as
a Continental officer, even after he gained no small amount of
fame as a partisan leader. He proved himself a good officer in the
regular army, following orders with dispatch and with a devotion
to both duty and discipline. Yet he demonstrated an almost vivid
imagination when forced to operate on his own as a guerilla
leader. In fact, he became almost too independent and, at times,
appeared to resent taking orders from superior Continental
officers, especially when they suggested that he take orders from,
and cooperate with, Thomas Sumter. Still, he appeard willing to
operate as an adjunct to the Southern Army once Nathanael
Greene indicated some appreciation of Marion's efforts.

Perhaps the best thing that could have happened to him was
jumping from the window at Captain McQueen's party and
breaking his ankle. Under none of the restrictions of a British
parole, Francis Marion, in the short space of three months in the
fall of 1780, grew from a name in occasional British intelligence
reports to a problem of major concern for the enemy.

He had entered into the second phase of his military career
with few men or arms, little ammunition, and limited military
resources. But he was a natural partisan leader and was able to
utilize a relatively small striking force to its greatest potential
—his primary weapon was the element of surprise. His greatest
strength was in keeping his men well mounted, thereby frustrat-
ing the designs of a superior force to bring him to a decisive
action and destroy him. Horses were so important to his operations that those taken or killed were emphasized as much in his

reports as either his own or the enemy's casualties. Because of his wide-ranging activities, the threat of Marion was ofttimes more effective than his actual presence, for the British were compelled to weaken their primary forces by detaching units to strengthen isolated garrisons, provide convoy protection, or just to limit his sweep of operations.

As he operated as a partisan leader, Marion painted his future in bold strokes. Although not so obvious as Sumter, he was just as ambitious. The actions of Thomas Sumter should not be discounted—he was cast in a different mold. Cornwallis considered Sumter to be his greatest plague, and he had been responsible for the partisan movement in South Carolina. He was a good leader of men, despite being so "Enchanted with the Splendor of victory, he would wade in torrents of blood to attain it." Despite Marion's abhorrence of "Sumter's Law," the idea was still a good field expedient in those times of uncertainty, for it enabled Sumter to maintain a considerable number of men in the field who could move into action quickly. In contrast, Marion was held back by the fickleness of his men and sometimes was delayed awaiting their coming into the field, which tended to diminish his effectiveness. Marion, on the other hand, was well aware of the importance of coordinating his movements with those of the Southern Army. Perhaps the difference between the two militia generals was best summed up by a contemporary, Robert Gray, who observed, "Sumpter was bold & rash, and run many risks from which his good fortune always extricated him. Marion was timid & cautious & would risk nothing, yet both succeeded in their attempts." [8]

Francis Marion was no knight in shining armor, for his operations often bore a stamp of ruthlessness when he considered such a course necessary. His emotional conflicts were great, yet he was able to temper the cruelty of war with the compassion of peace. In such turbulent times, Francis Marion was an anachronism, yet he was a leader of men.

Notes

CHAPTER I

1. J. W. Fortescue, A History of the British Army (London, 1899), III, 271; Annual Register, 1781, p. 81.

2. Peter Horry and M. L. Weems, The Life of Gen. Francis Marion, A Celebrated Partisan Officer in the Revolutionary War, against the British and Tories in South Carolina and Georgia (Philadelphia, 1845), p. 20.

3. John Lawson, A New Voyage to Carolina, ed. Hugh T. Lefler (Chapel Hill, N.C., 1967), p. 19.

4. William Willis Boddie, History of Williamsburg (Columbia, S.C., 1923), pp. 37, 87, 90.

5. Ibid., pp. 90–91.

6. Horry and Weems, Marion, pp. 20–21; William Dobein James, A Sketch of the Life of Brig. Gen. Francis Marion and a History of His Brigade (Charleston, 1821), p. 16.

7. South Carolina Historical and Genealogical Magazine, XXIII (July 1922), 93 (hereafter cited as SCHGM).

8. South Carolina Gazette (Charleston), 4 April 1761; SCHGM, III (October 1902), 205.

9. SCHGM, I (July 1900), 261; Edward McCrady, South Carolina under Royal Government (New York, 1897), pp. 349–52.

10. William Moultrie, Memoirs of the American Revolution, So Far as It Related to the States of North and South Carolina, and Georgia (New York, 1802), II, 223n.

11. James, Marion, p. 17.

12. David Duncan Wallace, South Carolina: A Short History, 1520–1948 (Chapel Hill, N.C., 1951), pp. 257–60.

13. David Ramsay, History of South Carolina, From Its First Settlement in 1670 to the Year 1808 (Newberry, S.C., 1858), I, 136; Edward McCrady, South Carolina in the Revolution, 1775–80 (New York, 1902), pp. 13–14, 14n.; Peter Horry to Nathanael Greene, 20 April 1781, Nathanael Greene Papers, William L. Clements Library, University of Michigan, Ann Arbor, Michigan.

14. David Ramsay, The History of the Revolution of South-Carolina,

300

From a British Province to an Independent State (Trenton, N.J., 1785), I, 116; Wallace, *South Carolina*, p. 259.

15. Francis Marion Orderly Book, Henry L. Huntington Library, San Marino, California (hereafter cited as Marion Ord. Bk., H.L.).

16. SCHGM, XVII (July 1918), 95–96, 100.

17. Marion Ord. Bk., H.L.

18. Moultrie, *Memoirs*, I, 90–91.

19. Marion Ord. Bk., H.L.; McCrady, *South Carolina in the Revolution 1775–80*, pp. 66–68; Moultrie, *Memoirs*, I, 86–91.

20. Wallace, *South Carolina*, p. 268.

21. Moultrie, *Memoirs*, I, 109–10, 109n.; Marion Ord. Bk., H.L., SCHGM, III (October 1902), 199; VI (January 1905), 8.

22. Marion Ord. Bk., H.L.

23. *Ibid.*; Moultrie, *Memoirs*, I, 124; McCrady, *South Carolina in the Revolution, 1775–1780*, p. 127n.; Thomas Pinckney to Harriet Horry, 24 December 1775, Pinckney Family Papers, Library of Congress, Washington, D.C.

24. *North Carolina Historical Review*, XXX (January 1953), 50–55.

25. Worthington C. Ford *et al*, eds., *Journals of the Continental Congress, 1774–1789* (Washington, 1904–37), III, 326.

26. R. W. Gibbes, ed., *Documentary History of the American Revolution* (New York, 1853–57), II, 5; *The Lee Papers: Collections of the New-York Historical Society for the Years 1871 . . . 1872 . . . 1873 . . . 1874* (New York, 1872–75), II, 66.

27. Gibbes, *Documentary History of the American Revolution*, II, 8; *The Lee Papers*, II, 8; John Drayton, *Memoirs of the American Revolution, From Its Commencement to the Year 1776, Inclusive: as Relating to the State of South-Carolina and Occasionally Referring to the States of North-Carolina and Georgia* (Charleston, 1821), II, 280; Moultrie, *Memoirs*, I, 14, 14n.; Richard Hutson to Isaac Hayne, 24 June 1776, Richard Hutson Papers, Duke University, Durham, N.C.; Thomas Pinckney to Eliza Pinckney, 9 June 1776, Pinckney Family Papers, Library of Congress; John Armstrong to John Hancock, 24 June 1776, Papers of the Continental Congress, National Archives, Washington, D.C.; Marion Ord. Bk., H.L.

28. Marion Ord. Bk., H.L.

29. Thomas Pinckney to Eliza Pinckney, 9 June 1776, Pinckney Family Papers, Library of Congress.

30. Henry B. Dawson, *Battles of the United States by Sea and Land* (New York, 1858), I, 136–38; Precis of the Expedition to the Southern Colonies, German Papers, William L. Clements Library; *South Carolina and American General Gazette* (Charleston), 2 August 1776; Drayton, *Memoirs*, II, 296, 299; Moultrie, *Memoirs*, I, 174–80; *Lee Papers*,

II, 91–92; John Richard Alden, *General Charles Lee: Traitor or Patriot?* (Baton Rouge, 1951), pp. 126–127; Gibbes, *Documentary History of the American Revolution*, II, 6, 9; Richard Hutson to Isaac Hayne, 24 June 1776, Richard Hutson Papers, Duke University; Robert Howe to ——, 29 June 1776, Robert Howe Papers, Southern Historical Collection, University of North Carolina, Chapel Hill, N.C.; SCHGM, LX (July 1959), 126.

31. Charles Lee to Edmund Randolph, 14 July 1776; Papers of Continental Congress, National Archives; *Lee Papers*, II, 139–40; Gibbes, *Documentary History of the American Revolution*, I, 5; Marion Ord. Bk., H.L.; Thomas Pinckney to Harriet Horry, 29 June 1776, Pinckney Family Papers, Library of Congress.

32. Moultrie, *Memoirs*, I, 180; Marion Ord. Bk., H.L.; William Gilmore Simms, *The Life of Francis Marion* (New York, 1844), p. 74n.

CHAPTER II

1. Alden, *General Charles Lee*, pp. 131–32; Robert Howe Orderly Book, William L. Clements Library; Moultrie, *Memoirs*, I, 184; Thomas Jones to James Iredell, 23 July 1776, Charles E. Johnston Collection, North Carolina Department of Archives and History, Raleigh, N.C.; *Lee Papers*, II, 114–17, 125, 129, 153, 157–60.

2. *Lee Papers*, II, 186–87; Drayton, *Memoirs*, II, 334–36; Marion Ord. Bk., H.L.

3. Walter Clark, ed., *The State Records of North Carolina* (Goldsboro, Winston, N.C., 1895–1914), XI, 344–45, 361–62; XV, 683; Extract from Council Minutes, 25 October 1776, Jethro Sumner Papers, Southern Historical Collection; Howe to President of Council, 6 November 1776, Robert Howe Papers, Southern Historical Collection; William L. Saunders, ed., *The Colonial Records of North Carolina* (Raleigh, Goldsboro, N.C., 1886–98), X, 928–29.

4. Robert Howe to Richard Caswell, 10 April 1777, Caswell Letterbook, North Carolina Department of Archives and History; Drayton, *Memoirs*, II, 336; Moultrie, *Memoirs*, I, 186; II, 336–37; Ford, ed., *Journals of the Continental Congress*, V, 638.

5. SCHGM, XII (April 1912), 89; Gibbes, *Documentary History of the American Revolution*, I, 45; Marion Ord. Bk., H.L.; McCrady, *South Carolina in the Revolution*, 1775–1780, p. 204.

6. Gibbes, *Documentary History of the American Revolution*, I, 46, 54–55; Robert Howe Ord. Bk., William L. Clements Library.

7. Moultrie, *Memoirs*, I, 189; Marion Ord. Bk., H.L.

8. Marion Ord. Bk., H.L.; Gibbes, *Documentary History of the American Revolution*, I, 59, 61.

9. Horry and Weems, *Marion*, p. 34; Marion Ord. Bk., H.L.; Moultrie, *Memoirs*, I, 96.

10. Marion Ord. Bk., H.L.; *SCHGM*, XIII (October 1912), 98.

11. *North Carolina State Records*, XIII, 224–26, 332–34; Testimonial of William Haslan, 6 December 1778, Governors' Papers, North Carolina Department of Archives and History; Benjamin Lincoln to Richard Caswell, 22 December 1778, Caswell Letterbook, North Carolina Department of Archives and History.

12. Edmund C. Burnett, ed., *Letters of Members of the Continental Congress* (Washington, 1921–36), III, 512; Richard Walsh, ed., *The Writings of Christopher Gadsden* (Columbia, S.C., 1966), pp. 124–25, 128, 135, 151; *North Carolina State Records*, XV, 766–67.

13. Ford, *Journals of the Continental Congress*, IX, 823; XIII, 951; Howe to John Hancock, 24 November 1778, Papers of the Continental Congress, National Archives; *Collections of the New-York Historical Society for 1879* (New York, 1880), pp. 241–42, 250–51, 265–67; Howe to Lincoln, 27 December 1779, Benjamin Lincoln Papers, Massachusetts Historical Society, Boston, Mass.; Dawson, *Battles of the United States*, I, 479; Archibald Campbell to Germain, 16 January 1779, Germain Papers, William L. Clements Library; David Ramsay, *The History of the American Revolution* (London, 1793), II, 130–31.

14. Moultrie, *Memoirs*, I, 270; Marion Ord. Bk., H.L.; Frederic R. Kirkland, ed., *Letters on the American Revolution in the Library at "Karolfred"* (Philadelphia, 1941), p. 62; Marion to Lincoln, 14 February, 19 February, 23 February 1779, Lincoln Papers, Massachusetts Historical Society.

15. Moultrie, *Memoirs*, I, 374–39, 403–13; Moultrie to Lincoln, 4 May 1779, Miscellaneous Papers, William L. Clements Library; Diary of John Graham, William A. Graham Papers, North Carolina Department of Archives and History; Lincoln to Henry Laurens, 23 June 1779, Papers of the Continental Congress, National Archives; Lincoln to John Rutledge, 2 May 1779, Moultrie to Lincoln, 30 April, 8 May 1779, Lincoln Papers, Massachusetts Historical Society.

16. Moultrie, *Memoirs*, I, 426–27; Dawson, *Battles of the United States*, I, 497–98; *North Carolina State Records*, XIV, 118–20; Diary of John Graham, William A. Graham Papers, North Carolina Department of Archives and History; Marion Ord. Bk., H.L.

17. Moultrie, *Memoirs*, I, 426–37; Henry Lee, *Memoirs of the War in the Southern Department of the United States*, ed., Robert E. Lee (New York, 1870), pp. 129–30; Oliver Hunt Diary (copy), Duke University; Moultrie to Lincoln, 16 May 1779, Miscellaneous Papers, William L. Clements Library.

18. Lee, *Memoirs*, pp. 128–30; Charles Stedman, *History of the*

American War (London, 1794), II, 116; Moultrie, *Memoirs*, I, 479, 488–91; Lincoln to John Jay, 21 June 1779, Papers of the Continental Congress, National Archives; Joseph Johnson, *Traditions and Reminiscences Chiefly of the American Revolution in South Carolina* (Charleston, 1851), p. 225; Ramsay, *Revolution in South Carolina*, II, 29; Lincoln to Rutledge, 19 June 1779, Moultrie to Lincoln, 19 June, 20 June, 26 June 1779, Return of the South Carolina Continental Brigade Commanded by Colonel Charles Cotesworth Pinckney, 4 July 1779, Return of a Detachment of the 2ᵈ South Carolina Continental Regiment in Garrison in Fort Moultrie, Lincoln Papers, Massachusetts Historical Society; Hugh F. Rankin, *The North Carolina Continentals* (Chapel Hill, N.C., 1971), pp. 204–06.

19. Christopher Ward, *The War of the Revolution*, ed. John R. Alden (New York, 1952), II, 688–89; Moultrie, *Memoirs*, II, 33; Marion Ord. Bk., H.L.; Henry Laurens to Lincoln, 15 May 1779, Laurens to Moultrie, 15 May 1779, Laurens to John Jay, 5 September 1779, Papers of the Continental Congress, National Archives.

20. Marion Ord. Bk., H.L.; Alexander A. Lawrence, *Storm over Savannah: The Story of Count d'Estaing and the Siege of the Town in 1779* (Athens, Ga., 1951), pp. 30–59; Charles C. Jooe, Jr., ed., *The Siege of Savannah in 1779, as Described in Two Contemporaneous Journals of French Officers in the Fleet of Count d'Estaing* (Albany, N.Y., 1874), pp. 51–61; Benjamin Franklin Stevens, ed., *Facsimiles of Manuscripts in European Archives Relating to America, 1773–1783* (London, 1889–95), XXIII, no. 2018; Robert Beatson, *Naval and Military Memoirs of Great Britain, from 1727 to 1783* (London, 1804), VI, 180–84; Marion to Lincoln, 5 September 1779, Miscellaneous Papers, New York Public Library, New York, N.Y.

21. Marion Ord. Bk., H.L.; Lawrence, *Storm over Savannah*, pp. 84–123; Lincoln to Samuel Huntington, 22 October 1779, Papers of the Continental Congress; Ward, *War of the Revolution*, II, 692; Moultrie, *Memoirs*, II, 37–41; Franklin B. Hough, *The Siege of Savannah, by the Combined American and French Forces, under the Command of Gen. Lincoln, and the Count d'Estaing* (Albany, N.Y., 1866), pp. 160–74; Alexander Garden, *Anecdotes of the American Revolution* (Charleston, 1822, 1828), I, 13; II, 25; SCHGM, LX (July 1959), 126.

22. Charles C. Pinckney to Eliza Pinckney, 9 October 1779, Pinckney Family Papers, Library of Congress; Captain John Henry to Admiral Arbuthnot, 8 November 1779, Public Record Office, London (hereafter cited as PRO)/AD I/486.

23. Marion to [Lincoln], 9 December 1779, 13 January 1780, Preston Davie Collection, Southern Historical Collection; Moultrie to Marion, 13 November 1779, Lincoln to Marion, 25 November, 15 December,

30 December 1779, "Horry Papers," Peter Force Transcripts, Library of Congress; Marion Ord. Bk., H.L.

24. Marion Ord. Bk., H.L.; Lincoln to Marion, 30 December 1779, 11 January 1780, "Horry Papers," Force Transcripts, Library of Congress; Horry to Lincoln, 9 November 1779, Lincoln Papers, Massachusetts Historical Society; Horry to Nathanael Greene, 20 April 1781, Greene Papers, William L. Clements Library.

CHAPTER III

1. Marion to Lincoln, 21 January 1780, Revolutionary Manuscripts, Duke University; Henry Clinton, *The American Rebellion: Sir Henry Clinton's Narrative of His Campaigns, 1775–1782*, ed. William B. Willcox (New Haven, Conn., 1954), pp. 156–60; Intelligence, n.d., Governors' Papers, North Carolina Department of Archives and History; Lincoln to Washington, 23–24 January, 28–29 January 1780, Papers of the Continental Congress.

2. McCrady, *South Carolina in the Revolution, 1775–1780*, p. 436; Lincoln to Marion, 31 January 1780, "Horry Papers," Force Manuscripts, Library of Congress; SCHGM, VI (January 1905), 15.

3. Marion Ord. Bk., H.L.; [Franklin Benjamin Hough,] *The Siege of Charleston, By the British Fleet and Army under the Command of Admiral Arbuthnot and Sir Henry Clinton* (Albany, N.Y., 1867), pp. 27, 30, 68–69; Lincoln to Huntington, 14 February, 22 February 1780, Papers of the Continental Congress, National Archives; Ramsay, *History of the American Revolution*, II, 151–52; *American Historical Review*, V (April 1899), 483–89; Simms, *Marion*, p. 93.

4. Wallace, *South Carolina*, p. 292; James, *Marion*, p. 30; John Laurens to Washington, 9 April 1780, George Washington Papers, Library of Congress; *North Carolina State Records*, XV, 353–54.

5. Lee, *Memoirs*, p. 174; Garden, *Anecdotes of the American Revolution*, I, 18n.; McCrady, *Revolution in South Carolina, 1775–1780*, pp. 568–59; James, *Marion*, p. 31; Horry and Weems, *Marion*, pp. 73–74.

6. John Lewis Gervais to Henry Laurens, 17 April 1780, George Washington Papers, Library of Congress; Journal of the Siege, Papers of the Continental Congress, National Archives; Moultrie, *Memoirs*, I, 222; [Hough,] *Siege of Charleston*, pp. 85, 115.

7. Horry to Greene, 20 April 1781, Greene Papers, William L. Clements Library.

8. Banastre Tarleton, *A History of the Campaigns of 1780 and 1781 in the Southern Provinces of North America* (London, 1787), pp. 27–32; *North Carolina State Records*, XIV, 821–24, 829–30, 823–33;

Rutledge to Abner Nash, Governors' Papers, North Carolina Department of Archives and History; James, *Marion*, p. 38.

9. *Royal Gazette* (Charleston), 17 June 1780; Alexander Innes to Cornwallis, 8 June 1780; George Turnbull to Cornwallis, 15 June 1780, Cornwallis Papers, PRO 30/11/2; Alexander MacDonald to his wife, 10 June 1780, Robertson-McDonald Manuscripts, National Library of Scotland, Edinburgh, Scotland; Charles Ross, ed., *Correspondence of Charles, First Marquis Cornwallis* (London, 1859), I, 48.

10. Tarleton, *Campaigns*, pp. 71–75; William B. Willcox, *Portrait of a General: Sir Henry Clinton in the War of Independence* (New York, 1964), p. 321; Ford, *Journals of the Continental Congress*, XVII, 554; Moultrie, *Memoirs*, II, 221; Francis, Lord Rawdon to Cornwallis, 7 July 1780, Cornwallis Papers, PRO 30/11/2.

11. Anne King Gregorie, *Thomas Sumter* (Columbia, S.C., 1931), pp. 74–85; Robert D. Bass, *Gamecock: The Life and Campaigns of General Thomas Sumter* (New York, 1961), pp. 53–61; Robert D. Bass, *The Green Dragoon* (New York, 1957), p. 90; James, *Marion*, p. 40; Cornwallis to William Cornwallis, 4 July 1780, Admiral William Cornwallis Papers, National Maritime Museum, Greenwich, England; Rawdon to Cornwallis, 10 July 1780, Cornwallis Papers, PRO 30/11/2.

12. James, *Marion*, pp. 42–43; Ramsay, *History of South Carolina*, I, 230–31; Heriot & Tucker to James Wemyss, 12 July 1780, Cornwallis Papers, PRO 30/11/21; *Harper's New Monthly Magazine*, XVII (October 1858), 53.

13. James, *Marion*, pp. 43–45; Ramsay, *History of South Carolina*, I, 231n.

14. Ross, *Cornwallis Correspondence*, I, 54.

15. Wemyss to Cornwallis, 28 July 1780, Cornwallis Papers, PRO 30/11/2; Rawdon to Cornwallis, 1 August 1780, Cornwallis Papers, PRO 30/11/63; Cornwallis to Alexander Innes, 30 July 1780, Cornwallis Papers, PRO 30/11/78; Cornwallis to Rawdon, 7 August 1780, Cornwallis Papers, PRO 30/11/79; Cornwallis to Clinton, 6 August 1780, British Headquarters Papers, Colonial Williamsburg, Williamsburg, Va.

16. Wemyss to Cornwallis, 11 July, 14 July, 17 July, 22 July, 25 July, 28 July, 30 July 1780; Rawdon to McArthur, 12 July 1780, Cornwallis Papers, PRO 30/11/2; Cornwallis to Wemyss, 15 July, 18 July, 23 July, 26 July, 28 July, 30 July 1780, Cornwallis Papers, PRO 30/11/78; Cornwallis to Rawdon, 4 August 1780, Cornwallis Papers, PRO 30/11/79; Wemyss to Cornwallis, 4 August 1780, Cornwallis Papers, PRO 30/11/63.

17. Tarleton to Cornwallis, 5 August 1780, Cornwallis Papers, PRO 30/11/63; Cornwallis to Rawdon, 30 July 1780, Cornwallis Papers, PRO 30/11/78; Cornwallis to Rawdon, 4 August 1780, Cornwallis Papers,

PRO 30/11/79; James, *Marion*, p. 45; Ramsay, *History of South Carolina*, I, 230.

18. Hugh Giles to William R. Davie, 12 August 1780, Cornwallis Papers, PRO 30/11/3; Gilbert Johnston to "Susanna," 8 March 1790, Johnston Papers, Southern Historical Association.

19. *North Carolina State Records*, XIV, 381–83, 843–44, 858–59, 865; Burnett, *Letters of Members of the Continental Congress*, V, 307, 314–16, 398; Alexander Graydon, *Memoirs of His Own Times with Reminiscences of the Men and Events of the Revolution*, ed., John Stockton Littell (Philadelphia, 1846), pp. 103n., 299; de Kalb to the Board of War, George Washington Papers, Library of Congress.

20. William Johnson, *Sketches of the Life and Correspondence of Nathanael Greene* (Charleston, 1822), I, 488; Peter Horry to Greene, 20 April 1781, Greene Papers, William L. Clements Library; de Kalb to Richard Caswell, 10 July 1780, De Kalb Papers, South Carolina Collection, University of South Carolina, Columbia, S.C.

21. George F. Scheer and Hugh F. Rankin, *Rebels and Redcoats* (Cleveland, 1957), pp. 404–06; Gates to Samuel Huntington, 20 July 1780, Papers of the Continental Congress, National Archives; Johnson, *Sketches . . . of Greene*, I, 487; Gates to Abner Nash, 3 August 1780, Governors' Papers, North Carolina Department of Archives and History.

22. Horry and Weems, *Marion*, p. 120; James, *Marion*, p. 46; Horry to Greene, n.d., "Horry Papers," Force Transcripts, Library of Congress; Horry to Greene, 20 April 1781, Greene Papers, William L. Clements Library; SCHGM, LX (July 1959), 122.

23. Johnson, *Sketches . . . of Greene*, I, 488.

CHAPTER IV

1. SCHGM, XXXVIII (July 1937), 83; XXXIX (July 1938), 127; McCrady, *South Carolina in the Revolution, 1775–1780*, p. 651; James, *Marion*, p. 45; Ramsay, *History of South Carolina*, II, 404.

2. James, *Marion*, appendix, p. 11; Johnson, *Sketches of . . . Greene*, I, 452; Lieutenant Haldane to Nisbet Balfour, 20 August 1780, George Turnbull to Patrick Ferguson, 20 August 1780, Cornwallis Papers, PRO 30/11/79; Cornwallis to Germain, 21 August 1780, Cornwallis Papers, PRO 30/11/76; Marion to Peter Horry, 17 August 1780, "Horry Papers," Force Transcripts, Library of Congress.

3. Horry and Weems, *Marion*, pp. 108–11; James, *Marion*, appendix, p. 12; Marion to Horry, 27 August 1780, "Horry Papers," Force Transcripts, Library of Congress.

4. James, *Marion*, pp. 48–49, 55, appendix, p. 12; Gregorie, *Sumter*,

p. 104; McCrady, *South Carolina in the Revolution, 1775–1780*, p. 700; Marion to Horry, 27 August 1780, "Horry Papers," Force Transcripts, Library of Congress; *North Carolina State Papers*, XIV, 771; SCHGM, XVII (October 1906), 139; Benjamin Franklin Stevens, ed., *Clinton-Cornwallis Controversy, Growing out of the Campaign in Virginia, 1781* (London, 1888), I, 263, 267; Ramsay, *History of South Carolina*, II, 399; Cornwallis to Germain, 19 September 1780, Cornwallis Papers, PRO 30/11/76; John Hamilton to Cornwallis, 28 August 1780, Cornwallis Papers, PRO 30/11/63; Cornwallis to John H. Cruger, 27 August 1780, Cornwallis Papers, PRO 30/11/79; *Harper's New Monthly Magazine*, XVII (July 1858), 153; Marion to Gates, 15 September 1781, Horatio Gates Papers, New-York Historical Society, New York, N.Y.

5. Robert D. Bass, *Swamp Fox: The Life and Campaigns of General Francis Marion* (New York, 1959), p. 47; Jenkins, *Experiences of . . . the Rev. James Jenkins*, p. 26.

6. Cornwallis to Clinton, 3 September 1780, Clinton Papers, William L. Clements Library; *Royal Gazette*, 20 September 1780; Cornwallis to Germain, 19 September 1780, Cornwallis Papers, PRO 30/11/76; Proclamation, 6 September 1780, Book D, Mackenzie Papers, William L. Clements Library; Stevens, *Clinton-Cornwallis Controversy*, I, 290–93; Moultrie, *Memoirs*, II, 162–63; Ross, *Cornwallis Correspondence*, I, 56; SCHGM, XXXIII (January 1932), 2–5; Ramsay, *History of the American Revolution*, II, 171–72; Alexander Gregg, *History of the Old Cheraws* (New York, 1867), p. 346.

7. Gregg, *History of the Old Cheraws*, pp. 346–48.

8. Marion to Gates, 15 September 1780, Letters of the Continental Congress, National Archives; William Gordon, *The History of the Rise, Progress, and Establishment of the United States of America* (London, 1788), III, 455; James, *Marion*, p. 46; *North Carolina State Records*, XIV, 383; Moultrie, *Memoirs*, II, 223; Marion to Gates, 15 September 1780, Gates Papers, New-York Historical Society.

9. John Money Diary, Cornwallis Papers, PRO 30/11/3; Cornwallis to Germain, 19 September 1780, Cornwallis Papers, PRO 30/11/76; Cornwallis to Wemyss, 15 July, 30 July 1780, Cornwallis Papers, PRO 30/11/78; Cornwallis to Wemyss, 28 August 1780, Cornwallis Papers, PRO 30/11/79; Ross, *Cornwallis Correspondence*, I, 56–57; Cornwallis to Clinton, 29 August 1780, Clinton Papers, William L. Clements Library; Cornwallis to Cruger, 18 August 1780, British Headquarters Papers, Colonial Williamsburg.

10. Ramsay, *History of the Revolution of South Carolina*, I, 156; Boddie, *History of Williamsburg*, p. 54; Clinton to Cornwallis, 3 December 1780, Clinton Papers, William L. Clements Library; Cornwallis

to Balfour, 24 August 1780, Cornwallis to De Peyster, 13 August 1780, Cornwallis Papers, PRO 30/11/79.

11. Marion to Gates, 15 September 1780, Letters of Continental Congress, National Archives; *North Carolina State Records*, XIV, 616–18; McCrady, *South Carolina in the Revolution, 1775–1780*, p. 702; James, *Marion*, pp. 55–57; Boddie, *History of Williamsburg*, p. 54; Marion to Gates, 15 September 1780, Gates Papers, New-York Historical Society.

12. James, *Marion*, pp. 57, 58; *South Carolina and American General Gazette*, 20 September 1780; *Royal Gazette*, 21 September 1780; Gregg, *History of the Old Cheraws*, pp. 302–03; Ramsay, *History of the Revolution in South Carolina*, II, 156, 188–89; John Money Diary, Cornwallis Papers, PRO 30/11/2; Wemyss to Cornwallis, 20 September 1780, Cornwallis Papers, PRO 30/11/3; Wemyss to Cornwallis, 30 September 1780, Cornwallis Papers, PRO 30/11/64.

CHAPTER V

1. Marion to Gates, 15 September 1780, Letters of Continental Congress; James, *Marion*, pp. 57–58; Horry and Weems, *Marion*, pp. 130–31.

2. James, *Marion*, p. 58; Moncrieff to Balfour, 20 September 1780, Cornwallis Papers, PRO 30/11/64.

3. James, Marion, pp. 58–60; Simms, *Marion*, pp. 138–39; James Jenkins, *Experience, Labours and Sufferings of Rev. James Jenkins, of the South Carolina Conference* (Spartanburg, S.C., 1842), p. 20; Johnson, *Traditions and Reminiscences*, p. 281; *North Carolina State Records*, XIV, 665–66; 683–84; Horry and Weems, *Marion*, pp. 118–19; Balfour to Cornwallis, 10 October 1780, Cornwallis Papers, PRO 30/11/3, Marion to Gates, 4 October 1780, Gates Papers, New-York Historical Society.

4. *North Carolina State Records*, XIV, 622, 666, 747; George Washington Greene, *The Life of Nathanael Greene, Major-General in the Army of the Revolution* (Boston, 1890), III, 127; Gregg, *History of the Old Cheraws*, pp. 334–36.

5. Gregg, *History of the Old Cheraws*, pp. 337–38; Gray to Cornwallis, 7 October 1780, Balfour to Cornwallis, 10 October, 26 October, 5 November 1780, John Money Diary, Balfour to Rawdon, 20 October 1780, Wemyss to Cornwallis, 4 October 1780, Turnbull to Cornwallis, 4 October 1780, Cornwallis Papers, PRO 30/11/3; Wemyss to Cornwallis, 30 September 1780, Gray to Cornwallis, 30 September 1780, Cornwallis Papers, PRO 30/11/64; Cornwallis to Turnbull, 27 Sep-

tember, 29 September 1780, Cornwallis to Wemyss, 26 September 1780, Cornwallis Papers, PRO 30/11/80; Cornwallis to Turnbull, 12 October 1780, Cornwallis Papers, PRO 30/11/81; *North Carolina State Records*, XIV, 666.

6. Balfour to Rawdon, 20 October 1780, Cornwallis Papers, PRO 30/11/3; Gates to Marion, 11 October 1780, Gates to Marion, 11 October 1780, Gates Papers, New-York Historical Society.

7. Moultrie, *Memoirs*, II, 223; McCrady, *South Carolina in the Revolution*, *1775–1780*, p. 751; James, *Marion*, p. 60; Simms, *Marion*, pp. 140–41.

8. Cornwallis to Clinton, 30 October, 3 December 1780, Clinton Papers, William L. Clements Library; Clinton, *American Rebellion*, p. 476; James, *Marion*, pp. 60–61; Ramsay, *History of the Revolution in South Carolina*, II, 409; Turnbull to Cornwallis, 29 October 1780, Cornwallis Papers, PRO 30/11/3; *North Carolina State Records*, XIV, 726; Marion to Gates, 4 November 1780, Gates Papers, New-York Historical Society.

9. W. Thomas Balch, ed., *Papers Related Chiefly to the Maryland Line During the Revolution* (Philadelphia, 1857), pp. 120–21; *North Carolina State Records*, XIV, 423, 652, 726; Turnbull to Cornwallis, 3 November 1780, Cornwallis Papers, PRO 30/11/4; Gates to Harrington, 6 August 1780, Gates Papers, New-York Historical Society.

10. Marion to Gates, 15 October 1780, Gates Papers, New-York Historical Society; *North Carolina State Records*, XIV, 621–22; Horry and Weems, *Marion*, pp. 136–37.

CHAPTER VI

1. Harrington to Gates, 25 September 1780, Gates Papers, New-York Historical Society; *North Carolina State Records*, XIV, 622, 666, 683–84, 747.

2. *South Carolina Gazette and American Journal*, 15 November 1780; Stedman, *History of the . . . American War*, II, 206n.; T. H. Edsall, trans., *Journal of Lieutenant John Charles Von Kraft of the Regiment Von Bose, 1776–78: Collections of the New-York Historical Society for 1882* (New York, 1883), p. 124; Ross, *Cornwallis Correspondence*, I, 67–68; John Money to Wemyss, 1 November 1780, Cornwallis to Tarleton, 2 November 1780, Cornwallis Papers, PRO 30/11/82.

3. Tarleton, *Campaigns*, p. 198; Ross, *Cornwallis Correspondence*, I, 65; SCHGM, XVII (October 1916), 52–53; Turnbull to Cornwallis, 3 November 1780, Tarleton to Cornwallis, 3 November 1780, 5 November 1780, 7 November 1780, Cornwallis Papers, PRO 30/11/4; Marion

to Gates, 9 November 1780, Letters of Continental Congress, National Archives; Balch, *Maryland Line*, p. 127; James, *Marion*, p. 71.

4. Tarleton, *Campaigns*, p. 172; James, *Marion*, p. 63; Garden, *Anecdotes of the Revolution*, I, 287; McCrady, *South Carolina in the Revolution, 1776–1780*, pp. 818–19; Turnbull to Cornwallis, 5 November 1780, Cornwallis Papers, PRO 30/11/4.

5. Tarleton, Proclamation, 11 November 1780, Tarleton to Cornwallis, 11 November 1780, Cornwallis Papers, PRO 30/11/4; Johnson, *Traditions and Reminiscences*, pp. 161–62; James, *Marion*, p. 63; *SCHGM*, XVII (October 1916), 146; Balch, *Maryland Line*, p. 127; Moultrie, *Memoirs*, II, 239–40; Garden, *Anecdotes of the Revolution*, I, 285; Marion to Gates, 9 November 1780, Letters of Members of the Continental Congress, National Archives; Tarleton, *Campaigns*, p. 174.

6. Stevens, *Clinton-Cornwallis Controversy*, I, 188–89, 304; Clinton, *American Rebellion*, pp. 476–77; Ross, *Cornwallis Correspondence* I, 71.

7. Rawdon to Cornwallis, 13 November 1780, Cornwallis Papers, PRO 30/11/4; Cornwallis to Clinton, 3 December 1780, Cornwallis Papers, PRO 30/11/72; Cornwallis to Tarleton, 8 November, 9 November 1780, Cornwallis to Turnbull, 9 November 1780, Cornwallis to Cruger, 11 November 1780, Cornwallis Papers, PRO 30/11/82; Gates to President of Congress, 14 November 1780, Letters of Continental Congress, National Archives; Stevens, *Clinton-Cornwallis Controversy*, I, 304–05; M. A. Moore, *The Life of Gen. Edward Lacey, with a List of Battles and Skirmishes in South Carolina, During the Revolutionary War* (Spartanburg, S.C., 1859), p. 22.

8. Hugh Giles to William R. Davie, 14 August 1780, Cornwallis Papers, PRO 30/11/3; *North Carolina State Records*, XIV, 746–47, 748; Jenkins, *Experiences . . . of Rev. James Jenkins*, p. 24; Horry and Weems, *Marion*, pp. 142–44; James, *Marion*, pp. 65–66; Marion to Gates, 21 November 1780, Gates Papers, New-York Historical Society.

9. *North Carolina State Records*, XIV, 746–47; Marion to Gates, 21 November 1780, Gates Papers, New-York Historical Society.

10. Tarleton, *Campaigns*, pp. 178–80; Ross, *Cornwallis Correspondence*, I, 70; Tarleton to Cornwallis, 24 November, 25 November 1780, Cornwallis Papers, PRO 30/11/4; Cornwallis to Tarleton, 13 November 1780, Cornwallis to Balfour, 25 November 1780, Cornwallis Papers, PRO 30/11/82.

11. Balfour to Cornwallis, 24 November 1780, Cornwallis Papers, PRO 30/11/4; Cornwallis to Balfour, 17 November 1780, Cornwallis to Rawdon, 20 November 1780, Cornwallis to Balfour, 22 November 1780, Cornwallis Papers, PRO 30/11/82.

12. Marion to Gates, 22 November 1780, Greene Papers, William L.

Clements Library; Marion to Gates, 21 November 1780, Harrington to Gates, 23 November 1780, Gates Papers, New-York Historical Society; *North Carolina State Records*, XIV, 746–47.

13. Marion to Gates, 7 December 1780, Marion to Greene, 27 December 1780, 5 January 1781, Greene Papers, William L. Clements Library; Balfour to Cornwallis, 4 November, 24 November, 29 November, 4 December 1780, Rawdon to Cornwallis, 2 December 1780, Cornwallis Papers, PRO 30/11/4; Cornwallis to Rawdon, 29 November, 1 December, 3 December 1780, Cornwallis to Tarleton, 4 December 1780, Cornwallis Papers, PRO 30/11/83.

14. James, *Marion*, p. 67; Bass, *Swamp Fox*, pp. 104–05.

15. Marion to Gates, 7 December 1780, Greene Papers, William L. Clements Library; *Collections of the New-York Historical Society for 1875* (New York, 1876), p. 475; Rawdon to Cornwallis, 5 December 1780, Cornwallis Papers, PRO 30/11/4.

16. Horry and Weems, *Marion*, p. 158–59.

17. Rawdon to Cornwallis, 8 December, 16 December 1780, Balfour to Cornwallis, 15 December 1780, Cornwallis Papers, PRO 30/11/4; Cornwallis to Balfour, 14 December 1780, Cornwallis to Rawdon, 16 December 1780, Cornwallis Papers, PRO 30/11/83; Marion to Greene, 22 December 1780, Greene Papers, William L. Clements Library.

18. Marion to Gates, 22 December 1780, Greene Papers, William L. Clements Library; SCHGM, XVIII (April 1917), 62; McCrady, *South Carolina in the Revolution*, 1775–1780, pp. 102–03; Rawdon to Cornwallis, 14 December, 16 December 1780, Coffin to Rawdon, 13 December 1780, Cornwallis Papers, PRO 30/11/4; Cornwallis to Rawdon, 3 December 1780, Cornwallis Papers, PRO 30/11/83.

CHAPTER VII

1. Rawdon to Cornwallis, 21 December 1780, 24 December 1780, Cornwallis Papers, PRO 30/11/4; Balch, *Papers of the Maryland Line*, p. 127; Marion to Greene, 22 December 1780, Greene Papers, William L. Clements Library.

2. Burnett, *Letters of Members of the Continental Congress*, V, 408; Robert Howe to Abner Nash, 23 October 1780, Robert Howe Papers, Southern Historical Collection; Harold C. Syrett, ed., *The Papers of Alexander Hamilton* (New York, 1961), II, 530; *The Portfolio*, 3rd Series (1813), I, 203–06, 290–91.

3. Greene to Marion, 4 December 1780, Greene Papers, Huntington Library; Marion to Gates, 6 December 1780, Marion to Greene, 22 December 1780, 28 December 1780, 9 January 1781, Greene Papers,

William L. Clements Library; *The Portfolio*, 3rd Series (1813), I, 290–91; *SCHGM*, XVIII (April 1917), 65.

4. Marion to Greene, 9 January 1781, Greene Papers, William L. Clements Library; Cornwallis to Rawdon, 21 December 1780, 25 December 1780, Cornwallis to Tarleton, 18 December 1780, Cornwallis to Leslie, 21 December 1780, Cornwallis Papers, PRO 30/11/83; John McKamara to Charles Mellish, 31 December 1780, Mellish Manuscripts, 172–111, University of Nottingham, Nottingham, England; Cornwallis to Clinton, 29 December 1780, Clinton Papers, William L. Clements Library.

5. Greene to Marion, 24 December 1780, 22 January 1781, 23 January 1781, Greene Papers, William L. Clements Library; Marion to [Greene], 8 January 1781, Marion Papers, South Caroliniana Collection, University of South Carolina, Columbia, South Carolina; James, *Marion*, appendix, pp. 14–15; Greene to Marion, 4 January 1781, Greene to Sumter, 8 January 1781, Bancroft Transcripts, New York Public Library, New York, New York; Gregg, *History of the Old Cheraws*, p. 352; *Publications of the Southern History Association*, XI (May 1907), 82–84, 186–87; Johnson, *Sketches . . . of Greene*, II, 256–57; James Graham, *The Life of General Daniel Morgan, of the Virginia Line of the United States* (New York, 1856), p. 285.

6. Stevens, *Clinton-Cornwallis Controversy*, I, 315; Rawdon to Cornwallis, 31 December 1780, Cornwallis Papers, PRO 30/11/4; Balfour to Clinton, 25 January 1781, Cornwallis Papers, PRO 30/11/5; Rawdon to Cornwallis, 28 December 1780, Cornwallis Papers, PRO 30/11/80; Cornwallis to Rawdon, 19 December 1780, Cornwallis Papers, PRO 30/11/83; Situation of the American Army, 2 January 1781, Cornwallis Papers, PRO 30/11/102; Balfour to Campbell, 11 January, 25 January 1781, Emmett Collection, New York Public Library.

7. Horry and Weems, *Marion*, pp. 135–37; Jenkins, *Experiences . . . of Rev. James Jenkins*, p. 19.

8. McCrady, *South Carolina in the Revolution, 1780–1783*, p. 82; James, *Marion*, appendix, pp. 14–15; Marion to Greene, 9 January 1781, 14 January 1781, Greene Papers, William L. Clements Library; Marion to John Postell, 16 January 1781, Marion to [Greene], 18 January 1781, Marion Papers, South Caroliniana Collection.

9. *SCHGM*, XVIII (April 1917), 63; Horry and Weems, *Marion*, pp. 124–25; James, *Marion*, p. 64; *Publications of the Southern History Association*, XI, 189; Marion to Greene, 16 January 1781, Marion Papers, South Caroliniana Collection.

10. George Campbell to Marion, 21 January 1781, "Horry Papers," Force Transcripts, Library of Congress; Marion to Greene, 14 January 1781, Greene Papers, William L. Clements Library; Marion to [Greene],

18 January 1781, Marion Papers, South Caroliniana Collection; Horry and Weems, *Marion*, pp. 191–92; Simms, *Marion*, pp. 201–02.

11. Henry Lee, Jr., *The Campaign of 1781 in the Carolinas with Remarks Historical and Critical on Johnson's Life of Greene* (Philadelphia, 1824), p. 81, appendix, p. vii; Lee, *Memoirs*, p. 223; *Publications of the Southern History Association*, XI, 190; Gibbes, *Documentary History*, III, 16; Marion to Greene, 9 January 1781, Lee to ————, 23 January 1781, Greene to Marion, 25 January 1781, Greene Papers, William L. Clements Library.

12. Lee, Jr., *Campaign of 1781*, appendix, p. vii; *Publications of the Southern History Association*, XI (May 1907), 166–67; Lee, *Memoirs*, pp. 223–25; James, *Marion*, pp. 90–91; Greene to James Campbell, 30 January 1781, Preston Davie Collection, Southern Historical Collection; Lee to Greene, 27 January, 30 January 1781, Marion to Greene, 27 January 1781, Lewis Morris to Abner Nash, 28 January 1781, Greene Papers, William L. Clements Library; Gibbes, *Documentary History*, III, 16–17; Balfour to Clinton, 31 January 1781, Emmett Collection, New York Public Library; Balfour to Cornwallis, 2 December 1780, Cornwallis Papers, PRO 30/11/70; *Year Book, Charleston*, 1899, pp. 79–80; Horry and Weems, *Marion*, pp. 196–97.

13. James, *Marion*, appendix, pp. 17–21; Lee, Jr., *Campaign of 1781*, appendix, pp. vii–viii; Greene to Marion, 23 January, 25 January 1781, "Horry Papers," Force Transcripts, Library of Congress; Marion to Greene, 27 January 1781, Greene Papers, William L. Clements Library; Gibbes, *Documentary History*, III, 18–19.

CHAPTER VIII

1. James, *Marion*, pp. 91–92; *Publications of the Southern History Association*, XI, 193–94; *Year Book, Charleston*, 1899, p. 82; Greene to Sumter, 9 February 1781, Bancroft Transcripts, New York Public Library; Balfour to Clinton, 31 January 1781, Emmett Collection, New York Public Library; Marion Ord. Bk., H.L.

2. Marion Ord. Bk., H.L.

3. Huger to Marion, 28 January 1781, Rutledge to Marion, 28 January 1781, "Horry Papers," Force Transcripts, Library of Congress; Marion to Huger, 6 February 1781, Marion Papers, South Caroliniana Collection; Gibbes, *Documentary History*, III, 22, 53, 56; Edward Eberstadt. *American Historical Documents & Manuscripts Offered for Sale*, Catalogue No. 129 (New York, 1951), p. 50; Rutledge to Marion, 28 January 1781, Kolb to Marion, 18 April 1781, Bancroft Transcripts, New York Public Library.

4. Marion to Saunders, 22 February 1781, "Horry Papers," Force Transcripts, Library of Congress; McCrady, *South Carolina in the Revolution, 1780–1783*, pp. 83, 151; Balfour to Clinton, 24 February 1781, Clinton Papers, William L. Clements Library; Snipes to Marion, 30 April 1781, Bancroft Transcripts, New York Public Library.

5. A. S. Salley, Jr., *The History of Orangeburg County South Carolina from Its First Settlement to the Close of the Revolutionary War* (Orangeburg, S.C., 1898), pp. 510–11n.; Marion to Sumter, 26 February 1781, Marion Papers, South Caroliniana Collection, McCrady, *South Carolina in the Revolution, 1780–1783*, pp. 107–08; Gibbes, *Documentary History*, III, 23, 81–83; Sumter to Marion, 20 February, 28 February, 4 March 1781, "Horry Papers," Force Transcripts, Library of Congress; Bass, *Gamecock*, pp. 133–35; Gregorie, *Sumter*, pp. 138–42; Balfour to Clinton, 24 February, 3 March 1781, Cornwallis Papers, PRO 30/11/5.

6. Rawdon to Cornwallis, 5 March 1781, Cornwallis Papers, PRO 30/11/69; Rawdon to Clinton, 14 February 1781, British Headquarters Papers, Colonial Williamsburg, Williamsburg, Virginia.

7. Charles I. Bushnell, ed., *Memoirs of Tarleton Brown, a Captain in the Revolutionary Army* (New York, 1862), p. 35; McCrady, *South Carolina in the Revolution, 1780–1783*, p. 113; James, *Marion*, pp. 98–99; Simms, *Marion*, pp. 214–16.

8. Marion to ———, 7 March 1781, Emmett Collection, New York Public Library; Marion to Watson, 7 March 1781, Marion to Saunders, 7 March 1781, Marion to Balfour, 7 March 1781, Watson to Marion, 9 March 1781, "Horry Papers," Force Transcripts, Library of Congress; Bass, *Gamecock*, p. 130; James, *Marion*, pp. 100, 113.

9. James, *Marion*, pp. 100–02; McCrady, *South Carolina in the Revolution, 1780–1783*, pp. 114–16; Simms, *Marion*, pp. 216–18; Ramsay, *South Carolina in the Revolution*, I, 236–37.

10. Marion to Watson, n.d., Marion's Pass, 16 March 1781, Watson to Marion, 15 March, 16 March 1781, "Horry Papers," Force Transcripts, Library of Congress; James, *Marion*, pp. 102–03, appendix, p. 28–29.

11. James, *Marion*, appendix, pp. 26–27; Balfour to Marion, 12 March 1781, Balfour to Saunders, 12 March 1781, "Horry Papers," Force Transcripts, Library of Congress.

12. James, *Marion*, pp. 99–104; Horry and Weems, *Marion*, pp. 179–80; Simms, *Marion*, pp. 219–21.

13. James, *Marion*, p. 104; Simms, *Marion*, p. 222; *Royal Gazette* (Charleston, S.C.), 4 April 1781.

14. Marion to Greene, 21 April 1781, Greene Papers, Huntington Library; *Publications of the Southern History Association*, XI, 195–96;

James, *Marion*, p. 105; Horry and Weems, *Marion*, pp. 184–88; Simms, *Marion*, pp. 223–25; Bass, *Swamp Fox*, pp. 160–61.

CHAPTER IX

1. Gibbes, *Documentary History*, III, 32–33; *American Review*, VI (September 1847), 279; *Year Book, Charleston*, 1899, pp. 6–7, 85–86; Rutledge to Marion, 8 March 1781, Sumter to Marion, 28 March 1781, "Horry Papers," Force Transcripts, Library of Congress.

2. Balfour to Cornwallis, 20 April, 21 May 1781, Cornwallis Papers, PRO 30/11/5; Jenkins, *Experiences . . . of Rev. James Jenkins*, p. 29; *SCHGM*, XI (July 1910), 152; Moultrie, *Memoirs*, II, 222–23; Lee *Memoirs*, p. 330; Johnson, *Sketches of . . . Greene*, II, 69; Greene, *Greene*, IV, 233–34; Lee to Greene, n.d., Greene Papers, William L. Clements Library; James, *Marion*, pp. 106–07.

3. *Annual Register*, 1781, p. 71; Greene to Marion, 4 April 1781, Congress to William Pierce, 24 April 1781, Greene Papers, William L. Clements Library; Marion to Greene, 21 April 1781, Greene Papers, Huntington Library; Gibbes, *Documentary History*, III, 489; *Year Book, Charleston*, 1899, pp. 81–86; Lee, *Memoirs*, p. 330.

4. Lee to Greene, n.d., Greene Papers, William L. Clements Library; Balfour to Clinton, 20 April 1781, Clinton Papers, William L. Clements Library; Rawdon to Balfour, 13 April 1781, Cornwallis Papers, PRO 30/11/5; James, *Marion*, p. 106.

5. James, *Marion*, pp. 109–10; Greene to Lee, 4 April 1781, Lee to Greene, 18 April, 20 April 1781, William Pierce to Eaton, 18 April 1781, Eaton to Greene, 29 April 1781, Marion to Greene, 23 April 1781, Terms of Capitulation, Fort Watson, 23 April 1781, Greene Papers, William L. Clements Library; Marion to Greene, 21 April 1781, Greene Papers, Huntington Library; Marion Ord. Bk., H.L.; Nathaniel Pendleton Orderly Book, Library of Congress; Rawdon to Cornwallis, 24 May 1781, Cornwallis Papers, PRO 30/11/6; *Year Book, Charleston*, 1899, p. 92; Gibbes, *Documentary History*, III, 58; *Publications of the Southern History Association*, XI, 196–97; Lee, *Memoirs*, pp. 331–33; Moultrie, *Memoirs*, I, 124.

6. Kolb to Snipes, n.d., Snipes to Kolb, n.d., Greene to Marion, 18 April 1781, Kolb to Marion, 18 April 1781, Snipes to Marion, 30 April 1781, Sumter to Marion, 30 April 1781, "Horry Papers," Force Transcripts, Library of Congress; Gibbes, *Documentary History*, II, 53, 56; *Year Book, Charleston*, 1899, p. 25.

7. Balfour to Moultrie, 30 March 1781, Clinton Papers, William L. Clements Library; Moultrie to Balfour, 31 March 1781, Emmett

Collection, New York Public Library; Moultrie to Marion, 16 April 1781, "Horry Papers," Force Transcripts, Library of Congress.

8. Lee to Greene, 20 April 1781, Greene to Marion, 24 April, 26 April 1781, Greene Papers, William L. Clements Library; Greene to Joseph Reed, 4 May 1781, Joseph Reed Papers, New-York Historical Society; Greene, *Greene*, III, 258; Lee, Jr., *Campaign of 1781*, appendix, p. xiii; Gibbes, *Documentary History*, II, 60.

9. Clinton, *American Rebellion*, pp. 95, 513; Rawdon to Cornwallis, 25 April 1781, Cornwallis Papers, PRO 30/11/6; Lee to Greene, 28 April 1781, Greene Papers, William L. Clements Library; Greene to Marion, 27 April 1781, Greene Papers, Huntington Library; Greene to Marion, 28 April 1781, "Horry Papers," Force Transcripts, Library of Congress; Gibbes, *Documentary History*, II, 60–63.

10. Harden to Greene, 12 May 1780, Revolutionary Papers, Duke University; James, *Marion*, p. 112.

CHAPTER X

1. Blackwell Robinson, *William R. Davie* (Chapel Hill, N.C., 1963), p. 111; Greene to Marion, 27 April 1781, Miscellaneous Papers, Library of Congress; Greene to Lee, 29 April 1781, Illinois State Historical Library, photostat in William L. Clements Library.

2. Moultrie, *Memoirs*, II, 340–41; McCrady, *South Carolina in the Revolution, 1780–1783*, p. 630; Greene to Marion, 6 May 1781, Bancroft Transcripts, New York Public Library.

3. Marion to Greene, 25 April, 6 May 1781, Green to Marion, 4 May 1781, Greene Papers, William L. Clements Library; Greene to Marion, 6 May 1781, "Horry Papers," Force Transcripts, Library of Congress; Gibbes, *Documentary History*, II, 66–67, 173–75; Greene, *Greene*, III, 291; George H. Richmond, *Letters by and to Gen. Nathanael Greene with Some to His Wife* (New York, 1906), p. 27.

4. Greene to Marion, 1 May, 6 May 1781, "Horry Papers," Force Transcripts, Library of Congress; Ervin to Greene, 6 May 1781, Marion to Greene, 6 May 1781, Greene Papers, William L. Clements Library; Rawdon to Cornwallis, 26 April 1781, Cornwallis Papers, PRO 30/11/6; Stevens, *Clinton-Cornwallis Controversy*, I, 482; Lee, *Memoirs*, p. 343.

5. Greene to Lafayette, 4 May 1781, Sumter to Greene, 7 May 1781, Greene Papers, William L. Clements Library; Balfour to Cornwallis, 21 May 1781, Cornwallis Papers, PRO 30/11/6; Lee, *Memoirs*, p. 345; *Royal Gazette*, 13–17 April 1782; SCHGM, XVII (January 1916), 3–4.

6. Greene to Marion, 4 May 1781, Lee to Greene, 8 May 1781, Greene Papers, William L. Clements Library; Greene to Marion, 9 May

1781, Greene Papers, Huntington Library; Balfour to Clinton, 23 March 1781, British Headquarters Papers, Colonial Williamsburg; Clinton, *American Rebellion*, p. 501; *Year Book, Charleston*, 1899, pp. 14, 95; Greene, *Greene*, III, 292.

7. Rawdon to Cornwallis, 24 May 1781, Cornwallis Papers, PRO 30/11/6; Gibbes, *Documentary History*, II, 67, 69; *Year Book, Charleston*, 1899, p. 99; Stevens, *Clinton-Cornwallis Controversy*, I, 482–83; Lee, Jr., *Campaign of 1781*, pp. 386–87; Ross, *Cornwallis Correspondence*, I, 98, 101; Lee, *Memoirs*, pp. 344–45; *Magazine of American History*, VII (December 1881), 431–32.

8. Nathaniel Pendleton to Marion, 10 May 1781, Marion to Greene, 11 May 1781, Greene Papers, William L. Clements Library; Rawdon to Cornwallis, 24 May 1781, Clinton Papers, William L. Clements Library; Lee, *Memoirs*, pp. 347–48; Horry and Weems, *Marion*, p. 221; Marion to Greene, 12 May 1781, Miscellaneous Papers, New York Public Library.

9. *Royal Gazette*, 13–17 April 1782; Horry and Weems, *Marion*, p. 223; Johnson, *Traditions and Reminiscences*, p. 101.

10. Greene to Marion, 9 May 1781, Marion to Greene, 11 May 1781, Greene Papers, William L. Clements Library; Greene, *Greene*, III, 293.

11. *Royal Gazette*, 13–17 April 1782; Lee to Maxwell, 14 May 1781, Lee to Greene, 15 May 1781, Sumter to Greene, 4 May, 7 May, 15 May 1781, Articles of Capitulation, Fort Granby, 15 May 1781, Greene Papers, William L. Clements Library; Greene, *Greene*, III, 280; Burnett to Marion, 18 May 1781, "Horry Papers," Force Transcripts, Library of Congress; Gibbes, *Documentary History*, II, 74; Lee, Jr., *Campaign of 1781*, appendix, p. xxxi; Bass, *Gamecock*, pp. 176–77; *Year Book, Charleston*, 1899, pp. 100–02.

12. Marion Ord. Bk., H.L.; Marion to Greene, 19 May, 20 May, 22 May 1781, Greene to Marion, 26 May 1781, Greene Papers, William L. Clements Library; *Year Book, Charleston*, 1899, pp. 103–04; Gibbes, *Documentary History*, II, 80–81.

13. Marion to Greene, 19 May, 20 May, 22 May, 5 June, 6 June 1781, Greene to Marion, 26 May, 10 June 1781, Edmund Hyrne to Greene, 30 May 1781, Maham to Greene, 1 June, 5 June 1781, Thomas Wade to Greene, 4 July 1781, Greene Papers, William L. Clements Library; *Publications of the Southern History Association*, XI, 197–98; *Year Book, Charleston*, 1899, pp. 106–07, 109–10.

14. Alexander McGregor to Marion, 5 June 1781, Greene to Marion, 10 June 1781, Pierce to Marion, 1 May 1781, Marion to Greene, 5 June, 16 June, 25 June 1781, Maham to Greene, 5 June 1781, Greene Papers, William L. Clements Library; Sumter to Marion, 9 June, 14 June, 15 June, 16 June 1781, "Horry Papers," Force Tran-

scripts, Library of Congress; Greene to Marion, 10 June 1781, Greene to Sumter, 17 June 1781, Greene Papers, Duke University; Greene to Abner Nash, 2 May 1781, Miscellaneous Manuscripts, Library of Congress; *Year Book, Charleston,* 1899, pp. 98–99, 106–07, 110–10, 113; Gibbes, *Documentary History,* II, 95–96, 97.

15. Articles of Agreement, 17 June 1781, "Horry Papers," Force Transcripts, Library of Congress; Marion to Greene, 16 June 1781, Wade to Greene, 4 July 1781, Greene Papers, William L. Clements Library; Ganey to Marion, 25 August 1781, Marion Letterbook (transcripts), Gibbes Collection, South Carolina Department of Archives, Columbia, South Carolina; Gibbes, *Documentary History,* II, 98.

16. Pendleton Orderly Book, Library of Congress; Balfour to Cornwallis, 27 June 1781, Cornwallis Papers, PRO 30/11/109.

17. Greene to Marion, 25 June 1781, Greene Papers, William L. Clements Library; Greene, *Greene,* III, 320.

CHAPTER XI

1. Greene to Maham, 21 June 1781, Maham Orderly Book, New York Public Library; Maham's Commission, 22 June 1781, Emmett Collection, New York Public Library; Greene to Maham, 21 June 1781, Greene to Horry, 28 June, 30 July 1781, Pierce to Horry, 14 September 1781, Ichabod Burnett to Horry, 2 July 1781, Horry to Greene, 28 June 1781, Greene Papers, William L. Clements Library; Lee, Jr., *Campaign of 1781,* p. 358; Gibbes, *Documentary History,* III, 172; Marion Ord. Bk., H.L.

2. Marion to Greene, 28 June 1781, Greene Papers, William L. Clements Library; Greene to Sumter, Greene Papers, Duke University; Washington Irving, *Life of George Washington* (New York, 1855–1859), IV, 88; *Year Book, Charleston,* 1899, pp. 35–36, 116.

3. Marion to Greene, 28 June, 7 July, 8 July 1781, Greene to Marion, 1 July, 2 July, 10 July 1781, Intelligence, 9 July 1781, Greene Papers, William L. Clements Library; Pierce to Marion, 10 July 1781, Greene Papers, Huntington Library; Marion to Greene, 10 July 1781, Preston Davie Collection, Southern Historical Collection; Rawdon to Cornwallis, 2 August 1781, Cornwallis Papers, PRO 30/11/6; Lee, *Memoirs,* pp. 264, 385n.; Greene, *Greene,* III, 331–32; *Historical Magazine,* IX (September 1865), 282–83.

4. Clinton, *American Rebellion,* p. 551; Kirkland and Kennedy, *Historic Camden,* I, 403; Sumter to Greene, 15 July 1781, Greene Papers, William L. Clements Library; *Historical Magazine,* IX (September 1865), 283; *Year Book, Charleston,* 1899, pp. 40–41, 41–44,

45–46; Lee, *Memoirs*, p. 388; William Pierce to St. George Tucker, 20 July 1781, Coleman-Tucker Papers, Colonial Williamsburg; *SCHGM*, XXXVIII, (January 1937), 4.

5. Marion to Greene, 19 July 1781, Greene Papers, William L. Clements Library; Sumter to Greene, 25 July 1781, Revolutionary Manuscripts, Duke University; *Historical Magazine*, IX (September 1865), 283; *Year Book, Charleston*, 1899, pp. 41–44, 45–46; Lee, *Memoirs*, pp. 388–89.

6. Marion to Greene, 19 June 1781, Greene Papers, William L. Clements Library; Marion Ord. Bk., H.L.; Garden, *Anecdotes of the American Revolution*, I, 30–31; Pierce to St. George Tucker, 23 July 1781, Coleman-Tucker Papers, Colonial Williamsburg; Jenkins, *Experiences . . . of Rev. James Jenkins*, p. 28; Lee, *Memoirs*, pp. 389–90; Sumter to Greene, 25 July 1781, Revolutionary Manuscripts, Duke University; *Year Book, Charleston*, 1899, p. 43; Draper Manuscripts, 16VV35, Wisconsin Historical Society, Madison, Wisconsin.

7. Lee, Jr., *Campaign of 1781*, p. 450; Kirkland and Kennedy, *Historic Camden*, I, 403; Marion to Greene, 19 July, 24 July, 1 August, 9 August 1781, Greene to Marion, 21 July 1781, Greene Papers, William L. Clements Library; Sumter to Greene, 25 July 1781, Revolutionary Manuscripts, Duke University; *Year Book, Charleston*, 1899, pp. 44, 48–50, 122, 128; Gregorie, *Sumter*, p. 179–80; Balfour to Clinton, 20 July 1781, Clinton Papers, William L. Clements Library; Clinton, *American Rebellion*, p. 551.

8. Marion to Greene, 24 July 1781, Henderson to Greene, 14 August 1781, Pierce to Marion, 18 August 1781, Hyrne to Marion, 18 August 1781, Greene Papers, William L. Clements Library; *American Review*, VI, 281–82; Rutledge to Marion, 1 September 1781, Marion Letterbook, Gibbes Collection, South Carolina Department of Archives; *The Public Acts of the General Assembly of North Carolina* (New Bern, N.C., 1804), p. 447; *Year Book, Charleston*, 1899, pp. 44, 53–54; Lee, Jr., *Campaign of 1781*, pp. 48–50; Gregorie, *Sumter*, p. 181; Johnson, *Sketches of Greene*, II, 215; Greene, *Greene*, III, 281, 343–44; Gibbes, *Documentary History*, II, 122–23, 126–27.

9. Pierce to Marion, 18 August 1781, Greene Papers, William L. Clements Library; Rutledge to Marion, 1 September, 2 September 1781, Marion Letterbook, Gibbes Collection, South Carolina Department of Archives; Rutledge to Marion, 13 August 1781, "Horry Papers," Force Transcripts, Library of Congress; Gibbes, *Documentary History*, II, 122–23, 126–27, 131; *American Review*, VI, 281–82.

10. Rutledge to Marion, 13 August 1781, Marion Letterbook, Gibbes Collection, South Carolina Department of Archives; Balfour to Clinton, 21 July 1781, Emmett Collection, New York Public Library; Balfour

to Clinton, 6 May 1781, Clinton Papers, William L. Clements Library; Greene to Balfour, 26 August 1781, Greene's Proclamation, 26 August 1781, Greene to Marion, 10 August 1781, Greene Papers, William L. Clements Library; *Royal Gazette*, 4–8 August 1781; Lee, Jr., *Campaign of 1781*, appendix, p. xxxv; Johnson, *Sketches of Greene*, II, 197; McCrady, *South Carolina in the Revolution, 1780–1783*, p. 399.

11. Marion Ord. Bk., H.L.; Hyrne to Marion, 18 August 1781, Greene to Marion, 20 August 1781, Marion to Greene, 20 August 1781, William L. Clements Library; *Journal of American History*, I (no. 3, 1907), 463; *Publications of the Southern History Association*, XI, 198–201.

CHAPTER XII

1. Lee to Greene, 13 August 1781, Greene to Marion, 5 September 1781, Greene Papers, William L. Clements Library; Rawdon to Cornwallis, 2 August 1781, Cornwallis Papers, PRO 30/11/6; Clinton, *American Rebellion*, p. 335; Lee to Greene, 11 August 1781, Siege of Yorktown Papers, Pierpont Morgan Library, New York, New York.

2. Stewart to Cornwallis, 13 August 1781, Cornwallis Papers, PRO 30/11/70.

3. Hyrne to Marion, 4 September 1781, Greene to Marion, 5 September 1781, Greene Papers, William L. Clements Library; Pendleton Orderly Book, Library of Congress; Osmond Tiffany, *A Sketch of the Life and Services of Gen. Otho Williams* (Baltimore, 1851), p. 231; Elizabeth Merritt, ed., *Calendar of the General Otho Williams Papers in the Maryland Historical Society* (Baltimore, 1940), pp. 48–49.

4. Tiffany, *Otho Williams*, pp. 23–24; 26; Dawson, *Battles of the United States*, I, 712; *Graham's Magazine* (December 1847), p. 258; *Pennsylvania Magazine of History and Biography*, XXX (1906), 359–61; *Southern Literary Messenger*, XXIX (October 1859), 291–92; *Magazine of History with Notes and Queries*, Extra Number 139, XXXV (1928), 74–75; *North Carolina State Records*, XXII, 153; Lee, *Memoirs*, pp. 466, 604; Gibbes, *Documentary History*, III, 141–42, 144; Pendleton Orderly Book, Library of Congress; Greene to Benjamin Lincoln, 11 September 1781, Greene Papers, William L. Clements Library; Stewart to Cornwallis, 9 September, 19 September 1781, Cornwallis Papers, PRO 30/11/73.

5. William Hooper to James Iredell, 1 October 1781, James Iredell Papers, Duke University; Stedman, *History of the . . . American War*, II, 420; Lee, *Memoirs*, pp. 466–68; Greene to Lincoln, 11 September 1781, Greene Papers, William L. Clements Library; Stewart to Cornwallis, 9 September, 19 September 1781, Cornwallis Papers, PRO

30/11/73; *Pennsylvania Magazine of History and Biography*, XXX (1906), 359–63; Gibbes, *Documentary History*, III, 144, 148–49, 150–51, 152–53; *North Carolina State Records*, XV, 638; *Southern Literary Messenger*, XXIX (October 1859), 291–92; *Magazine of History with Notes and Queries*, Extra Number 139, XXV (1928), 73–77; *Virginia Magazine of History and Biography*, LI (April 1943), 141–49; SCHGM, XVI (April 1915), 140; *Graham's Magazine* (December 1847), p. 257; Returns of the Killed, Missing & Wounded of the Southern Army Commanded by the Honourable Major General Nathanael Greene in the Action of the Eutaw, September 8th 1781, Miscellaneous Papers, 1770–1896, Southern Historical Collection; Pendleton Orderly Book, Library of Congress; Marion Ord. Bk., H.L.; Marion to Peter Horry, 14 September 1781, Marion Letterbook, Gibbes Collection, South Carolina Department of Archives; William Vaugh's Declaration, 7 June 1832, William Vaugh Deposition, 2 December 1833, William Vaugh Papers, South Caroliniana Collection; Royal Gazette, 26–29 September 1781.

6. Marion to Peter Horry, 14 September 1781, Balfour to Marion, 18 August 1781, Marion Letterbook, Gibbes Collection, South Carolina Department of Archives; Marion to Greene, 17 September 1781, Miscellaneous Manuscripts, New York Public Library; Marion to Greene, 20 August, 9 September, 13 September, 21 September, 25 September, 27 September 1781, Greene Papers, William L. Clements Library.

7. Greene to Eggleston, 25 October 1781, Whitaker-Meade Papers, Southern Historical Collection; Rutledge to Marion, 3 September, 6 September 1781, Greene to Peter Horry, 17 September 1781, Greene to Marion, 19 September 1781, "Horry Papers," Force Transcripts, Library of Congress; Rutledge to Marion, 26 September 1781, Marion Letterbook, Gibbes Collection, South Carolina Department of Archives; SCHGM, XVI (July 1915), 107–08; Marion to Greene, 23 September 1781, Greene Papers, Duke University; *American Review*, III, 179, VI, 284–85, 287; Gibbes, *Documentary History*, III, 167, 170, 179, 185–87, 188–89; *Year Book, Charleston*, 1899, pp. 124–26; *Pennsylvania Magazine of History and Biography*, XIV (1890), 83–84; Marion to Greene, 9 September, 13 September, 21 September, 25 September, 27 September 1781, Greene Papers, William L. Clements Library.

CHAPTER XIII

1. Maham Orderly Book, New York Public Library; Return of Lt. Col. Peter Horry's Regiment of Cavalry, 20 September 1781, Greene to Horry, 9 October, 18 October, 11 November 1781, 14 February

1782, Greene to Maham, 23 October 1781, Rutledge to Horry, 4 November 1781, Greene Papers, William L. Clements Library; Horry to Greene, 8 November 1781, Revolutionary Manuscripts, Duke University; Horry to Greene, 31 October 1781, Rutledge to Marion, 24 October 1781, Marion to Horry, 29 October 1781, Horry to Greene, 31 October 1781, Rutledge to Horry, 25 September 1781, "Horry Papers," Force Transcripts, Library of Congress; *American Review*, VI, 283–85; Gibbes, *Documentary History*, III, 198, 203–04, 206–07.

2. Greene to Marion, 15 November 1781, Greene Papers, William L. Clements Library; Greene to Marion, 30 October 1781, 15 November 1781, Greene Papers, Huntington Library.

3. Maham to Greene, 27 November 1781, Marion to Greene, 30 November 1781, Doyle to Marion, 20 November 1781, Greene Papers, William L. Clements Library; Greene to Marion, 16 October 1781, "Horry Papers," Force Transcripts, Library of Congress; Greene to Marion, 24 November 1781, Greene Papers, Huntington Library; Hector MacLean to Murdoch MacLean, 15 September 1781, MacLaine of Lockburne Muniments, no. 34, Scottish Record Office, Edinburgh, Scotland; Johnson, *Sketches of Greene*, II, 258; Moultrie, *Memoirs*, II, 296; *SCHGM*, VI (January 1905), 15.

4. Marion to Greene, 10 November, 25 November, 27 November, 1 December, 9 December, 12 December, 18 December, 21 December 1781, Greene to Marion, 25 November 1781, 3 December 1781, Greene Papers, William L. Clements Library; Marion Ord. Bk., H.L.; Extract from the Minutes of Congress, "Horry Papers," Force Transcripts, Library of Congress; *SCHGM*, XII (October 1910), 233; Leslie to Earl of Levin, 29 October, 14 December 1781, Levin and Melville Muniments, sec. N., 512., Scottish Record Office; Moultrie, *Memoirs*, II, 407; Johnson, *Sketches of Greene*, II, 258–59.

5. Gibbes, *Documentary History*, III, 78, 212, 215, 217, 219–20, 223; Greene to Marion, 12 December 1781, Greene Papers, Duke University; *Year Book, Charleston*, 1899, pp. 57–59, 64, 127, 130–31; Proclamation, 15 December 1781, Alexander Leslie Papers, North Carolina Department of Archives and History; *American Review*, VI, 288–89.

6. Greene to Marion, 27 December, 31 December 1781, 3 January 1782, Greene Papers, William L. Clements Library; Marion to Greene, 1 December 1781, Greene to Marion, 31 December 1781, Greene Papers, Huntington Library; Greene to Marion, 12 December 1781, Greene Papers, Duke University; Gibbes, *Documentary History*, III, 217, 219–20, 224–25, 226, 228; *Year Book, Charleston*, 1899, pp. 64, 130–31, 131–32; *Publications of the Southern History Association*, XI, 201; Rutledge to Marion, 23 November 1781, "Horry Papers," Force Transcripts, Library of Congress; *SCHGM*, XXVI (October 1925), 191–92; John Armstrong

to Jethro Sumner, 5 November 1781, Jethro Sumner Papers, Southern Historical Collection.

7. Marion to Greene, 5 January [1782], Greene to Marion, 15 January 1782, Greene Papers, William L. Clements Library; Leslie to Clinton, 29 January 1782, British Headquarters Papers, Colonial Williamsburg; Marion Ord. Bk., H.L.; James, *Marion*, p. 159; Maham Orderly Book, New York Public Library; Precis of Correspondence, 1782, Clinton Papers, William L. Clements Library; Marion to Greene, 30 December 1781, Charleston Museum Collection (copies), South Caroliniana Collection.

8. Marion to Greene, 2 January, 10 January 1782, Greene to Marion, 27 December 1781, William L. Clements Library; Bass, *Gamecock*, p. 217; *Year Book, Charleston, 1899*, pp. 131–32; Gibbes, *Documentary History*, III, 224–25, 226, 228; *Publications of the Southern History Association*, XI, 201; SCHGM, XXVI (October 1925), 210.

9. Greene to Marion, 27 December 1781, 15 January, 16 January, 26 January, 28 January 1782, Marion to Greene, 2 January, 15 January 1782, Horry to Greene, 13 January, 17 January 1782, Maham to Greene, 4 January 1782, Maham to Horry, 20 January 1782, Greene Papers, William L. Clements Library; Maham to Horry, 23 January 1782, "Horry Papers," Force Transcripts, Library of Congress; *Publications of the Southern History Association*, XI, 201; Gibbes, *Documentary History*, III, 249; Lee, Jr., *Campaign of 1781*, appendix, p. xxv.

10. Greene to Marion, 27 December 1781, Greene Papers, William L. Clements Library; Bass, *Gamecock*, p. 217; SCHGM, XXVI (October 1925), 210; *Year Book, Charleston, 1899*, pp. 131–32; Gibbes, *Documentary History*, III, 249, 280–81; Horry and Weems, *Marion*, p. 236; Pierce to St. George Tucker, 6 February 1782, Coleman-Tucker Papers, Colonial Williamsburg.

11. Marion to Greene, 25 January, 19 February 1782, Greene to Maham, 1 February 1782, Maham to Greene, 17 February 1782, Horry to Greene, 28 February 1782, Greene Papers, William L. Clements Library; Marion to Horry, 18 January, 20 January, 29 January, 3 February, 10 February 1782, Horry to Maham, 31 January 1782, "Horry Papers," Force Transcripts, Library of Congress; Simms, *Marion*, p. 298.

CHAPTER XIV

1. Horry to Greene, 20 February, 28 February, 1782, Marion to Greene, 1 March 1782, Greene to Marion, 1 February 1782, Greene Papers, William L. Clements Library; Marion Ord. Bk., H.L.; Thompson to Leslie, 24 February, 25 February 1782, British Headquarters

Papers, Colonial Williamsburg; Greene to Steuben, 12 March 1782, Steuben Papers, New-York Historical Society; James, *Marion*, pp. 162–63; *SCHGM*, XXVI (October 1905), 195; *Publications of the Southern History Association*, XI, 204–05; Gibbes, *Documentary History*, III, 261–62; Marion to Horry, 26 February 1782, "Horry Papers," Force Transcripts, Library of Congress; *Royal Gazette*, 27 February–2 March 1782.

2. Marion to Greene, 4 March, 8 March, 13 March, 19 March, 23 March, 5 April, 8 April 1782, Greene to Marion, 19 March, 27 March, 10 April 1782, Horry to Greene, 24 May, 28 May 1782, Greene to Horry, 27 March, 19 March 1782, Marion to Horry, 31 March 1782, Greene Papers, William L. Clements Library; Horry to Greene, 25 March 1782, Lloyd Smith Collection, Morristown National Historical Park, Morristown, New Jersey; Marion Ord. Bk., H.L.; Horry to Marion, 11 March, 1 April 1782; Marion to Horry, 7 March, 31 March, 9 April 1782, Mathews to Marion, 26 February, 12 March 1782, Horry to Greene, 1 April 1782, "Horry Papers," Force Transcripts, Library of Congress; James, *Marion*, p. 165; Gibbes, *Documentary History*, III, 163, 263, 276–77, 281–82, 284–85; Marion to Greene, 5 April 1782, Marion Papers, South Caroliniana Collection.

3. Maham to Greene, 20 May 1782, Greene Papers, William L. Clements Library; Johnson, *Traditions and Reminiscences*, p. 288.

4. Greene to Marion, 6 April, 12 April, 14 April, 15 April 1782, Greene Papers, William L. Clements Library; Gibbes, *Documentary History*, III, 150, 154–55, 156–57, 161, 165, 166–67, 171, 173–74.

5. Greene to Marion, 1 May 1782, Preston Davie Collection, Southern Historical Collection; Horry to Greene, 20 September 1781, Greene to Marion, 2 May 1782, Greene Papers, William L. Clements Library; John James to Marion, 20 September 1781, Greene to Horry, 24 September 1781, Marion to Horry, 3 May 1782, Articles of Agreement, 8 June 1782, Ganey to Marion, 8 September 1781, "Horry Papers," Force Transcripts, Library of Congress; Marion to Greene, 23 September 1781, Greene to Marion, 9 July 1782, Greene Papers, Duke University; Moultrie, *Memoirs*, II, 419–21; Greene to Marion, 12 April 1782, Greene Papers, Huntington Library; *North Carolina State Records*, XVI, 182–83, 283, 688–89, 690–91, 693; *SCHGM*, XI (July 1910), 156, XXVI (October 1925), 191–92, 197–202; William Henry Hoyt, ed., *The Papers of Archibald Murphey* (Raleigh, N.C., 1914), II, 309; Gibbes, *Documentary History*, I, 149, III, 172–73, 179; *Year Book, Charleston*, 1899, pp. 68–69, 92–93; Stedman, *History of the . . . American War*, II, 319n.

6. David Fanning, *The Narrative of Colonel David Fanning* (New York, 1865), p. 61; Leslie to Greene, 30 June 1782, Emmett Collec-

tion, New York Public Library; Garden, *Anecdotes of the American Revolution*, I, 25–26, 26–27; Marion to Horry, 9 June, 12 June 1782, "Horry Papers," Force Transcripts, Library of Congress; Greene to Marion, 9 July 1782, Greene Papers, Duke University; *SCHGM*, XXXVIII (January 1937), 9–10.

7. Greene to Horry, 10 August 1782, Marion to Greene, 8 July, 16 July, 5 August 1782, Conyers to Pierce, 6 July 1782, Greene Papers, William L. Clements Library; Marion Ord. Bk., H.L.; Burnett to Marion, 26 July 1782, Greene Papers, Duke University; Proceedings of the Consolidation of Col. Maham & Major Conyers Corps of Cavalry, 4 August 1782, Preston Davie Collection, Southern Historical Collection.

8. Marion to Greene, 8 July, 16 July, 5 August, 30 August 1782, Conyers to Pierce, 6 July 1782, Greene Papers, William L. Clements Library; Marion Ord. Bk., H.L.; Greene to Marion, 31 August 1782, "Horry Papers," Force Transcripts Library of Congress; Leslie to Guy Carleton, 8 September 1782, British Headquarters Papers, Colonial Williamsburg; Leslie to Doyle, 26 July 1782, Frazer to [Leslie?], 4 September 1782, Emmett Collection, New York Public Library; *SCHGM*, XII (April 1900), 44–51, XVII (October 1906), 176–77, XXVII (January 1926), 23; Gibbes, *Documentary History*, II, 202–05.

9. Marion to Greene, 30 August, 2 September 1782, Greene Papers, William L. Clements Library; Marion to Greene, 13 September 1782, Marion Papers, South Caroliniana Collection; Marion Ord. Bk., H.L.; Garden, *Anecdotes of the American Revolution*, I, 23; Marion to Greene, 31 October 1781, Greene Papers, Huntington Library.

10. Marion to Greene, 31 October, 24 November 1782, Greene Papers, William L. Clements Library; Greene to Marion, 13 November, 22 November 1782, Greene Papers, Huntington Library; *SCHGM*, XLI (April 1940), 55.

11. Marion Ord. Bk., H.L.

CHAPTER XV

1. Marion to Horry, 18 January 1783, "Horry Papers," Force Transcripts, Library of Congress; Gregorie, *Sumter*, pp. 202, 206, 206n.; North Carolina State Records, XXIV, 954; James, *Marion*, pp. 177–78; Simms, *Marion*, pp. 336–37; Horry and Weems, *Marion*, pp. 237–38.

2. Adele Stanton Edwards, ed., *Journals of the Privy Council, 1783–1789* (Columbia, S.C., 1971), pp. 119–20, 189; Simms, *Marion*, pp. 341–42; James, *Marion*, pp. 177–78; Horry and Weems, *Marion*, pp. 235–36.

3. *SCHGM*, XX (January 1919), 55–56, XLV (January 1944), 40;

Harper's New Monthly Magazine, XVII (July 1858), 170; James, *Marion*, p. 178; Simms, *Marion*, pp. 342–43.

4. Voucher, Commission of Public Works on Fort Johnson, 10 February 1787, Miscellaneous Papers, New York Public Library; Marion to Albert N. Muller, 24 August 1789, Marion Papers, South Caroliniana Collection; James, *Marion*, p. 179.

5. Johnson, *Traditions and Reminiscences*, p. 291; Garden, *Anecdotes of the American Revolution*, I, 29.

6. Pay Voucher, 4 June 1790, Marion to Francis Marion, 8 November 1794, Marion Papers, South Caroliniana Collection; J. Isaac Copeland, "The Movement for Free Public Schools in South Carolina, to 1868" (unpublished Ph.D. dissertation, University of North Carolina, 1957), p. 141; Horry and Weems, *Marion*, pp. 238–40, 242–47; SCHGM, XLIX (January 1968), 32; James, *Marion*, pp. 179–80; Testimonial, 15 November 1794, "Horry Papers," Force Transcripts, Library of Congress.

7. Marion to Francis Marion, 8 November 1794, Marion Papers, South Caroliniana Collection; Will of Francis Marion, 16 July 1794 (probated 16 March 1795), Will Book, Charleston County, XXV, Book A270, South Carolina Department of Archives; SCHGM, XXXIX (July 1939), 104; Benson J. Lossing, *Field Book of the American Revolution* (Philadelphia, 1851), II, 502; Horry and Weems, *Marion*, pp. 238–39; James, *Marion*, p. 182.

8. Wallace, *South Carolina*, pp. 312, 323; SCHGM, XI (July 1910), 144.

Bibliography

UNPUBLISHED PAPERS

Admiralty Papers. Public Record Office (PRO), London, Eng.

Bancroft Transcripts. New York Public Library, New York, N.Y.

British Headquarters Papers. Colonial Williamsburg, Inc., Williamsburg, Va.

Caswell, Richard, Letterbook. North Carolina Department of Archives and History, Raleigh, N.C.

Charleston Museum Collection (copies). South Caroliniana Collection. University of South Carolina, Columbia, S.C.

Clinton, Sir Henry. William L. Clements Library, University of Michigan, Ann Arbor, Mich.

Coleman-Tucker Papers. Colonial Williamsburg, Inc., Williamsburg, Va.

Continental Congress, Papers of the. National Archives, Washington, D.C.

Cornwallis, Charles. Public Record Office (PRO), London, Eng.

Cornwallis, William. National Maritime Museum, Greenwich, Eng.

Davie, Preston, Collection. Southern Historical Collection. The University of North Carolina at Chapel Hill, Chapel Hill, N.C.

DeKalb, Johann. South Caroliniana Collection. University of South Carolina, Columbia, S.C.

Draper, Lyman. Wisconsin Historical Society, Madison, Wisc.

Emmett, Thomas Addison, Collection. New York Public Library, New York, N.Y.

Gates, Horatio. New-York Historical Society, New York, N.Y.

Germain, Lord George. William L. Clements Library, University of Michigan, Ann Arbor, Mich.

Governors' Papers. North Carolina Department of Archives and History, Raleigh, N.C.

Graham, William A. North Carolina Department of Archives and History, Raleigh, N.C.

Greene, Nathanael. Duke University, Durham, N.C.

———. Henry L. Huntington Library, San Marino, Calif.

———. William L. Clements Library, University of Michigan, Ann Arbor, Mich.

"Horry [, Peter,] Papers," Peter Force Transcripts, Library of Congress, Washington, D.C.

Howe, Robert, Orderly Book. William L. Clements Library, University of Michigan, Ann Arbor, Mich.

————. Southern Historical Collection. The University of North Carolina at Chapel Hill, Chapel Hill, N.C.

Hunt, Oliver, Diary (copy). Duke University, Durham, N.C.

Hutson, Richard. Duke University, Durham, N.C.

Iredell, James. Duke University, Durham, N.C.

Johnston, Charles E., Collection. North Carolina Department of Archives and History, Raleigh, N.C.

Johnson Papers. Southern Historical Collection. The University of North Carolina at Chapel Hill, Chapel Hill, N.C.

Leslie, Alexander. North Carolina Department of Archives and History, Raleigh, N.C.

Levin and Melville Muniments. Scottish Record Office, Edinburgh, Scot.

Lincoln, Banjamin. Massachusetts Historical Society, Boston, Mass.

Mackenzie Papers. William L. Clements Library, University of Michigan, Ann Arbor, Mich.

MacLaine of Lockburne Muniments. Scottish Record Office, Edinburgh, Scot.

Maham, Hezikiah, Orderly Book. New York Public Library, New York, N.Y.

Marion, Francis, Letterbook (transcripts). Gibbes Collection. South Carolina Department of Archives, Columbia, S.C.

————, Orderly Books. Henry L. Huntington Library, San Marino, Calif.

————. South Caroliniana Collection. University of South Carolina, Columbia, S.C.

Mellish Manuscripts. University of Nottingham, Nottingham, Eng.

Miscellaneous Papers. Library of Congress, Washington, D.C.

————. New York Public Library, New York, N.Y.

————. William L. Clements Library, University of Michigan, Ann Arbor, Mich.

————, 1770–1896. Southern Historical Collection. The University of North Carolina at Chapel Hill, Chapel Hill, N.C.

Pendleton, Nathaniel, Orderly Book. Library of Congress, Washington, D.C.

Pinckney Family Papers. Library of Congress, Washington, D.C.

Reed, Joseph. New-York Historical Society, New York, N.Y.

Revolutionary Manuscripts. Duke University, Durham, N.C.

FRANCIS MARION:

Robertson-MacDonald Manuscripts. National Library of Scotland, Edinburgh, Scot.

Siege of Yorktown Papers. Pierpont Morgan Library, New York, N.Y.

Smith, Lloyd, Collection. Morristown National Historical Park, Morristown, N.J.

Steuben Papers. New-York Historical Society, New York, N.Y.

Sumner, Jethro. Southern Historical Collection. The University of North Carolina at Chapel Hill, Chapel Hill, N.C.

Vaugh, William. South Caroliniana Collection. University of South Carolina, Columbia, S.C.

Washington, George. Library of Congress, Washington, D.C.

Whitaker-Meade Papers. Southern Historical Collection. The University of North Carolina at Chapel Hill, N.C.

Will Book, Charleston County, XXV, Book A 270. South Carolina Department of Archives, Columbia, S.C.

DISSERTATION

Copeland, J. Isaac. "The Movement for Free Public Schools in South Carolina, to 1868." Ph.D. dissertation, University of North Carolina, 1957.

NEWSPAPERS

Royal Gazette (Charleston, S.C.), 1780, 1781, 1782.

South Carolina and American General Gazette (Charleston, S.C.), 1776, 1780.

South Carolina Gazette (Charleston, S.C.), 1761.

South Carolina Gazette and American Journal (Charleston, S.C.), 1780.

MAGAZINES AND JOURNALS

American Historical Review, V.

American Review, VI.

Annual Register, or a View of the History, Politics, and Literature for the Year 1781. London, 1781.

Graham's Magazine, 1847.

Harper's New Monthly Magazine, XVII.

Historical Magazine, IX.

Magazine of American History, VII.

Magazine of History with Notes and Queries, Extra Number 139, XXXV.

North Carolina Historical Review, XXX.
Pennsylvania Magazine of History and Biography, XIV, XXX.
Portfolio, The, 3rd Series, I.
Publications of the Southern History Association, XI.
South Carolina Historical and Genealogical Magazine, I, III, VI, XI, XII, XIII, XVI, XVII, XVIII, XXVI, XXXIII, XXXVIII, XLI, LX.
Southern Literary Messenger, XXIX.
Virginia Magazine of History and Biography, LI.

BOOKS

Alden, John Richard. *General Charles Lee: Traitor or Patriot?* Baton Rouge, La., 1951.
Balch, W.. Thomas, ed. *Papers Related Chiefly to the Maryland Line During the Revolution.* Philadelphia, 1857.
Bass, Robert D. *Gamecock: The Life and Campaigns of General Thomas Sumter.* New York, 1961.
———. *The Green Dragoon: The Lives of Banastre Tarleton and Mary Robinson.* New York, 1957.
———. *Swamp Fox: The Life and Campaigns of General Francis Marion.* New York, 1959.
Beatson, Robert. *Naval and Military Memoirs of Great Britain, from 1727 to 1783.* 6 vols. London, 1804.
Boddie, William Willis. *History of Williamsburg.* Columbia, S.C., 1923.
Burnett, Edmund C., ed. *Letters of Members of the Continental Congress.* 8 vols. Washington, 1921–36.
Bushnell, Charles I., ed. *Memoirs of Tarleton Brown, a Captain in the Revolutionary Army.* New York, 1862.
Clark, Walter, ed. *The State Records of North Carolina.* 16 vols. Goldsboro, Winston, N.C., 1895–1914.
Clinton, Sir Henry. *The American Rebellion: Sir Henry Clinton's Narrative of His Campaigns, 1775–1782,* ed. William B. Willcox. New Haven, Conn., 1954.
Collections of the New-York Historical Society for the Year 1875. New York, 1876.
Collections of the New-York Historical Society for the Year 1879. New York, 1880.
Dawson, Henry B. *Battles of the United States by Sea and Land.* 2 vols. New York, 1858.
Drayton, John. *Memoirs of the American Revolution, from Its Commencement to the Year 1776, Inclusive: as Relating to the State of*

South-Carolina and Occasionally Referring to the States of North-Carolina and Georgia. 2 vols. Charleston, S.C., 1821.

Eberstadt, Edward. *American Historical Documents & Manuscripts Offered for Sale.* Catalogue no. 129. New York, 1951.

Edsall, T. H., trans. *Journal of Lieutenant John Charles Von Kraft of the Regiment Von Bose, 1776–78: Collections of the New-York Historical Society for 1882.* New York, 1883.

Edwards, Adele Stanton, ed. *Journals of the Privy Council, 1783–1789.* Columbia, S.C., 1971.

Ford, Worthington C. et al., eds. *Journals of the Continental Congress, 1774–1789.* 34 vols. Washington, 1904–37.

Fortescue, J. W. *A History of the British Army.* 13 vols. London, 1899–1930.

Garden, Alexander. *Anecdotes of the American Revolution, Illustrative of the Talents and Virtues of the Heroes of the Revolution, Who Acted the Most Conspicuous Parts Therein.* 2 vols. Charleston, S.C., 1822, 1828.

Gibbes, R. W., ed. *Documentary History of the American Revolution.* 3 vols. New York, 1853–57.

Gordon, William. *The History of the Rise, Progress, and Establishment of the United States of America.* 4 vols. London, 1788.

Graham, James. *The Life of General Daniel Morgan, of the Virginia Line of the United States.* New York, 1856.

Graydon, Alexander. *Memoirs of His Own Times with Reminiscences of the Men and Events of the Revolution,* ed. John Stockton Littell. Philadelphia, 1846.

Greene, George Washington. *The Life of Nathanael Greene, Major-General of the Army of the Revolution.* 3 vols. New York, 1867–71.

Gregorie, Ann King. *Thomas Sumter.* Columbia, S.C., 1931.

Gregg, Alexander. *History of the Old Cheraws.* New York, 1867.

Horry, Peter, and M. L. Weems. *The Life of Gen. Francis Marion, A Celebrated Partisan Officer in the Revolutionary War, against the British and Tories in South Carolina and Georgia.* Philadelphia, 1845.

[Hough, Franklin Benjamin]. *The Siege of Charleston, by the British Fleet and Army under the Command of Admiral Arbuthnot and Sir Henry Clinton.* Albany, N.Y., 1867.

Hough, Franklin B. *The Siege of Savannah, by the Combined American and French Forces, under the Command of Gen. Lincoln, and the Count d'Estaing, in the Autumn of 1779.* Albany, N.Y., 1866.

Hoyt, William Henry, ed. *The Papers of Archibald D. Murphey.* 2 vols. Raleigh, N.C., 1914.

Irving, Washington. *Life of George Washington.* 4 vols. New York, 1855–59.

James, William Dobein. *A Sketch of the Life of Brig. Gen. Francis Marion and a History of His Brigade*. Charleston, S.C., 1821.

Jenkins, James. *Experiences, Labours and Sufferings of Rev. James Jenkins, of the South Carolina Conference*. Spartanburg, S.C., 1842.

Johnson, Joseph. *Traditions and Reminiscences Chiefly of the American Revolution in the South*. Charleston, S.C., 1851.

Johnson, William. *Sketches of the Life and Correspondence of Nathanael Greene*. 2 vols. Charleston, S.C., 1822.

Jooe, Charles C., Jr., ed. *The Siege of Savannah in 1779, as Described in Two Contemporaneous Journals of French Officers in the Fleet of Count d'Estaing*. Albany, N.Y., 1874.

Kirkland, Frederic R., ed. *Letters on the American Revolution in the Library at "Karolfred."* Philadelphia, 1941.

Kirkland, Thomas J., and Robert M. Kennedy. *Historic Camden*. 2 vols. Columbia, S.C., 1905.

Lawson, John. *A New Voyage to Carolina*, ed. Hugh T. Lefler. Chapel Hill, N.C., 1967.

Lee, Henry. *Memoirs of the War in the Southern Department of the United States*, ed. Robert E. Lee. New York, 1870.

Lee, Henry, Jr. *The Campaign of 1781 in the Carolinas: with Remarks Historical and Critical on Johnson's Life of Greene*. Philadelphia, 1824.

Lee Papers, The, in *Collections of the New-York Historical Society for the Year 1871 . . . 1872 . . . 1873 . . . 1874*. 4 vols. New York, 1872–75.

Lossing, Benson J. *Field Book of the American Revolution*. 2 vols. Philadelphia, 1851.

McCrady, Edward. *South Carolina in the Revolution, 1775–80*. New York, 1901.

———. *South Carolina in the Revolution, 1780–1783*. New York, 1902.

———. *South Carolina under Royal Government*. New York, 1897.

Merritt, Elizabeth, ed. *Calendar of the General Otho Williams Papers in the Maryland Historical Society*. Baltimore, Md., 1940.

Moore, M. A. *The Life of Gen. Edward Lacey, with a List of Battles and Skirmishes in South Carolina, During the Revolutionary War*. Spartanburg, S.C., 1859.

Moultrie, William. *Memoirs of the American Revolution, So Far as It Related to the States of North and South Carolina, and Georgia*. 2 vols. New York, 1802.

Public Acts of the General Assembly of North Carolina, The. New Bern, N.C., 1804.

Ramsay, David. *History of South Carolina: From Its First Settlement in 1670 to the Year 1808*. Newberry, S.C., 1858.

————. *The History of the American Revolution.* 2 vols. London, 1793.

————. *The History of the Revolution in South-Carolina, from a British Province to an Independent State.* Trenton, N.J., 1785.

Rankin, Hugh F. *The North Carolina Continentals.* Chapel Hill, N.C., 1971.

Richmond, George H. *Letters by and to Gen. Nathanael Greene, with Some to His Wife.* New York, 1906.

Robinson, Blackwell P. *William R. Davie.* Chapel Hill, N.C., 1957.

Ross, Charles, ed. *Correspondence of Charles, First Marquis Cornwallis.* 3 vols. London, 1859.

Salley, A. S., Jr. *The History of Orangeburg County South Carolina from Its First Settlement to the Close of the Revolutionary War.* Orangeburg, S.C., 1898.

Saunders, William L., ed. *The Colonial Records of North Carolina.* 10 vols. Raleigh, N.C., Goldsboro, N.C., etc., 1886–98.

Scheer, George F., and Hugh F. Rankin. *Rebels and Redcoats.* Cleveland, Ohio, 1957.

Simms, William Gilmore. *The Life of Francis Marion.* New York, 1844.

Stedman, Charles. *The History of the Origin, Progress, and Termination of the American War.* 2 vols. London, 1794.

Stevens, Benjamin Franklin, ed. *Clinton-Cornwallis Controversy Growing out of the Campaign in Virginia, 1781.* 2 vols. London, 1888.

————. *Facsimiles of Manuscripts in European Archives Relating to America, 1773–1783.* 25 vols. London, 1889–95.

Syrett, Harold C., ed. *The Papers of Alexander Hamilton.* 6 vols. New York, 1961–1963.

Tarleton, Banastre. *A History of the Campaigns of 1780 and 1781 in the Southern Provinces of North America.* London, 1787.

Tiffany, Osmond. *A Sketch of the Life and Services of Gen. Otho Williams.* Baltimore, Md., 1851.

Wallace, David Duncan. *South Carolina: A Short History, 1520–1948.* Chapel Hill, N.C., 1951.

Walsh, Richard, ed. *The Writings of Christopher Gadsden, 1746–1805.* Columbia, S.C., 1966.

Ward, Christopher. *The War of the Revolution,* ed. John R. Alden. 2 vols. New York, 1952.

Willcox, William B. *Portrait of a General: Sir Henry Clinton in the War of Independence.* New York, 1964.

Year Book City of Charleston, 1899. Charleston, S.C., 1899.

Index

Allston, Capt. William, 278
Alston, Col. William, 117
Amherst, Lord Jeffery, 5
Ami's Mill, 76, 87, 281
Andre, Maj. John, 234–235
Arbuthnot, Adm. Marriott, 45, 49
Ardesoife, Capt. John Plumer, 50–51
Armstrong, John, 244
Arnold, Benedict, 235
Ashe, John, 30
Ashley, Ferry, 33
Ashley River, 16, 45

Bacon's Bridge, 44, 279
Balfour, Lt. Col. Nisbet, 68, 72, 74, 89, 103, 110, 117, 121–122, 124–125, 135, 145, 167, 172, 191–192, 201, 234, 252
Ball, Col. John Coming, 54, 73–74, 83, 85, 87, 90
Barefield, Capt. Jesse, 69, 71, 117, 123
Barefield, Miles, 69
Bass's Mill, 152

Batt, Richard, ix
Baxter, Col. John, 106, 145, 148, 182, 229, 296
Bellesville, S.C., 197
Benbow's Ferry, 113, 136, 140
Benison, Maj. Lemuel, 66, 148, 198, 272–273
Bennett, Capt. Thomas, 272
Biggin's Bridge, 285
Biggin Swamp, 251
black dragoons, 284–286
Black Mingo, 120, 147
Black Mingo Creek, battle of, 83–84, 86–88
Black River, 103, 113, 117, 122, 145, 169, 181, 185, 200
Black River Church, 83, 87
Blakely's Plantation, 173
Bloom Hill, S.C., 193, 196
Blue Savannah, 71–72, 88
Bradley's Plantation, 164
Brandon, Thomas, 265
Brereton, Maj. William, 263-264
Brierly's Ferry, 111